Book 11

in the series

Free to be Holy

Living in the realm of

ROMANS REVEALED

You will never see yourself, or Sin in the same way

WENDY BARWEGEN

Free to be Holy: The Sin Within

ISBN-1-4196-9560-6

Most Scripture quotations are taken from the King James Version of the Bible. Others have been taken from The New Living Translation Edition 2, The New King James Version Edition 3, and the English Standard Version Edition 2.

All Hebrew and Greek definitions are taken from *Strong's Hebrew and Greek Dictionaries* Electronic Edition STEP Files Copyright © 2003, QuickVerse, a division of Findex.com, Inc., all rights reserved.

All English definitions are taken from the Encarta ® World English Dictionary © & (P) 1998-2004 Microsoft Corporation. All rights reserved.

All Charles Spurgeon quotes are taken from his devotional, *All of Grace*.

Cover design – Wendy Barwegen
Technical assistance –
Carol Kaufmann – Watseka Sign, Watseka IL

Cover photography –
Kathryn Northcott –
The Portrait Place, Onarga, IL

3 1558 00246 7405

T H A N K   Y O U

To my Father in Heaven,

You continue to amaze me.

To my sister, Tracy,

You have sailed these seas with me now
for many years, all the while
you have been both an excellent student
and an inspiration to me.
If only everyone had your valiant heart…

To my friend Joy,

Several years ago,
you gave me a living picture of trust
that I just cannot get out of my head.
What a wonderful thing.

To my dear friend in heaven, Dale Hauser,

God bless you for suffering through those early
manuscripts and graciously treating them as
though they had been written by Hemingway.
Your aid in these writings
has been beyond measure.

For additional copies visit
www.Booksurge.com,
www.BooksinPrint.com,
www.GlobalBooksinPrint.com,
www.Amazon.com,
www.Abebooks.com, or
www.Alibris.com

and select bookstores.

For information about other
books in this series, or scheduling
a speaking engagement, please
contact Wendy Barwegen
by calling or writing:

815.471.2986

wbarwegen@yahoo.com

CONTENTS

INTRODUCTION

Three years ago God began to give me the teachings that I shared in *Hell Bent*. By comparison with the balance of the *Free to be Holy* series, *Hell Bent* is relatively young. It was nearly eighteen years ago that God responded to the cry of my soul and began to teach me things I had never heard before. He has spent these many years building a case for them. Finally, after standing the tests of research, faith, and time, these teachings are ready to be revealed.

In *Hell Bent* we discovered that God purposed, for a myriad of reasons, to use sin in His plan for man. Now, working from that premise of truth, *The Sin Within* reveals Biblical secrets that teach how to live successfully in a body that is hell bent on sinning.

The aspect of sin and the idea of holiness are integral parts of every area of Scripture. In *Hell Bent* we saw how the book of Genesis laid a foundation of Truth concerning God and His plan for man. In *The Sin Within* we will see how the book of Romans does much the same for the message of grace found in the New Testament. Genesis created a problem that Romans fixes. When these foundations are) in place, the rest of the Bible becomes a great deal easier to read and understand; I can promise you that.

Simply Complex

From one end to the other we find the Biblical method of holiness to be simply receiving holiness by faith. We cannot add to this Gospel and we cannot take away from it. As you will soon see, the apostle Paul preaches this message repeatedly and in detail. It is for these reasons that ours should be an effortless task. But, because God muddied the waters a bit, we find that this effortless task has become a true struggle for every individual who has ever sought holiness.

This is as it should be. Anything worth having does not come easily. Holiness is no exception, *"Blessed are they which do **hunger** and **thirst** after righteousness: for they shall be filled." (Matt 5:6 KJV)* Those who hunger and thirst will be filled and will love these writings. Others who are fat and full will hate them. Still others, being lukewarm, will be strangely unaffected by them.

God is looking for sincerity and passion; He is as sober as a heart attack when it comes to the subject of holiness. To step into true holiness is to step into the vulnerable presence of God. When we are holy, we see and speak with Him face to face. We are told to enter the throne room boldly as we are washed in the blood of the Lamb. God is inviting us to get up close and personal with Him. It is for this reason that holiness is protected territory. Only the pure of heart can enter these gates, *"Blessed are the pure in heart: for they shall see God." (Matt 5:8 KJV)* To understand and experience holiness is to understand and experience God.

The Obstacle Course

Having said this, there are needless obstacles in our path that need to be addressed before we begin:

1. **False doctrine**
2. **Demonic trickery**
3. **Pride**
4. **Disrespecting the Holy Scriptures**

False Doctrine

False doctrine tops our list because in today's world, it is prevalent. Unfortunately, many Bible teachers do not completely understand the Scriptures as they pertain to sin and holiness. However, this does not stop them from attempting to teach on these subjects. It is not uncommon for the same preacher to set a congregation free on one day only to condemn them on another.

The Pharisees get their treat on Sunday morning while the sinners get theirs on Wednesday night. For two weeks we preach on television about the unmerited favor of God and then for two weeks we talk about the importance of behaving well and getting our act together so that we can obtain the (no longer unmerited) favor of God. This practice has led many to confusion and frustration. Messages of grace are beautiful, albeit temporary; they are only as effective as time will allow. Inevitably, a message of bondage will come in and begin to eat away at the message of grace until it fades into obscurity.

I am positive these teachers do not intend this confusion. Much of what they teach is spot on. However, when it comes to the doctrines involving holiness, many teachers are as confused as their students. The blind are leading the blind.

In our confusion we turn within and begin to reason things out in our natural minds. We come to the conclusion that it certainly can't hurt to try very hard to be good. And so, in the end, false doctrine teaches us to put our noses to the grindstone, obey the rules, knuckle down, do the right thing, toe the line, and otherwise kill ourselves to do what is right, because surely that is right…right?

Demonic Trickery

Demonic trickery is next in line. The devil loathes the Truth and he will do anything to stand in the way of it. The Truth exposes the devil for who he really is and he hates that more than anything. His entire purpose is found in painting false pictures in order to convince us of his fabrications.

Our enemy is very much like the wizard in The Wizard of Oz; he comes across all big and intimidating while he pathetically hides behind his screen of lies. The accuser of the brethren throws our sin up on the big screen and we jump and back away in fear. When we are frozen in terror and we don't know what to do, the devil has us right where he wants us. The average Christian becomes so focused on all the smoke and mirrors that he misses the Truth of the matter.

As long as we are focused on our sin we are not capable of seeing our holiness. We are going to learn how to shift our gaze from the sin of our flesh to the holiness of our spirit. Reading this book will get the devil's attention; following its precepts will get his goat.

As well, demonic trickery attempts to scare us into putting our noses to the grind-stone, obeying the rules, knuckling down, doing the right thing, toeing the line, and otherwise killing ourselves to do what is right because that is flat out wrong and the devil knows it.

Pride

Next we have pride. Humans, even Christian humans, do not easily admit defeat. Everyone wants a pat on the back. Everyone wants to think well of himself and have others think well of him too. Everyone wants to be fairly rewarded for being a good bloke.

Even those who try to be humble want to be acknowledged for their humility. No one wants to really embrace the Bible's definition of humility or humanity. When we get down to brass tacks, we all just want to do well and be recognized for it. This attitude does nothing but work against the program.

Pride, as well, prompts us to put our noses to the grindstone, obey the rules, knuckle down, do the right thing, toe the line, and otherwise kill ourselves to do what is right because "we can do it" and everyone will know it.

Disrespect of the Scriptures

Finally we have the most depressing obstacle to holiness: Disrespect of the Holy Scriptures. Rather than receiving the Bible as a whole message, we have a tendency to ignore many important passages of Scripture while we navigate toward familiar verses that seem easier for us to understand and embrace. Unfortunately, this only leads to half-baked ideas which sorely lack power and victory.

It is true; freedom is a difficult idea to apprehend. We have been living in bondage to someone or something from the moment we were born. We have difficulty wrapping our brains around the true notion of freedom. And although the Scriptures speak much of freedom, we tend to navigate over to the passages that speak about the law because we, being familiar with rules and regulations, can better relate to them.

However, we must respect the Scriptures enough to scrutinize them:

> *"Study to show thyself approved unto God,*
> *a workman that needeth not to be ashamed,*
> *rightly dividing the word of truth."*
> *(2 Tim 2:15 KJV)*

In the book of Acts, there was a particular group of believers from Berea who did this. The Bible refers to them as *noble*. These men did not take the word of man; they respected the Word of God enough to turn to it for wisdom:

> *"These were more noble than those in Thessalonica,*
> *in that they received the word with all readiness of mind,*
> **and searched the scriptures daily,**
> *whether those things were so.*
> *Therefore many of them believed; also of honourable*
> *women which were Greeks, and of men, not a few."*
> *(Acts 17:11-12 KJV emphasis mine)*

The Bereans received what the apostles were teaching with readiness of mind but they did not stop there. It is good that their hearts were open to the Gospel but these men took it a giant step further when they searched the Scriptures daily to see if these things were so.

Searching the Scriptures is exactly what we are going to do in *The Sin Within*. Soon we will begin to see the Bible as a whole message rather than several contradictory messages. And before too long we will begin to see the powerful message of grace that runs from the Book of Genesis all the way through to the Book of Revelation.

It is only when we do not "study to show ourselves approved" and "search the Scriptures to see if these things be so", that we end up settling into our fall back position of putting our noses to the grindstone, trying to obey the rules, trying to do the right thing, toeing the line, and otherwise killing ourselves to do what is right because that is what some of the Scriptures seem to be saying.

Labor

I am not suggesting that there is not a labor involved in obtaining Biblical holiness. As a matter of fact, we will not become holy until we are willing to labor like an ant on caffeine in the Mohave Desert. However, we will not labor by conventional methods; God is anything but conventional. Our labor will be in entering into God's rest. We will never work harder at anything in this life. Nevertheless, we must not worry…this is, and ever will be, the only task at hand.

Part I

Getting Real

"I could believe that Jesus would forgive sin," says one,
"but then my trouble is that I sin again,
and that I feel such awful tendencies to evil within me.
As surely as a stone, if it be flung up into the air,
soon comes down again to the ground, so do I,
though I am sent up to heaven by earnest preaching,
return again to my insensible state.
Alas! I am easily fascinated with the basilisk eyes of sin,
and am thus held as under a spell,
so that I cannot escape from my own folly."
Charles Spurgeon, All of Grace

1

THE INNER SINNER

Now that we know the sin nature was a necessary evil in God's big plan, let us take some time to get to know our inner sinner. We are living in a time when it has become very popular to discover our "inner worth" so that we might preserve our self-esteem. That may be okay for those of the world who are trying to survive by the world system, but it is not okay for the Christian.

So, if you are one who wants to feel good about yourself, close your ears, the apostle Paul is about to bare his soul to us in this seventh chapter of Romans. All pride is cast aside as Paul lays down every ounce of self-esteem to expose the utter worthlessness of a man born of the flesh.

Descending and Ascending

There are two mountains that are of great concern to God, and should be of great concern to us: The awful mountain of self, and the awesome mountain of God, *"Great is the LORD, and greatly to be praised in the city of our God, in the mountain of his holiness." (Psa 48:1 KJV)* The mountain of God is a mountain of holiness while the mountain of self is a heap of fleshly good works that put on a pretense of holiness.

While we are on the mountain of self, we are our own gods and we control our lives to the best of our ability; we look to ourselves, not God, to solve our problems. Whereas on the mountain of God, God is God and He has control of our lives according to His abilities. We look to Him to supply all things necessary for life and godliness.

Every human being begins on the mountain of self. From our very first cry in the delivery room, to the moment we fall on our knees before Jesus, we live on the mountain of self. That is as it should be; though all begin on the mountain of self, it is what is done when we realize this fact that makes all the difference.

As Christians, we want very much to be on the mountain of God; we are tired of struggling and losing the battle against sin and against the curse that was placed on this planet six thousand years ago. Unfortunately, even many who are avidly Christian do not know how to ascend the mountain of God, though it looms in front of them.

Descending

It is not possible to jump from one *abstract* mountain to the other anymore than it is possible to jump from one *physical* mountain to the other. It is necessary to descend one mountain before we can ascend the other. Between the two lies a dark and lonely valley that, as well, must be reckoned with. Thankfully, we don't have to stay in that valley long. As a matter of fact, our time there need not exceed a brief moment.

The work, for the most part, will be in climbing down that mountain of self. It is not a *selfish* mountain, as one might suppose; rather, it is a *self-reliant* mountain. Within each of us is a nasty "can-do" spirit. We mistakenly think that we *can* be good enough, we *can* please God, we *can* take care of ourselves, we *can* provide for ourselves, and we *can* protect ourselves. However, we "can-do" none of these things and the sooner we figure this out the closer we will be to the valley.

Unfortunately, humans are stubborn and usually have to be pitched into the valley several times before they no longer have the strength to trudge back up the mountain of self. We saw this evidenced in my son's valley story told in *Hell Bent*.

Ascending

We are going to watch the apostle Paul go through the process of descending the mountain of self. Paul notoriously invites his readers to join him and learn from him as he deals with his flesh. This seventh chapter of Romans is the mother ship of that teaching tool. In the first part, Paul unveils a mystery that most of us are reticent to embrace. Immediately following this revelation, Paul shows us how this mystery works by bringing it into his very present life.

Before he is finished, we will have watched the apostle Paul descend the mountain of self, enter the valley, and lay hold of the mountain of God. The wording in this chapter will surprise you. I know it surprised me. So, pay attention to the flow and watch Paul revolutionize before your eyes.

The Covenants

Before we begin we need to learn a little bit about the two Old Testament Covenants, the Mosaic Covenant and the Abrahamic Covenant, and the New Testament covenant, which is based on the Abrahamic Covenant. These Covenants are contracts that were made between God and men.

The Abrahamic Covenant

The first notable covenant made between God and man was the Abrahamic Covenant. The Abrahamic Covenant was a contract made between God and Abraham. This covenant was based on faith and promises. The Giver was God and the recipients were Abraham and his descendents. The Abrahamic Covenant was a one-way contract as God was the only One indebted to it. As Abraham simply trusted in God, God held up His end of the contract and blessed Abraham.

The Mosaic Covenant

The Mosaic Covenant was the second notable contract made between God and man. This covenant was a contract between God and the children of Israel, who were also the descendents of Abraham. This covenant was given on Mount Sinai and engraved on stone tablets by the finger of God. This, the Mosaic Covenant, had what is called a "mediator" between God and man: Moses. According to the Mosaic Covenant, the children of Israel were indebted to obey laws while God was indebted to bless the obedient. After summarizing this law, God said:

> *"I call heaven and earth to record this day against*
> *you, that I have set before you life and death,*
> *blessing and cursing: therefore choose life,*
> *that both thou and thy seed may live:"*
> *(Deut 30:19 KJV)*

We see that the Mosaic Covenant was a two-way contract; as the nation of Israel obeyed the Mosaic Law, God would hold up His end of the contract and bless them. Conversely, as the nation of Israel disobeyed the law, they were in line for trouble. Because God knew the children of Israel would be disobedient, (due to the fact that they had a sin nature), along with the Mosaic Law came the Levitical Priesthood.

The Levitical Priesthood, with its sacrifices and cleansing rituals, offered the children of Israel atonement for their transgressions. The blood of bulls and goats symbolized the blood of Christ and brought sure remission of sins. In this way the children of Israel could enjoy the benefits of being justified before God while also having sin.

The New Covenant

The third and final notable covenant made between God and man is the New Covenant. The New Covenant, sealed by the blood of Christ, disannuls the Mosaic Covenant while it embraces the Abrahamic Covenant. We are going to go into great detail about these covenants later, for now it is enough for us to keep the following words of Jesus in mind:

> *"Then said he, Lo, I come to do thy will, O God.*
> *He taketh away the first,*
> *that he may establish the second." (Heb 10:9 KJV)*

The Inner Sinner

Through the sacrifice of Christ, God took away the former Mosaic Covenant so that He could establish the present New Covenant, which is based on the Abrahamic Covenant and ratified by the blood of Christ. All the particulars of this New Covenant are covered in what we refer to as the *New Testament*, which is another way of saying *New Covenant*.

How to Break a Contract

Now that we are rehearsed in these covenants, we will better understand what Paul is trying to teach the church in Rome. In the first several verses Paul is speaking of a natural marriage...but not really. Paul is using the *example* of the marriage contract from the Mosaic Law to illustrate a point; he was not giving marriage advice as many suppose. Paul actually uses the Mosaic Law to demonstrate how the Mosaic Law is dead.

Keeping that in mind, let's read what he says:

> *"You shouldn't have any trouble understanding this,*
> *friends, for you know all the ins and outs of the law—*
> *how it works and how its power touches only the living.*
> *For instance, a wife is legally tied to her husband*
> *while he lives, but if he dies, she's free.*
> *If she lives with another man while her husband is living,*
> *she's obviously an adulteress.*
> *But if he dies, she is quite free to marry another man in*
> *good conscience, with no one's disapproval."*
> *(Rom 7:1-3 TMNT)*

Paul is using a Mosaic marriage legality as an example to show how a contract between two people becomes powerless when one of them dies. Paul is saying that in the event of a death, any contracts between the deceased and the ones left behind become null and void.

Although the Mosaic contract was legally binding, the moment either the nation of Israel, or God would die, the contract would be void of its power. We know that when a believer dies he is no longer under the Mosaic Law in that he is with the Lord. The contract is broken by death. In the same way, when Jesus died, God's end of the Mosaic contract was broken, which made our obligation null and void. The Mosaic contract has been broken by the death of Christ.

Both parties of a contract must be alive for a contract to be in force. That is why the following is true:

> *"Wherefore, my brethren, ye also are become dead to
> the law **by the body of Christ**; that ye should be married to
> another, even to him who is raised from the dead,
> that we should bring forth fruit unto God."*
> *(Rom 7:4 KJV emphasis mine)*

What Paul is saying is that when God, (in the Person of Jesus), died,
the law packed contract that was made between God and man
through Moses became null and void. And because this Mosaic Law
was disannulled through Christ's death, we are now dead to the law,
free from its restrictions, and in a position to be "married" to
Another, *"even to him who is raised from the dead, that we should
bring forth fruit unto God."*

A Natural Progression

This is one more example of how a thing begins in the spiritual
realm, is birthed as a natural example into the natural realm, and is
then brought back into the spiritual realm where it originated. God
made a spiritual covenant with Abraham based on faith and
promises:

> *"In the same day
> the LORD made a covenant with Abram, saying,
> Unto thy seed have I given this land,
> from the river of Egypt unto the great river,
> the river Euphrates:"*
> *(Gen 15:18 KJV)*

Although God had given this land to Abram, Abram never owned the
land in the natural. The blessing was in the form of a promise; it was
a spiritual gift that God gave to Abram for his seed. After this God
made a natural covenant with the children of Israel based on natural
laws, and physical blessings in a physical Promised Land through the
physical blood of natural bulls and goats:

> *"For when Moses had spoken every precept
> to all the people according to the law,
> he took the blood of calves and of goats, with water,
> and scarlet wool, and hyssop,
> and sprinkled both the book, and all the people,
> Saying, This is the blood of the testament*

The Inner Sinner

which God hath enjoined unto you.
Moreover he sprinkled with blood both the tabernacle,
and all the vessels of the ministry. "
(Heb 9:19-21 KJV)

Presently, God has made a *spiritual* covenant with all of mankind based on spiritual laws and a spiritual sacrifice:

"This is the covenant that I will make with them after those
days, saith the Lord, I will put my laws into their hearts,
and in their minds will I write them; "
(Heb 10:16 KJV)

"But Christ being come an high priest of good things to
come, by a greater and more perfect tabernacle, not made
with hands, that is to say, not of this building; Neither by
the blood of goats and calves, but by his own blood he
entered in once into the holy place, having obtained eternal
redemption for us. " (Heb 9:11-12 KJV)

So we see that God's covenants began in the spiritual realm with Abraham, were given a "body" in the natural realm through the Mosaic Law and Levitical Priesthood, and then were birthed back into the spiritual realm through Jesus Who is now the High Priest of a more perfect tabernacle *not made with hands; A holy place.* That is why the Abrahamic Covenant was considered an eternal covenant whereas the Mosaic Covenant was never meant to be more than a temporary natural example that demonstrated a spiritual Truth.

When God makes a covenant, He does not break it. The Abrahamic Covenant had to go the course of all things: It had to begin in the spiritual realm, be formed in the natural realm, and then be birthed back into the spiritual realm. Everything has to run this course and God's covenant with man was no exception to this rule.

An Everlasting Covenant

This is why God declared the Abrahamic Covenant an eternal covenant the moment He made it, *"And I will establish my covenant between me and thee and thy seed after thee in their generations for an everlasting covenant, to be a God unto thee, and to thy seed after thee." (Gen 17:7 KJV)* An everlasting covenant has no end. Our

New Testament Covenant is really not new at all; it is a continuation of the eternal covenant God made with Abraham:

"Even as Abraham believed God,
and it was accounted to him for righteousness.
Know ye therefore that they which are of faith,
the same are the children of Abraham.
And the scripture, foreseeing that God would
justify the heathen through faith, preached before the
gospel unto Abraham, saying,
In thee shall all nations be blessed."
(Gal 3:6-8 KJV)

The Fulfillment of the Everlasting Covenant

The only new thing about this covenant is that it replaces the Mosaic Covenant. We think that it is new and different in that it incorporated the Gentile nations. However, the very old covenant that God made with Abraham specifically stated that in Abraham, not just the nation of Israel, but *all nations* would be blessed. We have a New Covenant in that it is not the Mosaic Covenant, but we actually have a very Old Covenant that has reached its pinnacle.

Now we are living in a time when not only Jews are free from the Mosaic Law and are able to come back under Abraham's Covenant, but now *all nations* can be blessed by Abraham's covenant! We are seeing the Abrahamic Covenant fulfilled completely in these times. The Abrahamic Covenant was based on faith and promises and it was extended to all nations. We are living in the fulfillment of the Abrahamic Covenant.

We forget what a shocking blessing this was for the Gentile nations. For four thousand years the Israelites were the only ones who could get in on the blessings of God. A few Gentiles slipped in here and there, but by and large, this was all about the Israelites.

Can you imagine what this was like for the Gentile nations? They had heard about this God. Folklore concerning the nation of Israel was plenteous. Everyone knew about the God of the Israelites. They heard how He delivered the Israelites from their enemies, and how He allowed them to become captives of their enemies. They may have trusted Him or feared Him, but there was no questioning His reality. Now the nations of the world, formerly the very enemies

The Inner Sinner

of God, were being invited to become a child of Abraham just like the Israelites. This was huge.

Because the Old Mosaic Covenant that was sanctified by the blood of bulls and goats is no longer valid, *"In that he saith, A new covenant, he hath made the first old..." (Heb 8:13a KJV)*, God has brought everyone into the Abrahamic Covenant, not a two way covenant based on works of the law, but a one way covenant that is based on faith in Christ.

Jeopardy

Many years ago, in lieu of Halloween, I brought my children to a "Harvest Celebration" at a neighboring church. There were many games for the children, but one in particular stood out to me: Jeopardy. One of the contestants had to provide a question for the all-important answer, "This is what one must do to be saved." The child questioned, "What is being born again?" He was told that he was only half right. The opposing contestant sounded his buzzer and told them what they wanted to hear, "And obey the Ten Commandments!"

The game was aptly named; there *was* danger here. On the way home I had to explain to my children that what they had heard was incorrect. According to what Paul has told us, we are no longer under the requirement of the law. Our salvation is not contingent upon obedience to the Ten Commandments. Believers are not *required* to obey the Mosaic Law; however, they are *empowered* to obey the law through the Spirit of the New Covenant who came to lead and indwell us, *"But if ye be led of the Spirit, ye are not under the law." (Gal 5:18 KJV)*

No longer Law Abiders; now Fruit Bearers

While under the Old Mosaic Covenant, the best God could get out of mankind was pathetic human effort. However, under the New Covenant marriage contract, rather than through human effort, obedience to God becomes a natural result of a new birth. The fruit of the Spirit grows as believers of all nations are grafted into the Vine, *"I am the vine, ye are the branches: He that abideth in me, and I in him, the same bringeth forth much fruit: for without me ye can do nothing." (John 15:5 KJV)*

Through this new marriage we are brought into Christ, and by this action we will bear the fruit of holiness the way a tree bears fruit. Branches do not work to bear fruit; as long as they stay connected to the vine, they will bear fruit whether they like it or not. This is a spiritually instinctive process, and that is exactly in what we have been invited to partake. We are in the realm of the Spirit in this time of the fulfillment of the Abrahamic Covenant. We will not bear fleshly good acts; we will bear godly spiritual fruit.

Death to the Mosaic Law

When Jesus died He took the law with Him:

> *"Blotting out the handwriting of ordinances*
> *that was against us, which was contrary to us,*
> *and took it out of the way, nailing it to his cross;*
> *And having spoiled principalities and powers,*
> *he made a show of them openly,*
> *triumphing over them in it."*
> *(Col 2:14-15 KJV emphasis mine).*

First we get a picture of God dumping an inkwell across the parchment papers that contained the Law, and then we see Jesus grabbing the blotted paper and nailing it to His cross. Next we get a victory dance. How much more obvious can God get? We must know that the burden of the Mosaic Law has been annihilated.

By these acts, God spoiled all of Satan's fun and made a big show of it to boot. Satan, the accuser, can no longer hold our sin in front of our face. The handwriting of laws that was against us has been blotted out and nailed to the cross of death. It no longer exists. When Satan brings the obligation to the law to our attention, we can rightfully respond, "You got nothin' on me."

Now God is functioning with man under a new contract; He made a New Covenant with man through the life and death of His Son. And, the reason a New Covenant could even be made is because one of the participants of the Old Covenant died. God, in the Person of Christ, died so that we could legally be "married" to another, *"...that ye should be married to another, even to him who is raised from the dead, that we should bring forth fruit unto God."* *(Rom 7:4 KJV)*

A Natural Result

Showing us exactly how this new marriage plays out, Paul continues in the seventh chapter of Romans, *"For when we were in the flesh, the motions of sins, which were by the law, did work in our members to bring forth fruit unto death."* *(Rom 1:5 KJV)* Paul is saying that before we were born again, our sin nature, which gained power from the law, could only bring forth fruit unto death, just as it did with Adam. The lust within us, (a longing for that which is forbidden), was only *enticed* by the law; never *corrected* by the law.

Under the Mosaic law one does not even have to try to be bad; we bear bad fruit because that is what our hell bent flesh naturally produces the moment any law is introduced. No one sets out to be bad; it just comes naturally. It was not possible for us to do well under the Mosaic Law. God is not surprised by our behavior; He knows our frame, He remembers we are formed of dust.

Free at Last, Free at Last

But now, as we are set free from the law by the death of Jesus, we are in a position to bring forth fruit unto life. Hallelujah, the situation has reversed:

> *"But now we have been delivered from the law,*
> *having died to what we were held by,*
> *so that we should serve in the newness of the Spirit*
> *and not in the oldness of the letter." (Rom 7:6 NKJV)*

Now that we have entered the death of Christ and embraced our new marriage, we are free to obey the law in a *new* natural way, by the power of the Holy Spirit, and not in the old way that was laboring by rote obedience to letters on a page.

Lust has been Stymied

Do you remember what the Mosaic Law awakened in us? Lust -- that innate longing for all things forbidden. Guess what? There is nothing left that is forbidden. The Mosaic Law was nailed to the cross of Christ. How much more dead can a thing be? Now that we are free to do as we please, we no longer have the law of lust working against us.

God, at first, wrote His laws upon stone tablets; now He has written them upon our hearts, *"This is the covenant that I will make with them after those days, saith the Lord, I will put my laws into their hearts, and in their minds will I write them;" (Heb 10:16 KJV).* Now we contain the law of God written in our minds and in our hearts...not as commandments...but just as trees contain the design of fruit. What this means is that we who are the children of God *know* what to do, yes, but we also contain the *desire and the power* to perform it.

Paul spoke the following to the church in Corinth, *"All things are lawful unto me, but all things are not expedient: all things are lawful for me, but I will not be brought under the power of any." (1Cor 6:12 KJV)* What a statement! Now that all things are lawful, our inner lust has been stymied. Nothing is forbidden. Now we are free from the law that compelled us to evil so that we are able to serve in newness of the spirit and not in the oldness of the letter.

Is the Law Sin?

Understanding that we are now out from under the obligation of the law, a serious question begs to be asked. Paul was reading our minds when he broaches this question in our verses from Romans, *"What shall we say then? Is the law sin?"* Paul answers, *"God forbid." (Rom 7:7a KJV)* No, the law is not sin. But listen to Paul's reasoning as to *why* the law is not sin, *"Nay, I had not known sin, but by the law: for I had not known lust, except the law had said, Thou shalt not covet." (Rom 7:7b KJV)*

What Paul is saying is that the law, rather than being the *cause* of sin, was simply the vehicle by which *sin was exposed.* The law was not sin; the law was the *revealer* of sin; light reveals darkness. Paul didn't even know he had lust until he was told not to covet. Lust is a longing for that which is forbidden. Tell Paul not to covet, and Paul will want to covet because of the lust that resides in him. Paul's sin nature turned the law, whatever it was, into a piece of forbidden fruit.

The Law exposes the Hell Dust Factor

The law exposed the fact that Paul was hell bent. Now that Paul is told to not covet, Paul wants to covet. And it is <u>through this realization</u> that Paul sees that there is something wrong with him, *"But sin, taking occasion by the commandment, wrought in me all manner of concupiscence." (Rom 7:8a KJV)* Sin, having access through the law, caused every kind of perversion in Paul.

The law awakened in Paul his sin nature, which created every variety of ugly lust in him ("concupiscence" means lust and sexual sin). All self-esteem melts away as Paul discovers his inner sinner. Incredibly, this man of God says that sin gained an opportunity through the law to work in him *all manner* of lust. Paul is not holding back; he is being very honest with his audience. How many of us would address a church by saying that the law awakened within us every type and degree of lust?

The apostle goes on to say, *"For without the law sin was dead. For I was alive without the law once: but when the commandment came, sin revived, and I died." (Rom 7:8-9 KJV)* If there were no law, sin would not even have the ability to live. Paul thought he was fine until he was given a law. Once that commandment came, sin came alive and then Paul died. Through the law's exposure of his sin nature, Paul considered himself dead in the water; he discovered something inside of him that was at war with the law, and worthy of death. Sounds like Paul and Adam were cut from the same cloth.

Law Brings Death

Before his knowledge of the law, Paul thought he was just fine (mountain of self-reliance). But when the law came, sin awakened and Paul died, *"And the commandment, which was ordained to life, I found to be unto death." (Rom 7:10 KJV)* The law did exactly what it was intended to do: It exposed the sin nature and its proclivity to death.

We initially think that the law was intended to make men good, (just as Paul thought) when in all actuality, the law was brought in to expose man's evil and condemn it to death, *"For sin, taking occasion by the commandment, deceived me, and by it slew me." (Rom 7:11 KJV)* The law awoke lust, lust enticed sin, and sin brought death. Adam and Paul experienced the exact same thing.

Although God shackled us to a sin nature, there are those who are still trying to convince themselves that if they work hard enough they can be good. The law stands as a constant reminder to all of us that this is an impossible task.

The Purpose Spelled Out

"Wherefore the law is holy, and the commandment holy, and just, and good. Was then that which is good made death unto me? God forbid. But sin, that it might appear sin, working death in me by that which is good; that sin by the commandment might become exceeding sinful."
(Rom 7:12-13 KJV)

This is it in a nutshell: The law, in and of itself, is holy and good, but because the sin nature needed to be exposed, sin worked death in Paul through the law so that sin would become exceedingly sinful. God took a very holy law and used it to shine a flashlight on our sin nature and expose its existence through the manifestation of exceeding sin. God wanted us to get this picture.

God wanted our sin to become so bad that we would realize we had a problem, just as Paul is realizing he has a problem right in front of us. The purpose of the law was to force the issue of sin. The sin nature had to be exposed and the law was given for the sole purpose of exposing it, *"Moreover the law entered, that the offence might abound..." (Rom 5:20a KJV)*. For every law there is a forbidden piece of fruit waiting to entice us.

Through the commandment, sin became exceedingly sinful. The reason the commandment causes sin to become exceedingly sinful is because it mixes with the lust that is in us and causes us to sin even more than we would have without the law. We remember from <u>Hell Bent</u> that Adam had no other evil desire but to eat what had been forbidden. Adam was formed with sin; however, his sin became exceedingly sinful when a certain fruit was waved under his nose. It was then that Adam saw his nakedness. This is simply how it works. God needed Adam to discover the fact that he was created in such a way that he would be a complete failure without God. Adam needed to see his inner sinner. God formed Paul and us in the same way.

Sold Under Sin

Paul resigns himself, *"For we know that the law is spiritual: but I am carnal, sold under sin." (Rom 7:14 KJV)* Paul doesn't just say that he does bad things; he emphatically states that he is *sold* under sin. Sin owns him. This is the exact place that we must also land.

We do not just make mistakes...no...we are complete failures. We are hopelessly sold under sin. That is why it is downright futile to put our noses to the grindstone, knuckle down, toe the line, and otherwise kill ourselves to do what is right. It won't work...it will never work...it was not designed to work this way.

Bad to the Bone

Paul goes on to painstakingly describe how this utter malfunction manifested in his life, *"For that which I do, I allow not: for what I would, that do I not; but what I hate, that do I." (Rom 7:15 KJV)* Poor Paul doesn't want to be bad; we see here how he worked very hard to be good. However, the things Paul *wanted to do* escaped him while the things he *did not want to do* haunted him. In the end Paul *hated* the very things he did. Paul had been living under the devilish doctrine that suggests that, given enough effort, one could do well. His failure left Paul in a nasty predicament.

Those of us who are comfortable with our level of sin are far from the Truth. The mountain of self-reliance is the furthest point from God. When we have either been falsely indoctrinated, deceived by the devil, or we have allowed our pride to deceive us into thinking that we aren't so bad after all, we are truly delusional. The cold hard fact is that it is not possible for us to do the slightest good thing outside of the specific work of the Holy Spirit in us, *"…for without me ye can do nothing."*

A Black Crayon

The best thing to which we must liken ourselves is a black crayon. Peel off the paper and you will find nothing but black through and through. Cut it, slice it, shred it, melt it; when you get to the bottom of it, you will still find black.

A black crayon can draw flowers or it can draw a skull with crossbones but both pictures will be black because no matter what a black crayon draws, it will come out black. No matter how good our fleshly works may look, they are still dead and black:

> *"Behold, thou hast made my days as an handbreadth;*
> *and mine age is as nothing before thee: verily*
> ***every man at his best state is altogether vanity. Selah.***"
> *(Psa 39:5 KJV emphasis mine)*

The Hebrew word *"Selah"* is an instruction to pause. The Psalmist is saying, "Stop for a moment and ponder this thought: **Every man at his very best state is altogether worthless**. Wow. Every single man, even at his very best, is completely worthless. What can we say to this?

Not that I don't have a problem with that…

Now we are about to enter a pivotal area of Scripture. After Paul tells us that he disagrees with his very own behavior, he draws the following conclusion, *"If then I do that which I would not, I consent unto the law that it is good." (Rom 7:16 KJV)* Paul is basically saying this:

*"Hey, just because I act wrong does not mean that I am okay with that. I just told you that the very things I **don't** want to do are the things that I do, and I don't do the things that I **do** want to do! So, if I don't agree with my lawless actions, then I must agree with the law and believe it to be good. If I do those things I don't want to do then I have to agree that the law, in and of itself, is good. I have no issues with the law."*

Though Paul is a professed sinner, he is not a willing one. Paul agrees with the law, while at the same time disagrees with his behavior. That is a key element. While Paul was trying to be good, he was on the mountain of self. Now that Paul has gotten in touch with his inner sinner, he is in the valley between the mountains.

Don't look at me!

I hope you are sitting down for this next one. Paul wrenches himself from the mountain of self and from the base of the valley of wretchedness makes this declaration:

> *"Now then it is no more I that do it,*
> *but sin that dwelleth in me."*
> *(Rom 7:17 KJV)*

Hey, hold on there, Paul. It is no longer you who sins, but it's the sin that dwells *in you* that is sinning? What are you saying Paul? Are you telling us that you no longer take responsibility for your own actions? *It is no more you who sins?* You are washing your hands of your sin and placing the blame *and* the responsibility of it on your sin nature?!

Yes, he is. Here is Paul's reasoning, *"For I know that in me (that is, in my flesh,) dwelleth no good thing* (black crayon)*: for to will is present with me; but how to perform that which is good I find not." (Rom 7:18 KJV parentheses mine)* Let's read the same thing in The Message Bible, *"I realize that I don't have what it takes. I can will it, but I can't do it."* Paul has given up and washed his hands of the whole mess.

Logic prevails

Paul is an intelligent man. He is looking at this situation logically and seeing that there is no possible way to win. The law has exposed a part of him that he didn't even know existed. Paul finds himself enslaved to a sin nature that is bent on the fires of hell. He has every desire to be good but doesn't have the faintest idea how to pull it off. Been there; done that.

Paul's not talking about struggling and having a tough time; he is talking about complete and utter inadequacy when it comes to obeying the law. Paul says that after looking high and low, he found not one good thing about his flesh. Being the sharp guy that he is, Paul concludes that, given the circumstances, he could not possibly be responsible for his actions. If it were up to him, he *would* do better; hence, obviously it was *not* up to him. Paul takes himself out of the race. At some point in time, each one of us must take ourselves out of the race against the sin nature as it is a race that cannot be won.

Paul Becomes a Real Boy

Keep in mind that Paul is discovering the hell dust factor that the law exposed. We know from studying earlier that we were subject to sin, not willingly, but by God Who had hope to deliver us from the bondage of this corruption into the glorious liberty of the children of God. Paul knew this; he wrote it in the very next chapter! Paul is well aware that his contrary nature is part of the plan, and that plan had a deliverance clause. Therefore, Paul safely, and Biblically, separates himself from his sin nature.

Again, I tell you

I guess because he knew it would be hard for us to swallow, Paul repeats, even more emphatically, the two verses that are the most audacious, *"For the good that I would, I do not: but the evil which I would not, that I do." (Rom 7:19 KJV)* "I don't do the things I want to do, but I do the very evil that I do not want to do." Here Paul condemns himself further by calling what he does "evil"! If only we could be as honest.

Now look what *else* Paul repeats, *"Now if I do that I would not, it is no more I that do it, but sin that dwelleth in me." (Rom 7:20 KJV)* This time Paul specifically says that the evil that he manifests **is not done by him**, but by the sin that dwells in him. Paul bases his logic on the fact that he does not agree with his actions.

If Paul doesn't agree with his actions, he cannot possibly be the one instigating them. If Paul had the control, he would just fix the problem of sin. That's just it; Paul didn't have control over his sin anymore than we have control over ours. That is what convinced Paul that his bad behavior was not his responsibility.

It's a Law

This is such an important observation. Paul was not seeing himself as evil. Satan is evil; he enjoys doing evil things. Conversely, Paul *didn't like* the evil that was coming out of him; he didn't agree with it. We are not the same as the devil. Because Paul was born again, his new man was not in agreement with this evil; Paul was simply struggling against an unwilling hell bent disposition. Paul was seeing that he contained an evil element that had ultimate power over him, *"I find then a law, that, when I would do good, evil is present with me." (Rom 7:21 KJV)*

Paul isn't saying that his efforts to be good are in vain; he says that they are actually **counterproductive**. Paul didn't weigh the odds and say that it was difficult to do well; he said that he found a *law* that proved that it was impossible to do well. The property of this law is that when one makes an effort to do well, evil immediately shows up for work. Not only were Paul's efforts futile, they were dangerous to the cause. By laboring to be good, Paul was extending an invitation to evil.

Yes, Paul was a Christian when he wrote this

"For I delight in the law of God after the inward man:
But I see another law in my members,
warring against the law of my mind,
and bringing me into captivity
to the law of sin which is in my members."
(Rom 7:22-23 KJV)

Many will teach that in this chapter, Paul is speaking of his life before he received Christ. This verse argues that thought. Anyone who delights in the law of God after the inward man has been born again. One cannot even have an "inward man" unless he has first been born of God. And it was while Paul delighted in the law of God after the inward man that he saw another law working in his members that brought him into captivity.

When Paul was a Pharisee, he delighted in the law after the outward man. That is what Pharisees were known for. Paul saw absolutely nothing wrong with killing Christians because his "law" told him that they were worthy of death. Paul had no "inward man" to struggle with before he became born of God. The unregenerate man is in agreement with his sin. Only the born again man has a new inner man that has the law of written on his heart, thus the struggle begins the moment this new man arrives. This chapter in Romans was written to, for, and about a man who is born of God.

As a Christian, Paul loves the way he feels on the inside; being born of God, he is in complete agreement with God concerning all things! But as he looks at what is going on through the members of his own body, not only does Paul remove himself from the place of blame where his sin is concerned, but he also sees himself as a victim of his sin nature. Paul sees that there is a law that is contained in his members that brings him into a true sin clad prison sentence. He didn't know what was going on, but Paul knew something needed to be fixed because he was in bondage to sin through no fault of his own.

Not only does Paul take himself out of the place of responsibility where his sin is concerned, he is obviously a bit perturbed about the fact that he has been imprisoned in evil. Paul sees himself as a victim of an evil that has taken him captive.

No Apologies

This is a desperate situation! Does Paul cry, "Oh God, I'm so sorry!"? No. Paul does not feel responsible for his sin nature; therefore he does not apologize for it. Rather, Paul cries out for a Deliverer, *"O wretched man that I am! who shall deliver me from the body of this death?" (Rom 7:24 KJV)* Look at the separation! Please notice this! Paul was in the valley, hopelessly trapped in death. Even though this death was manifesting in his very own actions, he still saw it as a separate entity. Someone may as well have been poking Paul's brain and making him do things he did not want to do.

In anguish, Paul cries out, *"O wretched man that I am! who shall deliver me from the body of this death?"* Notice that Paul isn't asking for generic deliverance; he is specifically asking to be delivered from his body of death! "I am hopelessly enslaved to a body of sin! Who can help me?!" Paul knows that he needs help; he isn't trying to give excuses for a sin nature he cannot control, he is simply seeing it for what it is and recognizing that he needs divine intervention. In my opinion, this is the cleanest Biblical example of repentance. Now watch Paul do a complete about face.

The New Marriage Realized

Without missing a beat, Paul ascends the mountain of God by grabbing hold of what he spoke of earlier when he said, *"Wherefore, my brethren, ye also are become dead to the law by the body of Christ; that ye should be married to another, even to him who is raised from the dead, that we should bring forth fruit unto God." (Rom 7:4 KJV)* Paul recognized his inability to do good, washed his hands of the responsibility of the sin of his members, separated himself from his sin, cried out for a Savior, and then embraced the true way to bring forth fruit unto God and was married to Another.

Once Paul looked with repulsion upon the vileness of his flesh and entered the valley of wretchedness, he immediately called out for a Deliverer. What does Paul do now? Does he continue to worry and fret about his situation? Does he continue to try to be good in his own effort? No way. Paul only stayed in that valley for a moment in time before he thanked God, *"I thank God through Jesus Christ our Lord." (Rom 7:25a KJV)*

Paul Plants his Flag

Paul immediately ascended the mountain of God. He thanked God because Paul knew God would be faithful to perform that which he had promised (Rom 4:21). Paul obtained freedom from his flesh by turning his attention away from himself and his efforts (self-reliance), and set his face like flint toward God. Now that Paul is married to Another, he will be in a position to bring forth fruit unto God by a new and living way.

In the flesh, Paul very naturally bore bad fruit. Now that he is married to Another, Paul is attached to the Vine and just as naturally as he sinned, he will now, just as naturally, bring forth fruit unto God. Through the sin nature God bent Paul toward sin. Now, through the new nature, this same God will bend him toward holiness. We were created perfect in the spiritual realm, formed hell bent in the natural realm, and then recreated perfect in the spiritual realm: Spiritual, natural, spiritual.

A Done Deal

As far as Paul was concerned, once he cried out for deliverance, it was a done deal. Paul asked and then he thanked. Paul then stepped into the spiritual realm of Truth and began to communicate with God according to this Truth. The answer to his problem was so completely received by Paul that he could make this third startling declaration:

> *"So then with the mind I myself serve the law of God;*
> *but with the flesh the law of sin."*
> *(Rom 7:25b KJV)*

With his mind, Paul purposed to be a perfect, law-abiding citizen, even while with his flesh he would continue to serve the law of sin. As far as he is concerned, Paul has done all he can do: He acknowledged that his efforts worked against him, he looked for a Deliverer Who delivers from sin, he cried out for that deliverance, and then received the answer to that thing before it even manifested.

The Inner Sinner

In the second chapter of Genesis, Jehovah Elohim wanted fruit so He planted a seed and trusted that a tree would eventually spring forth and bear fruit in this natural realm. Jehovah Elohim waited and received. Paul wanted the fruit of holiness so he planted the dead seed of his old man, cried out for a Deliverer, and then trusted that deliverance would eventually come and bring the fruit of righteousness. Paul waited and received.

Manifestation Will Come

Consider Paul's words, *"I will serve the law of God with my mind even while I continue to serve the law of sin with my flesh."* Paul said this *after* he thanked God for Jesus Christ his Lord. When we listen to our present day Bible teachers we hear them say that after we receive our Deliverer we must try even harder to be good! Paul, after receiving deliverance, knew that fruit takes time to develop so he resigned himself to staying true to God in his mind while he waited out the manifestation in his body.

Paul will be content to serve the law of God with his mind even while his flesh continues to serve the law of sin. In this way, he has become dead to the law so that he can be married to Another; even to Him Who is raised from the dead, the Lord Jesus Christ.

We, as well, must become dead to the law so that we can be married to "Another", *"that we should bring forth fruit unto God."* Paul let go of his fleshly efforts and threw himself headlong into faith in Christ for the manifestation of the fruit of holiness. That is amazing.

Remember When?

Just as an interesting note, Paul, when speaking with the Galatians (which we will study at length in a later book) says this:

"Brethren, I beseech you, be as I am;
for I am as ye are: ye have not injured me at all.
Ye know how through infirmity of the flesh
I preached the gospel unto you at the first.
And my temptation which was in my flesh
ye despised not, nor rejected;
but received me as an angel of God,
even as Christ Jesus."
(Gal 4:12-14 KJV)

Evidently, when Paul first stepped out into this and was serving the law of God with his mind while with the flesh the law of sin, he didn't (or couldn't) hide it from those to whom he preached. He said that the Galatians **knew** how he preached the Gospel through the infirmity of his flesh. No, this was not an illness. Paul clearly refers to this infirmity as, *"my temptation which was in my flesh."*

Paul's followers would have no reason to treat him in a negative fashion if he simply had a health problem. Paul was praising them for the way they treated him even while he was manifesting sin. So, even though Paul was still manifesting sin, it was not being accounted to him because he was believing God to perform that which He had promised, *"Whereby are given unto us exceeding great and precious promises: that by these ye might be partakers of the divine nature, having escaped the corruption that is in the world through lust."* (2 Pet 1:4 KJV)

Paul was now a fruit bearer, not a law abider, and fruit takes time to develop. Paul was waiting for the supernatural manifestation of the promise of God and he wasn't going to let the "sin that dwelled in him" slow him down. Nothing could stop him -- not even sin -- from sharing this awesome Truth with a lost world. The Bible says that we abide with Him in our calling, we bear fruit when we abide, and we can ask whatever we wish when we abide. Paul was in the perfect place as he went forward in his calling, even while in sin.

And because Paul had to *remind* the Galatians about his former sinful condition, we rest assured that Paul received the manifestation for which he believed; he was obviously not preaching in an infirmity of his flesh anymore. Paul was reminding the Galatians of how he *preached* (past tense) the Gospel; not how he *presently* preaches it. Paul is encouraging these believers to be like he is because he is just like them and being just like them, he still boldly went forward even while manifesting sin. And, consequently, Paul eventually began to bear the very fruit of holiness. *Be as I am.*

In Summation

The first step in getting over sin is realizing that it cannot be done by our own power. We must climb down off the mountain of self-reliance. We have nothing to offer in the way of holiness, *"...for without me ye can do nothing...the flesh profits nothing."* There is a law at work that ushers in evil through our every good attempt.

Through recognition of our utter wretchedness, we enter the valley and cry out to God. Now, in order to ascend the mountain of

The Inner Sinner

God, we must separate ourselves from our hell dust sin nature and begin to serve the law of God with our mind even while we are yet serving the law of sin with our flesh. This is how one walks in faith.

The mountain of God is a faith mountain; therefore following Paul's example takes faith. Nothing outside of faith can step out in this way. Paul refused to look any further to himself; he left that mountain of self-reliance behind. All eyes are now on God and His divine deliverance through Jesus Christ. That is where it ended for him. That is exactly why Paul received such an acute manifestation of holiness that he had to remind the church in Galatia of how he used to be. This thing works.

The Rest of the Story

We have been taking in a lot of information that is somewhat new to us. After eighteen years of study, this Truth still reels me. We are now going to take a trip through the sixth chapter of Romans to learn more about Paul's all-important death to sin.

The Sin within

If, however, you are troubled about the power of sin,
and about the tendencies of your nature,
as you well may be, here is a promise for you.
Have faith in it, for it stands in that covenant of grace
which is ordered in all things and sure.
God, who cannot lie, has said in Ezekiel 36:26:
A new heart also will I give you, and a new spirit will I put
within you: and I will take away the stony heart out of your
flesh, and I will give you an heart of flesh.
You see, it is all "I will," and "I will."
"I will give," and "I will take away."
This is the royal style of the King of kings,
who is able to accomplish all His will.
No word of His shall ever fall to the ground.

The Lord knows right well that you cannot change
your own heart, and cannot cleanse your own nature;
but He also knows that He can do both.
He can cause the Ethiopian to change his skin,
and the leopard his spots.
Hear this, and be astonished:
He can create you a second time;
He can cause you to be born again.
This is a miracle of grace,
but the Holy Ghost will perform it.

Charles Spurgeon, All of Grace

For as in Adam all die,
even so in Christ shall all be made alive.
1 Corinthians 15:22

2

-- -- -- -- -- -- -- -- -- -- --

DEAD MEN WALKING

There are some things about Christianity that are what I like to call *imperatives*; the things that a Christian *must* do. Admittedly, there are a fair amount of these, but there is one that stands head and shoulders above the rest. In the words of Jesus, *"Ye must be born again."*

Yes, you are an axe murderer.

In getting to the bottom of things I have often asked people where they felt they were going to spend eternity. The reply almost always begins on this sentiment, "Well, it's not like I'm an axe murderer." O, contraire. We are all axe murderers. If we have broken the law in one place we are guilty of all. We are not measured according to how well we tamed our flesh; we are either guilty of all, or guilty of none. That is why it is imperative that we be born again. God does not give birth to imperfection.

Free to be Holy 31

More than a Catch Phrase

Over the years the expression "born again" has become little more than a Christian catch phrase to describe one who prays the prayer of salvation and becomes saved. As a matter of fact, for a long time, and even still in some circles, the term "born again" carries a negative connotation.

Those who refer to themselves as "born again" are considered to be overly religious and a little bit loopy. So controversial was this term that the following question was posed by Fred Barnes to both candidates at the First 1984 Mondale/Reagan Presidential Debate:

> *"Mr. President, would you describe your religious beliefs,*
> *noting particularly whether you consider yourself*
> *a born-again Christian...?"*

Why *in particular* would they need to know whether one would refer to himself as "born again"? There is no way they knew the real meaning of these words. They asked this question because they believed the catch phrase and knew that someone who professed to be a born again Christian was also admitting that he was overly religious.

The world sees this wording as a description of someone who takes his religion just a bit too far. The "born again" one is capable of anything – both good and bad – but especially odd. You'll have to keep one eye open with this guy.

Neither of these candidates was willing to admit they were "born again" though they both convincingly explained how they were "just fine and perfectly Christian" without being born again. If they had known what the words meant, they would have answered differently.

And so, the declaration of being born again is met with a roll of the eyes and an *"Oh, you're one of those..."* mumbled under the breath. Unfortunately, the world has had its impact on the church and many who have been born again still associate the idea of being "born again" with the idea of being avidly Christian. For the most part, the church does not seem to understand what it truly means to be born again.

Very simply, to be born again literally means to be *born again;* hence, when we are born again, we are actually born a second time. First we were born of our natural parents into the natural realm, next we are *born again* of our spiritual Parent into the spiritual realm.

Dead Men Walking

Ye Must be Born Again

Jesus said this very succinctly to Nicodemus:

"...Verily, verily, I say unto thee,
Except a man be born of water and of the Spirit,
he cannot enter into the kingdom of God.
That which is born of the flesh is flesh;
and that which is born of the Spirit is spirit.
Marvel not that I said unto thee,
Ye must be born again."
(John 3:5-7 KJV)

Jesus, very clearly, answered Nicodemus by saying *"Ye must be born again."* This was a very literal instruction. Jesus did not say to Nicodemus, *"Ye need to act like you are new"* or *"Ye must become zealous."* No, He said, *"Ye **must** be **born again**."* If we are to enter the kingdom of God, we must be born a second time.

We must be born of water (natural birth) and born of the Spirit (spiritual birth) if we are to enter the kingdom of God. Jesus said, *"That which is born of the flesh is flesh; and that which is born of the Spirit is spirit."* Jesus was not speaking about an attitude; He was speaking about two different beings, one born of the flesh, and one born of the Spirit.

Jesus is speaking of two different beings that are the result of two different births and two different parents, *"that which is born of the flesh is flesh and that which is born of the Spirit is spirit."* Jesus said, *"Marvel not"* because if we were to really think about what it is He is saying, we *would* marvel. He is telling us, *"Yes, it is marvelous, but it is also true. You can be born anew of the Spirit of God!"* We can be – yes – we *must* be born of the eternal Almighty God. What a privilege. If a true Christian who is born of God is asked whether he is born again, he must certainly answer with an emphatic, "Yes!"

So we see that the term "born again" does not exist simply to describe a Christian way of thinking or acting. Just as a new being exists when he is conceived of man, so a new being exists when he is conceived of the Holy Ghost through the born again experience. The moment one becomes born again, we find that the newborn person is very different from the one who had been born of natural parents.

From Bad to Good

Corruptible, or natural man can only give birth to hell-bent creatures, *"Behold, I was shapen in iniquity; and in sin did my mother conceive me." (Psa 51:5 KJV)*, whereas our incorruptible God gives birth to a perfect creature, *"Whosoever is born of God doth not commit sin; for his seed remaineth in him: and he cannot sin, because he is born of God." (1 John 3:9 KJV)* All things considered, it is a wonder we can walk upright.

The wording in these verses explicitly says that those who are born of man are innately sinful, while those who have been born of God are innately holy. So we see that there is a diametric difference between those who are born of man and those who have been born of the Spirit of God. Mankind is not a muddy conglomeration of good and bad; we are TWO. We do not have to root around in trash to find an element of God. He has made us brand new!

This is a marvelous thing, but do not marvel. We have been born of God and we have a new life. Many Christians do not know or understand this! If we are not born again, we are only born of man, thus locked into a deadly sin nature, and destined to spend our days sinning and our eternities in hell with no hope of being saved outside of this experience. To be born again is to escape the clutches of the sin nature by beginning a brand new life that does not include a sin nature.

When God looks at man, He sees one of two beings: Either He will see one who has been born of Him and is perfect, or He will see one who is born of man and is locked into sin and death. There is nothing in the middle.

We *must* be born again. This is not an option. If we want to enter God's salvation and God's spirit life, we must be born again. There is no other way in. That which is born of flesh is flesh and will always be flesh. That which is born of the Spirit, or *born again*, is spirit and is one with God eternally.

Had Mr. Mondale or Mr. Reagan known what it meant to truly be born again, they would have had a tougher time answering their question. If they had answered, "No", as they did in the debates, they would have willingly placed themselves outside of salvation. I believe at least one of these men would have admitted to being "born again" -- had he known what it meant.

Dead Men Walking

"Cover me -- I'm going back in"

Now when one becomes *born again*, that means that an entirely different person has come into existence; the same person cannot be born twice from the same source, *"Nicodemus saith unto him, How can a man be born when he is old? can he enter the second time into his mother's womb, and be born?" (John 3:4 KJV)* Of course a man cannot enter the womb a second time and be born. Even if he could, he would never find a woman who would allow it.

We will not be born again of *men*; we will be born anew of the Spirit of God. When a person is born of God he is born a new creature; Jesus did not tell Nicodemus that he needed to be *cleansed* again. Many believe that to be a Christian is to clean up the original man and make it behave more like something new. That is incorrect. Consider the words of Charles Spurgeon in *All of Grace*:

"To put the matter very simply—did you ever hear of Mr. Rowland Hill's illustration of the cat and the sow? I will give it in my own fashion, to illustrate our Saviour's expressive words—"Ye must be born again." Do you see that cat? What a cleanly creature she is! How cleverly she washes herself with her tongue and her paws! It is quite a pretty sight! Did you ever see a sow do that? No, you never did. It is contrary to its nature. It prefers to wallow in the mire. Go and teach a sow to wash itself, and see how little success you would gain. It would be a great sanitary improvement if swine would be clean. Teach them to wash and clean themselves as the cat has been doing! Useless task. You may by force wash that sow, but it hastens to the mire, and is soon as foul as ever. The only way in which you can get a sow to wash itself is to transform it into a cat; then it will wash and be clean, but not till then! Suppose that transformation to be accomplished, and then what was difficult or impossible is easy enough; the swine will henceforth be fit for your parlor and your hearth-rug. So it is with an ungodly man; you cannot force him to do what a renewed man does most willingly; you may teach him, and set him a good example, but he cannot learn the art of holiness, for he has no mind to it; his nature leads him another way. When the Lord makes a new man of him, then all things wear a different aspect."

The apostle Paul tells us, *"Therefore if any man be in Christ, **he is a new creature**: old things are passed away; behold, all things are become new." (2 Cor 5:17 KJV emphasis mine.)* The reason all things become new is because a new baby is a new baby; we are born first of man and then born *again* of God.

Nicodemus, the physical man, who stood before Jesus, was already born of a human parent and could not be born of a human parent a second time. If there is to be a second birth, there must also be a second "Parent." Two separate parents gave birth to two separate beings. Both of these beings inhabit the same natural body. And this is where we find one of the greatest mysteries of God.

Back in the Image

Look what Paul says about these two entities:

> *"Lie not one to another, seeing that ye have put off the old*
> *man with his deeds; And have put on the new man,*
> *which is renewed in knowledge*
> *after the image of him that created him:"*
> *(Col 3:9-10 KJV)*

We have put off the sinful old man who was born of man, and have put on the new man *"which is renewed in knowledge after the image of Him that created him."* Hmmm. This new man is renewed, or brought back to the image of Elohim Who created him in the spiritual realm to begin with: Spiritual, natural, spiritual.

Elohim created man in His image in the spiritual realm, Jehovah Elohim formed man to be hell bent in the natural realm, now through Christ, man has been invited to be born back into the spiritual realm as a new man who is now exactly according to how he was created to begin with: The very image of God! Surely a man with a sin nature is not in the image of God! The new man *is* created in this very image. We have been born back into the original image of God from creation. This is where God knew us first and this is where He receives us forever. Everything has its beginning and finds its end in the spiritual realm. This natural life is no more than a camping trip away from our original home (1Pet 1:14).

This is why, in the first chapter of Genesis, Elohim could look at His created man and say, "Behold, it is very good." This was no hell bent creature He was referring to. God would not call the sin nature "very good". Elohim created us perfect, it was Jehovah Elohim Who later formed us with a sin nature in the natural realm. Now the Spirit of God is offering to birth us back into the spiritual realm where we can be perfect again. The logic of this thing is spellbinding.

Dead Men Walking

And Baby makes Two

Paul makes it clear there are two men: The old man with his deeds and the new man who, amazingly, is after the image of God. The old man was *"conceived in sin and shapen in iniquity"* and the new man is born of God and His seed remains in him and he cannot sin because he is perfectly born of God: Two men.

According to the Greek definition, to "put off" the old man means to "sink out of, unclothe, separate and depart from oneself." To "put on" the new man means to "sink into, and clothe oneself." Paul is not offering us the option of remaining two entities; one of them has to go. We cannot wear two different kinds of clothing at once unless we are a punk rocker. We can either put on the one outfit or the other. Paul would have us to slide out of our death suit and clothe ourselves with the new man who was born of God.

We mistakenly believe that to "put off the old man" means to beat him into submission. A lovely thought, but again, an impossible task. The only way we can "put off the old man" is to separate ourselves from him in the exact same way Paul separated himself from his old man in the seventh chapter of Romans. The same Paul who wrote those words wrote these words. Paul taught us by dragging us through this death with him. If he was willing to throw himself out there for us, we must at least learn from his example.

Die Hard

So we see that although this born again experience offers a great reward, we are left with the task of putting off the old man, *"put off the old man with his deeds."* This is easier said than done -- though it is doable. Thankfully, the apostle Paul rides this subject like a mule. He knew that learning to die was a deeply spiritual concept that could not be easily understood, so he did his level best to help us through it.

It is due to its abstract quality that putting off the old man and putting on the new man can be a difficult spiritual discipline to appropriate. Over the years we have become a lazy people who rely on the studies of others as our sole provision of Godly wisdom. We have paid a high price for this. The Holy Spirit is the best Teacher for any concept, but especially so when we seek to understand the idea of spiritual death. You will learn the concepts of dying here but you will only understand them as the Spirit of God quickens them to your heart. He will surely be found by those who diligently seek Him.

Disillusioned:

Attempting to Live without Dying

Because the church proper struggles to understand spiritual death, we are left a confused and disillusioned body. Many try to live the Christian life without ever putting off the old man. These whole-heartedly agree with Paul's assertion, *"For that which I do I allow not: for what I would, that do I not; but what I hate, that do I." (Rom 7:15 KJV)* Unfortunately, this is generally where the buck stops. These people do not understand their death to sin and their born again creature. Because they have not separated themselves from their sin, they tend to live in a vicious cycle of trying, failing, repenting, and trying ever harder.

However, the two entities lie naked before us in this verse: I do, yet I allow not; I would, yet I do not; I hate, yet I do. This is why Paul said, *"For I know that in me (that is, in my flesh,) dwelleth no good thing: for to will is present with me; but how to perform that which is good I find not." (Rom 7:18 KJV)* Paul spoke of his "flesh" as though it was a separate entity from his new self, *"something in me is no good."*

This spiritual aspect is so acute in Paul that he saw his "new man" as an actual prisoner of the "old man", *"For I delight in the law of God after the inward man: But I see another law in my members, warring against the law of my mind, and bringing me into captivity to the law of sin which is in my members." (Rom 7:22-23 KJV emphasis mine)* The new Paul was losing against the old Paul. However, Paul did not stop here; he moved on in his knowledge. Paul was able to shift himself from this hopeless hell-bent state into freedom because of what he knew and wrote earlier in this very letter to the Romans. Paul knew how to die.

It's a Spiritual Thing

It is not that we must figure out a way to die; it is that we must figure out that we are already dead and then appropriate that death:

> *"Wherefore, as by one man sin entered into the world, and death by sin; and so death passed upon all men, for that all have sinned:" (Rom 5:12 KJV)*

Sin entered the world through Adam, and death was a result of this sin. This death passed on to all men because sin passed on to all men. Paul is not here referring to physical death, as physical death is only a natural manifestation of spiritual death. We are not dying naturally because Adam sinned; we are dying naturally because we first died spiritually in sin. Whatever happens in the spiritual realm manifests in the natural realm. In Adam we died spiritually and our natural bodies will bear this out.

Spiritual death passed to all men because all have sinned. The man who is only born of man will suffer the manifestation of his spiritual death in hell because in Adam all have already died. The old man with his sin nature is already dead. The minute we are born into the natural realm we begin to manifest this natural death.

Every day that we are here it can be medically said that we are dying. Our skin cells die and slough from our bodies. Do you think skin cells will die in eternity? Of course not. Just the fact that we are shedding these cells from the moment we are born proves that we are living in a body that is dying. Spiritual death is the penalty for sin and natural death is the manifestation of that spiritual death. So we must understand that the moment we were born naturally, we were born into death. We were spiritually killed by sin before we ever saw the light of day. Our natural bodies will bear this out.

This sounds like bad news, but it is really very good news. When Adam ate of the forbidden fruit, spiritual death was brought into all of hell-bent humanity, *"I was shapen in iniquity and in sin did my mother conceive me."* It was over for the old man before he ever made it out of the birth canal. God fixed it so that the sin nature would absolutely be blotted out forever through eternal death, *"for in the day that thou eatest thereof thou shalt surely die."* In the same moment that God instituted sin, He eradicated it. God has had this thing figured out right from the beginning.

Because we have been brainwashed to believe that Adam's disobedience was an evil thing, we also see his ensuing death as a bad situation. However, Adam's spiritual death was the best thing that could have happened to him. Adam's death was prerequisite to his new life. Adam was a hell-bent creature and in order for a new creature to be born, the hell-bent creature had to die.

Spiritual Death

We know that God was referring to a spiritual death because of His wording, *"in the day that you eat thereof...ye shall surely die."* Adam did not physically die in the day that he ate that fruit; Adam went on to physically live for hundreds of years.

However, God had said that in the *day* Adam ate, he would *surely* die. What this means is that in the day that Adam ate that fruit he surely *did* die; he simply died spiritually. Adam's disobedience killed his hell-bent flesh in the only way it *could* be killed: Spiritually. Now it will be manifested in the natural. The old man is dead in the spiritual realm and this is manifesting in the natural realm. The new man is born anew in the spiritual realm and this will also begin to manifest in the natural realm.

A Lineage of Sons

I would like to show you why I believe Adam was "born again" in the only way one *could* be born again under the Old Testament. This is important because it shows that God's plan worked from Adam right on up to the present.

No one was referred to as the "son of God" in the Old Testament except Jesus when Nebuchadnezzar saw Him in the burning fiery furnace. Twice the "*sons* of God" are referred to in the Old Testament; however, these are referring to demons (Gen 6 & Job 1). Never is a person given the title "son of God" in the Old Testament.

However, when we are given the lineage of Jesus Christ, God puts Himself as the final "Father" of Adam as He calls him the "son of God", *"Which was the son of Enos, which was the son of Seth, which was the son of **Adam, which was the son of God.**" (Luke 3:38 KJV emphasis mine.)*

The fact that Adam was the son of God is not written expressly in the original text. The original Greek text reads like this: *"And Jesus himself began to be about thirty years of age, being (as was supposed) **the son** of Joseph, which **was** of Heli, which **was** of Matthat, which **was** of Levi, which **was** of Melchias...which **was** of Seth, which **was** of Adam, which **was** of God."*

The list began with the words *"...which was the son of..."* and then continued, omitting the words *"the son"*: "Which was *of* so-and-so, which was *of* so-and-so, which was *of* so-and-so...". Therefore, we can make the safe assumption that all names following are assumed to be *"**the sons** of so-and-so."*

God would not have placed Himself in this list if He did not consider Himself the actual Father of Adam. It would have been sufficient to simply end the genealogy at Adam -- unless, God was trying to get a message across. Things are not written in the Bible to take up space; God wanted us to be aware of the fact that He considered Adam His son. From this we can assume that Adam was born again.

No Son; no sons

My point is this: The reason no one could be called the son of God in the Old Testament is because Jesus had not yet been born into the earth as the Son of God. Jesus is called the *Firstborn* among many brethren. As a matter of fact, up until His death and resurrection, Jesus is referred to as the *Only* Begotten Son of God. Until Jesus was born, no one was a son of God in this natural realm.

So why does our genealogy in Luke call Adam the son of God? Because the book of Luke was written after the death and resurrection of the Messiah, and the crucifixion worked backward as efficiently as it works forward (Heb 9:15). The moment God sacrificed an animal for the purpose of making "clothing" for Adam and Eve in the Garden of Eden, their sonship through Christ was a done deal in the spiritual realm. Once Jesus shed His blood and died in the natural realm, Adam became a manifested son of God and could be called thusly in the genealogy of Christ.

The wording of our Messianic genealogy shows the fulfillment of God's purpose of sonship in Adam according to the eighth chapter of Romans:

> *"For the creature was made subject to vanity,*
> *not willingly, but by reason of him who hath subjected the*
> *same in hope, Because the creature itself also shall be*
> *delivered from the bondage of corruption*
> *into the glorious liberty of the **children** of God."*
> *(Rom 8:20-21 KJV)*

God did not treat Adam any differently than anyone else. If the creature was made subject to vanity so that he could be delivered into sonship, then Adam was made subject to vanity so that he could be delivered into sonship. Adam began as a *creation* of God in the spiritual realm, went on to become a *formation* of God in the natural realm, and finally his standing culminated in the death and resurrection of Christ by becoming a *son of God* in every sense just as God had purposed:

> *"Therefore as by the offence of one*
> *judgment came upon all men to condemnation;*

> *even so by the righteousness of one the free gift came*
> *upon **all men** unto justification of life."*
> *(Rom 5:18 KJV)*

The free gift came upon all men; that included Adam. And what was this free gift?

> *"But as many as received him, to them gave he power to become the sons of God, even to them that believe on his name:" (John 1:12 KJV).*

Life, Death, Life

Adam was alive just as Paul, *"For I was alive without the law once…"* and then, like Paul, he sinned, died, and brought death into all of mankind, *"…but when the commandment came, sin revived, and I died."* Finally, Adam and Paul were resurrected back into life through the death of Christ. All of mankind is spiritually dead in Adam and, therefore, all need to be born again in Christ. From this we know that it is not that we need to die; it is that we need to recognize that our hell-bent creature is already dead in Adam and we are made alive again through Christ, *"For as in Adam all die, even so in Christ shall all be made alive." (1 Cor 15:22 KJV)*

Since the old man with his body of sin is dead, we need a new man and a new body. Otherwise we will have no body in heaven, *"…we long for the day when we will put on our heavenly bodies like new clothing." (2 Cor 5:2 NLT)* When we are given new incorruptible bodies in eternity, they will be nothing more than a physical manifestation of our spiritual born again creature; we will have manifested perfect bodies in heaven only after we have been born spiritually of a perfect God on earth.

This is why those who have never been born of God on earth will not have a spiritually alive body in eternity. Those who have never been born again have nothing but a physical body that has been condemned to hell and death. A thing cannot manifest in the natural realm until it has first gained truth in the spiritual realm.

At the end of the day, we must accept the fact that we are dead men walking and work from this premise. It is not our responsibility to die, as sin took care of that for us. It is our responsibility to appropriate this death so that we can go on to live our new life in Christ. And that is where the next chapter picks up.

3

--- --- --- --- --- --- --- --- --- --- ---

DEATH
BECOMES YOU

In this chapter we are going to learn how to walk in our spiritual death to sin. In taking this crucial step, all conventional methods must be set aside. Our death is absolutely real in the spiritual realm and it absolutely determines our final outcome. It is only when we appropriate our present death that we can begin to appropriate our new life.

We remember that it is perfectly okay that we are dead in sin. Our death is just as necessary to our resurrection life as the death of Christ was necessary to His resurrection life. Spiritual death was orchestrated by God, carried out by Adam, and remains an integral part of humanity. To be ignorant of our spiritual death is to miss an essential step in our pursuit of true holiness. We must take the apostle Paul's lead and learn to deal properly with this death.

Dear friend,

Salvation would be a sadly incomplete affair
if it did not deal with this part of our ruined estate.
We want to be purified as well as pardoned.
Justification without sanctification
would not be salvation at all.
It would call the leper clean,
and leave him to die of his disease;
it would forgive the rebellion
and allow the rebel to remain an enemy to his king.
It would remove the consequences
but overlook the cause,
and this would leave an endless and hopeless task before us.
It would stop the stream for a time,
but leave an open fountain of defilement,
which would sooner or later break forth with increased power.
Remember that the Lord Jesus
came to take away sin in three ways;
He came to remove the penalty of sin,
the power of sin, and, at last, the presence of sin.
At once you may reach to the second part—
the power of sin may immediately be broken;
and so you will be on the road to the third,
namely, the removal of the presence of sin.
"We know that he was manifested to take away our sins."

Charles Spurgeon, All of Grace

Death Becomes You

Sin hath Reigned unto Death

Our study will begin in the fifth and continue through the sixth chapters of Romans. Paul begins by taking us back to the Garden of Eden where everything began:

> *"Therefore, just as sin came into the world through one man, and death through sin, and so death spread to all men because all sinned—for sin indeed was in the world before the law was given, but sin is not counted where there is no law. Yet death reigned from Adam to Moses, even over those whose sinning was not like the transgression of Adam, who was a type of the one who was to come."*
> *(Rom 5:12-14 ESV)*

Sin came into the world through Adam and then death spread to all men simply because all men were just as prone to sin as was Adam, *"...death spread to all men because all sinned."* We do not all have sin because Adam sinned; rather, we all have sin because we all have been formed just as Adam was formed, therefore we will all behave as Adam behaved. Adam was simply the prototype.

These verses say that Adam was a type of Christ (the One Who was to come). I believe Adam was a "type" because he was the vessel God used to bring sin into the world the way Jesus was the Vessel God used to take sin out of the world, *"Behold the Lamb of God, which taketh away the sin of the world." (John 1:29 KJV)* God could not sin; man was needed for this. Man could not deliver from sin; God was needed for this. God wanted the element of evil without the element of bondage; He accomplished this through the blending of God and man. Our type was Adam and as surely as he brought sin into the world, Jesus took it out.

Paul goes on to show us how the sin of Adam was a good thing in that it instigated something quite wonderful:

> *"But the free gift is not like the trespass.*
> *For if many died through one man's trespass, much more have the grace of God and the free gift by the grace of that one man Jesus Christ abounded for many.*
> *And the free gift is not like the result of that one man's sin.*
> *For the judgment following one trespass brought*

*condemnation, but the free gift following many trespasses
brought justification." (Rom 5:15-16 ESV)*

The free gift we have received is not like Adam's sin. Many, indeed, *all* have died through Adam's sin, but the grace of God and the free gift through Jesus abounded for many. Adam's sin killed all but the gift through Jesus brought justification, though there were many sins. So we see that Paul is showing us the good news in all of this. He sums up his thoughts in this vein:

> *"If, because of one man's trespass, death reigned through
> that one man, much more will those who receive the
> abundance of grace and the free gift of righteousness reign
> in life through the one man Jesus Christ. Therefore, as one
> trespass led to condemnation for all men, so one act of
> righteousness leads to justification and life for all men.
> For as by the one man's disobedience the many were made
> sinners, so by the one man's obedience the many will be
> made righteous." (Rom 5:17-19 ESV)*

Paul clearly states that death reigned through Adam and that the abundance of grace and the free gift of righteousness reigns in life through Christ. And, just as one sin led to the condemnation of all men, so one act of righteousness leads to justification and life. Now, just as Adam's disobedience made many sinners, through Jesus' obedience many will be made abundantly righteous.

What we see here is a lot of parallelism. Death is continually associated with Adam while life is continually associated with Jesus. Everyone is ready to jump into our resurrection life, but God began in Adam with death and He will work with us likewise. We must pass through death to get to life. We cannot get around this aspect of death. We must understand that the moment Adam consumed that fruit death was brought into humanity through sin. If we do not take part in this death, we cannot reap its benefits. Death is prerequisite to life; if we want to learn to live, we must first learn to die.

The Tool of the Law

Paul is about to show us the role the law played in the lives of Adam and Eve:

Death Becomes You

"Moreover the law entered, that the offence might abound.
But where sin abounded, grace did much more abound:
That as sin hath reigned unto death,
even so might grace reign through righteousness unto
eternal life by Jesus Christ our Lord."
(Rom 5:20-21 KJV)

We know that Paul is here referring to the original law given to Adam and Eve because Paul has been referring to Adam's disobedience to this law for the last several verses. So we see that God gave Adam a law so that *Adam's* sin would abound. Adam was naked, being formed of hell dust, and he needed a law to awaken him to this fact. Why was this so important? Because where sin abounded, grace did much more abound. In other words, God instigated a problem through Adam that He had already solved through Christ in a way that went well beyond what was even possible before sin entered the picture: Where sin abounded, grace *much more abounded.* God increased humans through sin and death.

This is the premise from which we must work: The law entered so that sin would abound. God gave Adam a law and sin abounded. The very name of the tree that contained the forbidden fruit exposes the fact that sin was destined -- not to just exist -- but to abound: The Tree of the Knowledge of Good and Evil. This tree did not teach a man how to steal; it taught a man how to steal a million different ways. This was the knowledge of *all* good and evil.

The law did not come to make man good; it came so that sin would abound, *"The sting of death is sin; and the strength of sin is the law." (1 Cor 15:56 KJV)* Listen to the wording of this verse! The sting of death is sin. Death is the result of sin. God knew this when He gave man the capacity to sin. God knew that sin ended in death. Add to this, *"the strength of sin is the law."* The strength of sin is the Law! Sin's beginning is the law and sin's end is death. God knew this before He even made man. God knew that if he gave man a law, sin would be strengthened, *"the strength of sin is the law."* God provided Adam the perfect ingredients to perform sin: A sin nature and a law.

The whole point of any law, from the forbidden fruit to the Mosaic Law, was to entice sin out in the open where God could get a good shot at it. God had already removed the power of sin before the first sin was committed. We cannot do anything about sin except receive the Truth and let it set us free. It is only when we understand that we have lost the battle against sin that we are in a position to win the battle against sin. The law works endlessly to bring us into this realization.

Although we are hell bent toward sin we can still rejoice. Paul tells us that where sin abounds, grace much more abounds. It is for this reason that abounding sin is not a problem; God's answer far outdistances the problem of sin. God purposes not to *tolerate* sin, but to increase us through sin. It is **where** sin abounds that grace much more abounds. In order for grace to *more* abound, sin must first abound. We must not allow our sin to intimidate us; it is our bridge to grace.

Not just Unmerited Favor

So what is this grace? Normally when we think of grace, we think of the concept of unmerited favor. But, God's grace is all that and more. The Greek word for grace is *charis,* which *does* mean unmerited favor, but it also has this meaning: *the divine influence upon the heart, and its reflection in the life.*

To influence a thing is to change it. When we say that television has influenced society, we are also saying that it has *changed* society. When we say a teacher influenced us, we are saying their teachings have somehow changed us. So if grace is a divine *influence* upon our hearts then we must see that grace divinely *changes* our hearts. But that is not all. Grace does not stop at making us *think* differently or *feel* differently; grace changes our hearts in such a way that this change is *reflected in our lives*. To reflect means to give an indication. When God's grace is working, we will be able to look at our lives and see that a miraculous change is indeed taking place.

So, when the Bible says, *"Where sin abounded did grace much more abound"*, it is actually saying "When sin reaches its pinnacle, God's grace will far outdistance sin as it divinely changes our hearts to the extent that our very manifested lives will give indication of that change."

It was necessary for sin to become so entirely out of control that we would send up the white flag of surrender. In <u>Mere Christianity</u>, C.S. Lewis refers to this practice as "throwing up the sponge." When we come to the end of our striving and embrace our need for grace, grace will abound. So the law entered that the offence may abound, and where sin abounded, grace did much more abound.

Death Becomes You

Now we have come to a pivotal place in the Scriptures. Paul has just explained to the believers in Rome that the law was used by God to cause sin to abound. God bristled the sin nature to the surface through the law so that man would be forced to give up his own efforts, embrace his death, and begin to live by an amazing life-changing grace.

If we are to accept this way of thinking, a valid question needs to be addressed. Romans chapter six opens by posing this question:

> *"What shall we say then? Shall we continue in sin,
> that grace may abound?" (Rom 6:1 KJV)*

If sin causes grace and grace causes true repentance, which subsequently leads to death and then life, then shouldn't we sin more so that we can get more of this grace? Well that is a good question.

Embracing Death

The apostle Paul answers this question with another question, *"God forbid. How shall we, that are dead to sin, live any longer therein? (Rom 6:2 KJV)* Paul informs us that this is not about whether or not we are to sin; this is about whether or not we are sinners. Paul asks, "How can those who are dead to sin continue to live in sin? How is that even possible?" In the seventh chapter of Romans we watched Paul come to the realization that he was dead in sin. Then we watched him cry out for his Savior. Then we watched Paul begin to act as though he was dead to sin even while he continued to manifest sin. Paul walked in the spiritual reality of his death to sin well before he ever walked in the manifestation of it.

To ask Paul if it is a good thing to sin is to ask Paul if it is a good thing to let pigs fly. How can a wingless pig fly? We need not worry whether or not we should *let* pigs fly because a pig couldn't fly if he tried. With this thought in mind, it should not matter to us whether or not it is a good thing to sin because perfect beings are not *able* to sin. How can a perfect being sin? We need not worry about sinning because, *"Whosoever is born of God doth not commit sin; for his seed remaineth in him: and he cannot sin, because he is born of God." (1 John 3:9 KJV)* According to John, the act of sinning is not possible for those who have been born of God. <u>That</u> is the thought that must become predominant in our minds. Thinking of sin will only cause us to sin all the more, *"As a man thinkest in his heart, so is he."*

Paul knew he was born of the Spirit of God and that his old man was dead, therefore, it was no longer possible for him to sin. He knew that there could not be two of him; there must either be the one or the other. Paul identified with the new man and he did this, not by trying hard to be good, but by *"putting on the new man, which after God is created in righteousness and true holiness." (Eph 4:24 KJV)*

How do we do this? How do we "put off" the old man and "put on" the new? It is difficult to put into words how to employ this spiritual exercise. The very first step is in becoming completely convinced that we are indeed dead to sin. Once we wrap our brains around this Truth, we must continually think upon it. The Bible makes an iron clad case for our very true death. What Paul is about to share with us in the sixth chapter of Romans absolutely closes the lid on the subject. Knowing that we are dead to sin is the very first step to putting off the old man.

The second step is equally important. We must use our mouths to begin to inhabit this land. Paul is a master at speaking spiritual realities as though they were already manifested facts. That is why in this sixth chapter of Romans Paul is about to, not so much *tell* us, but *show* us how to use our mouth to instigate the manifestation of our death to sin.

Paul does this by using a technique he taught the church of Corinth. If we don't understand his method, we will miss Paul's message. I use Paul's method all day, every day. The moment I stop using it, I begin to regress. So before we continue with Paul's example in this sixth chapter of Romans, we are going to go to the tenth chapter of the book of Second Corinthians to learn the method of Paul's technique. This method is what I affectionately refer to as:

Flaying the Devil

Lands are always involved in warfare. The Bible says that we have everything we need in heavenly places. This is referring to the spiritual realm. We must "inhabit" these heavenly places. Death to sin is a heavenly place. Holiness is a heavenly place. We must take our places just as the children of Israel had to take their places in the Promised Land. The land of Canaan *spiritually* belonged to Abraham's descendents long before his actual descendents took it through warfare. The Canaanites legally owned the land but the Israelites spiritually owned it and spiritual ownership took precedence over legal ownership. Satan legally owns our blessings because of sin but we spiritually own them because of the death of

Death Becomes You

Christ. The Israelites, being our natural example, warred in the natural realm and gained their spiritual lands in the natural realm. We must use that natural example to help us to do the same. We must war in the spiritual realm in order to secure our "lands" in the natural.

Paul gives us the Biblical battle plan for taking spiritual lands, *"For though we walk in the flesh, we do not war after the flesh:" (2Cor 10:3).* Paul is in warfare and the land of holiness is at stake. Because this is spiritual warfare, Paul does not fight the way a natural man would fight. A natural man would use a natural weapon to conquer a natural land; a spiritual man uses a spiritual weapon to conquer a spiritual land, *"(For the weapons of our warfare are not carnal, but mighty through God to the pulling down of strong holds;)" (2Cor 10:4).* Our weapons are not worldly weapons; they are spiritual weapons that are mighty, or powerful.

These powerful weapons that we have through God, will pull down our strong holds. We were bent toward sin and that is what Satan uses to forge strongholds in our life. Everyone has to deal with strongholds. One person does not care one way or another about food while another is addicted to it. One is not prone to gossip while another can't seem to stop. One has a positive attitude while another struggles futilely against a sour disposition. A stronghold is anything that seems to have built an inescapable fortress in our lives. We need not despair; we have weapons that we can use against these strongholds! These weapons are not carnal or weakened by sin; they are mighty through God to the pulling down of these strongholds. These weapons work. So, what are these weapons?

The Weapon of our Warfare

In describing the armor that is to be worn by the Christian warrior in the sixth chapter of Ephesians, Paul speaks of only one weapon; *"...the sword of the Spirit which is the Word of God..." (Eph 6:17)* When we picture a man dressed in armor, we do not picture him with many weapons; we picture him clothed from head to toe in a metallic covering while he wields just one weapon. It only takes one weapon to kill.

Our deadly weapon is the Sword of the Spirit, which is the Word of God. This is the mighty weapon that we must use to pull down the strongholds of sin. So we do not use our fleshly strength to fight our battle against sin; we use the Word of God. That means that when the sin nature rears its ugly head, rather than putting our nose to the grindstone to try to push our flesh harder, we must pick up our sword, (which is what the Word of God says concerning sin), and begin to use it! The Bible says that we are dead to sin and alive to God. The Bible does not lie. We must speak these words in the face of sin, thereby using our one weapon: The Sword of the Spirit. A sword does not kill on its own; it needs to be picked up and used.

"And out of his Mouth

Went a Sharp Two-edged Sword"

The Sword of the Spirit is a spiritual weapon and it comes with its own special attributes. Carnal weapons are carried in the hand -- not so with this spiritual weapon. It is not enough to simply *possess* the Sword of the Spirit. Consider the description of Jesus who was our Forerunner, *"...and out of his mouth went a sharp twoedged sword..." (Rev 1:16)*. The Sword of the Spirit came out of Jesus' mouth, which means the Word of God came out of His mouth. As Jesus spoke the Words of God, they were sharp and they were double edged; they cut between two things. We see how Jesus wars with His tongue as He speaks the Word of God to the church of Pergamos:

> *"...These things saith he which hath the sharp sword with*
> *two edges; I know thy works...But I have a few things*
> *against thee...Repent; or else I will come unto thee quickly,*
> *and will fight against them with the sword of my mouth."*
> *(Rev 2:12-14&16 KJV)*

Jesus fought His battles with the sword of His mouth; therefore, we must fight our battles with the sword of our mouth, which is exactly what Paul is teaching us to do. The Sword of the Spirit, which is the Word of God on our tongue, is the only weapon we have in our war against sin. If we do not use this weapon, we will not win the battle.

Oh, it Cuts like a Knife and it Feels so Right

Now let us see exactly how this sharp, two-edged sword operates, *"For the word of God is quick, and powerful, and sharper than any twoedged sword, piercing even to the dividing asunder of soul and spirit, and of the joints and marrow, and is a discerner of the thoughts and intents of the heart." (Heb 4:12 KJV)* The Sword of the Spirit makes very important cuts. The blade, inserted between two things, will cut and divide. This is the Sword's only job.

Death Becomes You

Soul and Spirit

First of all, we see that the Word of God divides between the **soul** and the **spirit**. This is an important division. It is the spirit portion of a man that is born again and perfect. The soul of the man, which is made up of his mind, will, and emotions, is not always going to be perfectly in line with the spirit until *"corruption has put on incorruption"* and we are taken to our final home. While we remain on earth, the soul will always be the "X" factor in our equation. We know that the old man is sinful and dead and the new man is perfect and alive, however, the *soul*, made up of our mind, will, and emotions, hangs in the balance.

Our mind is comprised of our thoughts, our will is made up of our desires, and our emotions are composed of our feelings. Although our spirits are perfect due to the fact that we were spiritually birthed by God, our thoughts will dart here and there, our desires will change from time to time, and our feelings will surely fluctuate.

This is why the Sword of the Spirit is handy in that it makes a distinction between the soul and the spirit: The Word of God is only concerned about what is true in the spiritual realm. When we use it, it will not take into consideration what we may desire, what we may think, or how we may feel. The Sword of the Spirit cuts all that out and only concerns itself with the spiritual Truths that have been received by faith and spoken. When we purposely take the Word of God and speak it in the face of sin regardless of what we think, desire, or feel, it will make the proper division and cut accordingly to bring down those strongholds.

That is why when we experience a *thought* to sin, we use the Sword of the Spirit, the Word of God, and it divides the thought from the Word we are speaking. When we *desire* to sin, we use the Sword of the Spirit, the Word of God, and it divides the desire from the Word we are speaking. When we *feel* like sinning, we use the Sword of the Spirit, the Word of God, and it divides the feelings from the Word we are speaking. Once that Sword divides the things of the soul from the things of the spirit, the Word can go forth, unencumbered, to break down those strongholds.

This is where a man exercises his free will. We are left to make the choice of whether we are going to fight for our land or learn to live outside of it. If we want to inhabit the land of holiness, we must not cower in the face of sin; we must pick up our weapon in the face of sin!

Joints and Marrow

Our verse from Hebrews says that the Sword of the Spirit also divides between the joints and the marrow. The joints are a part of the vessel of the physical body; it is the marrow within the joint that contains the life. The Sword of the Spirit will divide between the vessel (our body) and the creative life (new creature in Christ) that is within the vessel. The Sword of the Spirit will cut between the motions of the flesh and the new life that was birthed into us, *"with my mind I will serve the law of God while with my flesh the law of sin."* Thank You God! The Sword divides and conquers!

Thoughts and Intentions

Finally, the Sword of the Spirit divides between the thoughts and intents of the heart. Randy Travis wrote a song that contained the following lyrics, *"I hear tell the road to hell is paved with good intentions."* That may be true for the world, but it is not true for the Christian. We can have evil thoughts and good intents all the way to heaven.

We watched Paul go through this, *"I hate the very things I do."* Paul's behavior went one way while his intent went another. This word "intent" means moral understanding. Our thoughts do not always contain moral understanding; however, our intents as a Christian do, as we have been given new hearts in which the Word of God has been inscribed. Christians have every intention of doing the right thing. It is the carrying out of this task that proves difficult. The Sword of the Spirit divides between these two and considers the intent of the heart. What a wonderful God.

Jesus had evil thoughts. If, as it says in Hebrews, Jesus was tempted in all ways just as we were, then when the devil came to Him in the wilderness, he came to His mind with thoughts. These were evil thoughts. What did Jesus do? He pulled out the Sword of the Spirit and began to fight with His tongue. This Sword divided between the evil thoughts and the intents of His heart and delivered our Lord from the temptation of the devil.

If Jesus thought it necessary to speak the Word of God in the face of temptation, so must we. Jesus did not begin to apologize to God for thinking about abusing His gifts, committing suicide, and worshipping Satan. Jesus didn't even consider these thoughts outside of how they looked in the light of God's Word. Jesus used the Sword of the Spirit and divided His devilish thoughts from the intents of His heart.

I knew a woman who stayed away from the Lord for several years because she had a thought to denounce Christ! She took ownership of that thought and allowed this evil thought to rule her life. She needed the Sword of the Spirit to divide between that devilish thought and the true intent of her heart.

The Sword of the Spirit, which is the Word of God, will divide between the soul and the spirit, the joints and the marrow, and the thoughts and intents of the heart. The order of this verse is precise; *soul, joints, thoughts*, then, *spirit, marrow, and intents of the heart*. The first group has no life while the second group has Spirit life. We began as one, we became two, and now we must be one again. We must divide the dead man from the new man with the Sword of the Spirit.

Take the Sword

Being what it is, it is downright shameful that our sword so often remains sheathed at our side. What we *normally* do when the sin nature rears its ugly head is ignore the Sword of the Spirit, which is the Word of God, and grab the lying sword of the devil and begin to stab ourselves in the chest.

Let me show you what I mean. Let's consider a Christian who is addicted to obsessive gossiping. She has prayed about this sin and received forgiveness and cleansing and then she steps out in faith. However, while visiting a friend she falls to the temptation to gossip. On her way home the devil begins to accuse her of her sin. Many times Christians respond to these satanic accusations by orally stabbing themselves to death:

> "I am such a loser! I swear...I will never get over this! It is just too hard. I don't know how I can call myself a Christian. If I don't stop doing this, God will never be able to bless me.

> "I don't know what to do! This is crazy. Someone is going to hear something I have said and I am going to get called out on the carpet; I just know it! Why am I such a bad person? If people knew who I really was they would hate me. I swear, I will never get it right."

And he Spoke with a Forked Tongue

What we must understand is that those words are Satan's words. That is exactly what *he* says about us. They are *his* "swords". This is what we must notice about the devil: He is a serpent and he has a serpentine tongue. Out of the mouth of Jesus comes a sharp *two-edged* sword, but out of the mouth of the serpent comes a *forked* tongue. Although the Sword of the Spirit *divides* Truth from lies, the *forked tongue of the serpent <u>combines</u> truth and lies*. When Satan opens his mouth, truths mixed with lies come pouring out. This is what makes the devil so dangerous.

A snake has an organ in the roof of its mouth that helps him smell. By darting his forked tongue, he picks up bits of dust and brings them to this organ where he "tastes" them to find a trail of prey. When he is finished testing this dust, he clears his palate for more, thus he swallows, or "eats the dust" just as he was cursed to do. And, as usual, this has a spiritual parallel.

Using his forked tongue, Satan looks for our "hell dust" so that he can find his prey. If we are not walking according to our sin nature, the devil will find no dust to track him to us. Satan is equipped to find hell-dust, not a child of the living God. When the devil finds the hell-dust, he will have found his prey. It is imperative that we not walk according to the flesh.

The devil uses words just as God uses Words, but while God's Words appeal to our spirits, Satan's words appeal to our flesh. Satan would have us to think we can have it both ways: "You can eat the forbidden fruit and live!" Adam could either eat the forbidden fruit or he could live; he could not do both. Truth and lies mixed together like this show us that the devil is in the neighborhood.

Our enemy is doing the same thing today. The devil will tell us that we are to be good, which is true, but he will also bring us under condemnation and tempt us to be good by our own power. While it is true that we must be holy, it is a lie to think that we can do this by the power of the flesh. The devil is mixing the truth with a lie in order to appeal to our flesh. The devil has complete power over our flesh and that is why he is always trying to involve it. However, our spirit man has complete control over the devil and that is why we must learn to involve our born anew spirit man.

Every single thing that the gossiper said to herself was a lie of the devil mixed with a contorted truth. We *were* losers, but we are not losers now; we are children of God. It is true that we cannot get over sin *in our own power*, but as Christians we will get over sin because we are promised victory over sin through the blood of Jesus. It is true that *in our flesh* we are not good people, but we call ourselves Christians because we first trusted in Christ, not because we are good people.

It is true that we do not have *good behavior*, but God blesses us because He has a covenant with us based on His promises, not our behavior. It is true that we sometimes do not know what to do, but God has promised to give us wisdom and we who are born of God are not crazy; we have the mind of Christ. It is true that we sometimes *feel* fear because of our sin, but we have not been given a spirit of fear and the blood of Jesus has covered our sin. It is true that we *were* bad people, but we are now born of God and we are not bad people because a perfect God cannot give birth to an imperfect creature.

Do you see how the satanic lies have been intermingled with truth? The power of division is found in the Word of God. Satan has a forked tongue; we have a sharp two-edged sword. God's Word is the ultimate Truth regardless of what may or may not be happening in this natural world. The Sword of the Spirit, which is the Word of God, will cut to the core by making key divisions to bring down those strongholds.

Satan is the accuser of the brethren. Must we join in his tirade and begin to flay ourselves into a bloody mess? What is the point of that? That bloody mess is just going to get up and act stupid again because the devil remains whole, smiling, and ready for another attack. If God were to come upon this gruesome scene and ask the devil what he did, the devil could rightfully answer, "I didn't do a thing; he did this to himself."

Divide and Conquer

Now let's go back and replay this scenario. Let's reconsider the Christian who is addicted to obsessive gossiping. She has prayed about this sin and received forgiveness and cleansing according to the Word of God. She steps out in faith but while visiting a friend she falls to the temptation to gossip.

On her way home, the devil begins to use his forked tongue to accuse her of her sin. But the Christian who knows the Word of God opens her mouth and in a flash the Sword of the Spirit, which is the Word of God, comes flying out in the devil's face and begins to divide the soul from the spirit, the joints from the marrow, and the thoughts from the intents:

> *"I am born of God and I cannot sin."* **Slash!** *"I am dead to sin and no longer live in it."* **Slash!** *"It is no longer I that do it but the sin that dwells in me."* **Slash!** *"I am the righteousness of God in Christ Jesus."* **Slash!** *"I have been delivered from the bondage of corruption and into the glorious liberty of the sons of God."* **Slash!** *"He Who began a good work in me will be faithful to complete it in Christ Jesus."* **Slash!** *"I am made a partaker of the divine nature through His great and precious promises."* **Slash!** *"He perfects that which concerns me and He will perfect me in this area because it concerns me."* **Slash!** *"I thank God through Jesus Christ my Lord so with my mind I serve the law of God even when, with my flesh I serve the law of sin."* **Slash!** *"There is, therefore, no condemnation for me because I am in Christ Jesus and I do not walk according to the flesh but according to the Spirit because the law of the Spirit of life in Christ Jesus hath made me free from the law of sin and death."* **Slash!** *"Jesus paid the penalty for my sin and cleansed me of it the moment I confessed it."* **Slash!** *"God has separated my sin from me as far as the east is from the west."* **Slash!** *"Let God be true though every man be a liar."* **Slash!** *"God's Word is sure and I will not look at things that I see because they are TEMPORARY! I will not look at sin! I will look on things that I don't see because they are ETERNAL! I choose to look at my deliverance from this sin."* **Slash!** *"Now I rebuke you, Satan, in the name of Jesus!"* **Slash, slash, slash**.

Now who's the bloody mess? If God were to come upon this gruesome scene (and He will), and ask us what we did, we could rightfully smile from ear to ear and say, "I pulled down my stronghold, Father." Well done. After this tirade against the devil and the sin nature, the days of gossiping are numbered, if not over. The Sword of the Spirit *will* pull down strongholds. God's Word does not lie.

Now that we have won this battle, we will be stronger and wiser. We have sowed the Word of God and we will reap a harvest. The

Death Becomes You

seed will produce the tree of righteousness. The more we hear ourselves speaking the Word, the more it will become ingrained in us. By speaking in this way, we are burying that word in our heart and it is there that it was intended to grow. God planted a garden and sent Adam in to tend it. God plants His Word into our hearts but we must tend that garden with our mouths and cut away at that problem so that the Word can take root and become established.

Not our Problem Anymore

If this thing doesn't work, it is not our fault. The Word has taught us that it *will* work and we either believe in this God or we don't. As we partake in this practice of speaking God's Word in the face of sin, it will only be a matter of time before we will find ourselves using our sword before we sin! But, we must always begin where we are; it does us no good to look backward. The starting point needs to be in the face of sin. We must speak to our strongholds with the creative and powerful tongue God placed in our mouths.

Trust me, Satan will not soon recover from a good tongue-lashing. And, when he does recover, he may think twice before he comes back for more. You see, Satan is a spirit being and is subject to the spiritual realm. Aptly named, the Sword of the Spirit does its work in the spiritual realm. We don't see Satan fall to the ground, but he does. We do not see his grimace of pain, but it is there. We don't see how he cowers and begs, but he does. He is a spirit being and he is subject to our spiritual weapon. In our physical realm, this sword is nothing more than intangible words in the air, but in the spiritual realm, this sword is razor sharp and it cuts.

Choose your Weapon

Satan only laughs when we plead, *"Leave me alone...I can't take it anymore!"* But, he is picked up and thrown backward when we say *"I rebuke you in the name of Jesus!"* We must consider the spiritual realm in all we do. We must choose our weapon, and choose it carefully: Will we speak with the forked tongue of the devil and mix God's Truth with the lies of the devil, or will we use our sharp two-edged sword and divide what we see, think, and feel from the Truth of God's Word? The weapon we choose will be working for us or against us, but mark my words, as long as we use our mouths, it will be working.

Paul's Example

Now that we understand Paul's method of victory over the
strongholds of sin we will better understand his diatribe concerning
death at the mere mention of sin in the sixth chapter of Romans.
You see, Paul knew God's Word and that means he knew the
following about himself:

> *"I am crucified with Christ: nevertheless I live;*
> *yet not I, but Christ liveth in me:*
> *and the life which I now live in the flesh*
> *I live by the faith of the Son of God,*
> *who loved me, and gave himself for me."*
> *(Gal 2:20 KJV)*

Paul knew he was dead even though he lived which means that Paul
knew there were two realities from which to choose. Paul chose to
live in his spiritual reality. That is exactly why he speaks confidently
about who he is when he is encountered with the question, *"What
shall we say then, shall we sin so that grace will abound?"* Rather
than answer this absurd question, Paul pulls out his sword,
sssshhhhing, and begins to speak his spiritual reality into existence:

Shall we Sin so that Grace will abound?

> *"Don't you know that anyone who has been baptized into Jesus*
> *Christ has been baptized into His death?*
> *Now we are buried with Jesus by baptism into death so that just as*
> *Christ was raised up from the dead by the glory of the Father,*
> *we also will walk in newness of life.*
> *For if we have been planted together in the likeness of his death,*
> *we shall be also in the likeness of his resurrection.*
> ***The knowledge that our old man is crucified***
> ***destroys the body of sin.***
> *Now we are delivered from the bondage of sin,*
> *because he that is dead is free from sin.*
> *Now if we are dead with Christ, we believe that we shall also live*
> *with him. We know that Christ dies no more in that He became*
> *victorious over death when He was raised from the dead. In that He*
> *died, He died unto sin once: but in that he lives, he lives unto God."*
> *(Rom 6:2-10 paraphrase)*

Death Becomes You

Go Paul! At the mere mention of sin, Paul does not discuss whether one should or should not sin; rather, he declares who we are in Christ. He did not give sin the slightest opportunity. Paul went in there and used his sword and cut the sin nature to pieces. The stronghold of sin is being pulled down before our eyes. The hell dust is nowhere to be seen as the devil slithers hopelessly around searching for it.

Please know: This is the key to Paul's success. He does not play games. He is a warrior and he knows how to use his weapon. This is the reason Paul had to remind the church in Galatia of a time when he *used to* have a temptation of sin in his flesh. Paul got victory over his sin by using the Sword of the Spirit in the face of sin, and so shall we.

Baptized into His Death

What does it mean to be baptized into Christ's death? We have churches that mandate baptism, others that mandate immersion baptism, others still that mandate sprinkling baptism, and still others that ignore baptism altogether. Leave it to the devil to ritualize one of the most important spiritual lessons we have to learn. God did not give us baptism as a "thing to do"; He gave us the rite of baptism as a *visual aid*. We must accept the fact that the Bible is packed with visual aids.

When I get baptized, I go under water. This act symbolizes my very real spiritual death to sin. When we die physically, we go underground, when we die spiritually, we go under water. This is how we are "buried by baptism." Now that I am under the water, I must come up from the water. This act symbolizes my spiritual rising in Christ. When one comes out of the ground, it is because he has been resurrected. This is why when we are buried by baptism we are resurrected in newness of life:

> *"Therefore we are buried with him by baptism into death:*
> *that like as Christ was raised up from the dead*
> *by the glory of the Father,*
> *even so we also should walk in newness of life"*
> *(Rom 6:4 KJV)*

Now I have a natural visual, which shows me a spiritual Truth. That is all. If this thing was about the act itself, all who have been under water have been saved. We have been given the rite of baptism because God knew this was a difficult thing to understand and thought it would be a good idea to give us a mental image of what has actually happened.

We can better wrap our brains around "going under" as one person, and "raising up" as another when we can see this action in our head. Jesus died bearing the sin of the world, as though He had committed it Himself, but He was raised a perfect God Who had no sin. As well, we have died in sin so that we can be raised in Christ. We must let our baptism remind us of this amazing truth.

To be baptized into Christ's death is to identify with our spiritual death that has already taken place. And because Jesus actually *did* die, we know that if we are to be baptized into *His* death, we have to understand that a very real death has taken place in the spiritual realm. And if a real death has taken place, then it is a very real death into which we must be baptized! We must consider ourselves very truly dead to sin because we are! The Truths of the spiritual realm take precedence over the manifestations of the natural realm. Knowledge brings deliverance; the Truth shall set you free.

In the spiritual realm we are dead to sin, so we enter this death and, *"...like as Christ was raised up from the dead by the glory of the Father, even so we also should walk in newness of life."* We cannot walk in newness of life until we have walked in the reality of the actual spiritual death, *"For if we have been planted together in the likeness of his death, we shall be also in the likeness of his resurrection:"* (Now I know why Paul said, *"Notice what large letters I use as I write."* Paul was writing in large letters so that his readers would get the importance of what he was saying. These things need emphasis!) *If, and only if,* we accept our spiritual death for the true death that it is, we will begin to walk in newness of life.

Knowing This

It is important to *know* this, *"Knowing this, that our old man is crucified with him..."* Why do we need to *know* this? So that, *"...the body of sin might be destroyed."* To know and accept this death as a reality is to *destroy* the body of sin! Isn't that what we are after? When the body of sin is destroyed, it follows *"...that henceforth we should not serve sin."* Again, why? Because *"...he that is dead is freed from sin."*

This is all about a very real death that has already taken place, *"Now if we be dead with Christ, we believe that we shall also live with him:"*. Once we enter into this death, we enter into the belief that we will live with Him! Why? Because, *"Knowing that Christ being raised from the dead dieth no more; death hath no more dominion over him. For in that he died, he died unto sin once: but in that he liveth, he liveth unto God."* Do not miss the finality of this declaration. Die once; live forever unto God. Jesus died once; we are buried with him by baptism into death. Our body of death is dead forever, it lives no more! Now it is all about life with God.

No Metaphor

Please do not make the mistake of thinking this is a metaphor. When instructing us concerning this death, Paul goes on to say, *"Likewise reckon ye also yourselves to be dead **indeed** unto sin..."* (Rom 6:11a). Dead *indeed*. That means *actually dead*, not metaphorically dead. Grab that death...it is there for you!

The Word of God says that we are dead to sin. However, if we are dead to it, how is it then possible for us to sin? Paul is saying, "Hey, you aren't thinking right. The idea is not about sinning, but about being dead to sin. Why would you even identify with sin? How can a person who is dead to sin live any longer in sin? Get your head out of the gutter! Rather, keep your mind on the fact that you are dead to sin."

Perfect Paul?

Do we think Paul is proclaiming he is dead to sin because he doesn't sin anymore? No. Just one chapter later this same Paul said, *"With my mind I will serve the law of God, while with the flesh the law of sin."* Paul is not stating a manifested fact when he says, *"How can we who are dead to sin live any longer therein"*; rather, he is wielding his sword in the face of temporary facts so that he can pull down that stronghold of sin! Don't miss his example!

It is a *fact* that Paul is sinning, but it is a *Truth* that Paul is dead to sin. ***The Truth will never change...the fact has to change.*** That is why we don't base our Christian lives on facts. We must take God's Word as the undeniable Truth because it is the only reality that can change natural facts!

The Day of Reckoning

Paul knows that <u>initially</u>, we will not *actually* experience a manifestation of this death to sin, so he tells us what to do. He says, "Hey, even though you are dead to sin in the spiritual realm, I know it has not yet manifested in the physical realm. This is what you need to do, *'Likewise **reckon** ye also yourselves to be dead indeed* *unto sin, but alive unto God through Jesus Christ our Lord.'" (Rom 6:11 KJV)* I love that word reckon; it has saved my life numerous times. It means to count or regard. The Greek definition adds, "to suppose, conclude, and think on". This word is used more commonly in the South.

Let's say, on an episode of the Andy Griffith Show, Aunt Bea was being short with Opie and Opie brought his concern to his dad, "Pa, Aunt Bea is mad at me and I don't know why." Andy knows his Aunt Bea well and responds by saying, "Aw, she aint mad at you, Ope. If Aunt Bea is actin' funny I reckon somethin' else is probly bother'n her. Let's find out what's goin' on."

Andy had a fact: Aunt Bea is acting like she is mad at Opie. And he had a persuasion based on truth: Something must be bothering Aunt Bea. Andy knew his aunt and knew that she would not purposely make Opie feel like she was mad at him. Andy was so convinced of the character of his aunt that he pronounced a reckoning about her based on what he *knew* rather than what he *saw*. He reckoned the situation according to his heart right in the face of contradicting evidence. As Andy *reckoned*, he showed the direction he was leaning. To reckon is to consider, deem, and think.

This is what we must do concerning our spiritual death to sin. We must reckon ourselves dead to sin as though we really are! It matters not what we see with our eyes. What we see and experience must bow to the persuasion of our heart concerning the Word of God. We must reckon ourselves dead indeed unto sin, even while we sin. After all, what need is there for faith if we only believe what we see and experience? *"Blessed are they that have not seen, and yet have believed."* We must at once come to a place where we believe God's Word enough to exalt it above what we perceive with our sensory system.

Time is of the Essence

We have learned that our old man is dead. We don't have to try to kill him; Adam did just fine. The problem is not with death; the problem is with time. The manifested facts that lie before us betray us and convince us of their truths. If my old man with his sin nature is dead, why am I still sinning?

We saw where Elohim moved very quickly as He created all things in the spiritual realm in six days. Then we saw Jehovah Elohim birth those creations into the natural realm where much more time was in use. There is a very good reason for this. In the spiritual realm everything is eternal which means that everything is instantly now. There is no concept of time; all is what it is. What is meant by the usage of the word "day" in the first several verses of Genesis is unknown because God was calling certain periods "days" before He had created the sun and the moon, which established the concept of a natural day.

It is difficult to even begin to understand eternity, but what we have to understand is that Elohim **said** and it *instantly* was, whereas Jehovah Elohim **planted** and **built** and **formed** and *then* it eventually was. Elohim said, "Trees be!" and then He saw trees alive and mature in the spiritual realm. Jehovah Elohim saw an empty garden in the natural realm and provided a mist, formed a man, planted seeds, and grew trees. This natural realm employs a thing called "Time"; it is a natural realm where things grow naturally. Jehovah Elohim worked in the natural realm and took advantage of time to birth Elohim's creations. A baby is conceived instantly, however, time is employed to get that baby to the place where it can be birthed. This is our natural example.

The second chapter of Genesis does not say that Jehovah Elohim *saw* plant life after He planted seeds. What it *does* say is that after Jehovah Elohim planted the garden, He set His man in there to tend it. In the natural realm, a garden *grows*. A thing can be absolutely true, complete, and mature in the spiritual realm even while it is yet in a state of transition in the natural realm. A baby is a human being the moment it is conceived but it remains in a state of transition up until the moment it is born. This baby is no less real before it is born than it is after it is born. Plant life existed in the first chapter of Genesis just as sure as it ever would, even while that ground appeared barren in the second chapter. The plant life did not become more real when it manifested than it had been when Elohim created it in the spiritual realm.

To say that a thing become more real when it manifests here on earth is to say that a rocket becomes more real when it enters space. That is ridiculous. We are absolutely perfect in the spiritual realm. That is the only realm that matters. That is why the work of the cross works backward and forward. The Lamb was slain from the foundation of the earth. Once it was done it was done. If we have been created and birthed by God and are His perfect children indeed in the spiritual realm, then that is the predominant Truth we must be reckoning in this natural realm.

That is how our old man can be dead even while the natural realm says he lives. If we find ourselves looking at barren ground, it is time to peer into the spiritual realm and claim its possessions. Once we do, we consider them done in the only place where it matters. Now we wait for that thing to grow. Time.

We need to look into that spiritual realm where our old man is dead in Adam and plant that dead seed in this natural realm and allow time to work in this natural realm to bring forth the fruit of this act, *"For if we have been planted together in the likeness of his death, we shall be also in the likeness of his resurrection:" (Rom 6:5 KJV). We shall be…*future tense. It will take time to completely manifest holiness…probably the rest of our lives.

Do not despair…this is God's way of doing things. All the while that we are in an imperfect state in the natural, we are at the same time in a perfect state in the spiritual realm. The spiritual realm is the realm that counts; it is the realm of Truth. The spiritual realm is an eternal realm that does not change and does not die. So what if the natural realm employs time? God is the One Who created it this way. If the Almighty God is okay with waiting for the natural manifestation of our spiritual holiness, I think we can be okay with waiting for it. We must learn to rest in Him. Resting is our only job.

Two Trees

Something that will help us walk in our spiritual death is to remember that we are trees that bear fruit. And, according to Jesus, a born again person is not capable of bearing anything but good fruit. Jesus helps us understand the distinction between the old man and the new as He informs His disciples that, *"A good tree cannot bring forth evil fruit, neither can a corrupt tree bring forth good fruit. Every tree that bringeth not forth good fruit is hewn down, and cast into the fire." (Matt 7:18-19 KJV)*

I remember the days when I would read this and shake my head. I bring forth good fruit and evil fruit! How is it that Jesus can say that if I am a good tree I cannot bear evil fruit and if I am an evil tree I cannot bear good fruit? I have proven that I can do both! Am I good or evil? Surely there is no perfect being that bears not one bad fruit. Could there possibly be?

The only explanation is the idea of there being more than one tree. If we have more than one fruit and a tree can only bear one type of fruit, there must be two trees. The old man and the new man are the two trees. We will either identify with the old man and bear evil fruit, or we will identify with the new man and bear good fruit. One man will not produce both kinds of fruit.

Trees that do not produce good fruit will be cut down and thrown into the fire. Our "old man evil tree" is destined for the fire. God cannot throw that old man in the fire until that new man has detached himself from it and embraced God. This is how we destroy our body of death – we believe God's Word and reckon our flesh dead so that God can get rid of it! Now we live as the new man who is a good tree that produces good fruit and we ignore the rest. We are to interact with God as though we are perfectly holy even before we are physically acting that way.

The Fruits of our Trees

The purpose of a fruit tree is to bear fruit. However, even a tree that bears good fruit will at times display bad "behavior". My good fruit bearing tree may prevent my flowers from getting needed sun, it may get a disease I have to treat, it will drop its leaves for me to rake and clean out of my gutters, it will drop branches I have to collect from my yard, it may even drop a large branch onto my house causing a great deal of damage. However, if it bears the fruit that I want, I will tolerate its bad behavior.

God does not judge the tree; He judges the fruit. God, in the Person of the Holy Spirit, will help the tree through sickness, disease, and trials. During these times the fruit harvest may diminish in size, but the tree will not produce a different type of fruit while it goes through these times. The same tree cannot produce two different kinds of fruit. Our born again tree is a good tree and it bears good fruit, sometimes little, other times much, but always the same fruit.

So we see that we must identify with our new man and realize that we have been planted as a tree that bears good fruit. We don't focus on the evil tree that bears bad fruit, as that tree is dead. Hence, it is not possible for the born again man to bear bad fruit. God is looking for good fruit. As long as we have faith in these sayings and do not try to make things happen in the flesh, we will bear that good fruit. When we identify with the old man by focusing on him and trying to get him in line, we are going to bear evil fruit because an evil tree (man with a sin nature) can only bear evil fruit. The flesh profits nothing.

If it isn't faith; it's sin

We are never going to get it perfectly right in this life. That is an inconceivable goal. But *something* must be perfect; a good tree cannot bear evil fruit. Our tree must be consistently good in some way. The perfection God seeks in us is a perfection of faith. We must learn to live our lives wholly and completely by faith. We must live as though we are perfect even while we are yet imperfect. This is a conceivable goal.

It is a verse we commonly overlook, but it conveys a sobering message, "*...for whatsoever is not of faith is sin.*" *(Rom 14:23b KJV)* Paul says these words after he explains what sin really is:

"For meat destroy not the work of God.
All things indeed are pure;
but it is evil for that man who eateth with offence.
It is good neither to eat flesh, nor to drink wine,
nor any thing whereby thy brother stumbleth,
or is offended, or is made weak.
Hast thou faith? have it to thyself before God.
Happy is he that condemneth not himself
in that thing which he alloweth.
And he that doubteth is damned if he eat,
because he eateth not of faith:
for whatsoever is not of faith is sin."
(Rom 14:20-23 KJV)

Let me see if I can paraphrase with the help of the original Greek:

"Mere food cannot stand in the way of God's work.
Although all things are pure and clean
it is evil for a man to eat anything that vies with his faith.
As well, it's not a good idea to eat, drink, or do anything
that places a stumbling block and weakens another.
Do you have faith about eating that thing?
That is between you and God.
Happy are you when you don't condemn yourself
in those things that you allow.
But if you doubt, you will be damned in the eating
because you do not eat by faith.
For whatsoever is not of faith is sin.

Death Becomes You

The message is this: What we do cannot stand in God's way because all things are pure and clean in His realm because God, through Jesus took sin out of the world. It doesn't matter whether or not it is a good idea to eat a particular kind of food. What matters is whether you are eating by faith. We must be careful to not flaunt our freedom around when younger ones are present. They are impressionable and if they feel that they should eat a particular food in obedience to God, then eat that food with them! This is not about food; this is about faith! Everything is about faith!

Conversely, when we doubt, or refuse to exercise our faith, we are damned no matter what we do because whatsoever is not of faith is sin. If I eat a thing in fear I am sinning. If I abstain from eating the same thing in fear I am sinning. Yet I can both eat or abstain from eating and be perfectly holy if I eat in faith. We will either be creatures of fear or creatures of faith. This is what God has set before us. We cannot beat our flesh into submission but we can choose to believe in God and all He says.

The Way it Was

I remember how powerless I used to feel before God taught me these Truths. Every morning I got up with great resolve to behave well. I purposed to be patient, kind, and loving with everyone. I was intent on keeping an organized home and spending quality time with God. I set out to break every bad habit and develop a few good ones. Every night I went to bed with these words on my lips, "Oh God, I'm so sorry. I don't know what is wrong with me. Why do I have to screw up so thoroughly every stupid day? Why is it not enough to just want to do well? Why must I struggle against myself every moment of every day? Forgive me. I have no idea what to do." I was a Christian, I loved the Lord, and He was surely at work in my life but, behaviorally, I was a failure.

It was only when I began to learn of my death to sin that I began to come out from under the tyranny of the sin nature. When I discovered Paul's method of destroying the body of flesh with the Sword of the Spirit, I used it with my children. I didn't like how impatient I was with the boys. I didn't like the anger I displayed or the way I spoke to them. I began to do what Paul did and shed the entire responsibility of it and speak Truth in the face of my sin.

I told the boys that I loved them and I did not agree with some of the ways that I treated them. I explained that my flesh was dead and that I was going to reckon it so every time I saw it. I'm not sure how much they understood (they were very young) but it worked. Right after I would act unbecoming toward them I would look up to God and say, "I'm so glad she's dead." I would return to the boys and say, "You know I love you. That was just my flesh, so ignore it; it's dead."

It's funny because they would answer me back with a very bored, "We know" as they had grown accustomed to hearing that. But before long, I wasn't yelling anymore. I wasn't getting angry. Instead, I was treating them with love and talking to them with respect. I turned out to be a pretty good mom. I became a peculiar person, zealous of "good mom" works. Today, if you were to ask my sons, they would tell you they have no remembrance of me acting inappropriately toward them. That is a miracle. I have had the privilege of raising my sons in a godly fashion, not because I worked very hard at being a good mother, but simply because I dared to believe God's Word even while it stood in direct contradiction with what I saw with my eyes.

The things for which I believed came to be for me. I became a better wife in the same way. I became a better person all around when I gave up my own efforts and began to look at my propensity toward sin as non-existent. It wasn't me that did wrong things; it was the sin that dwelled in me. As I focused on the promises found in God's Word and reckoned my flesh dead I found my freedom.

Go ahead and hate them

I had a friend who had been seriously abused by the hierarchy of her church. As she relayed the story to me several months after the fact, I had to pass her a box of tissues. My friend was obviously still very upset about the ordeal. Several times she returned to her church only to leave with a great deal of bitterness in her heart. Because she was a Christian, she hated the fact that she still felt the way she did. As well, she hated the fact that she was still talking about this problem months after the fact. This thing was plaguing her. Finally she gave up and began searching for a new church.

After talking with me she read *Hell Bent* and then *The Sin Within* all in a matter of a couple of weeks. When she was done I asked her how she did with the chapters that taught on death. She answered hesitatingly, *"I don't know..."* I completely understood her response. I have found that although these concepts are *taught* through word, they are only "caught" through experience.

Death Becomes You

A couple of weeks later she came into my office and said, "Funny thing happened. I ran into someone from the church. He wasn't involved in the problem but I found myself talking to him about it. The more I talked the madder I got. I was mad at the ones who had done this, and mad at myself for talking about it...again! When I was left alone I began to condemn myself. Even as I hated myself for what I had just done, I found myself hating them even more. I sat and fought with myself when I heard the Lord say, 'Go ahead and hate them.' I stopped for a moment, quit fighting my feelings, and then just released myself to them.

"All of a sudden my bitterness disappeared. I sensed a great burden lift from my shoulders. So sudden was this deliverance that I felt I had to test it so I went back to church the following Sunday. I was amazed. All feelings of hatred and bitterness were gone and I found myself loving these people more than I ever had!"

In allowing herself to "hate" with abandon my friend was serving the law of God with her mind while with her flesh she served the law of sin:

"I Thank God through Jesus Christ our Lord.
So then with the mind I myself serve the law of God;
but with the flesh the law of sin.
There is therefore now no condemnation
to them which are in Christ Jesus,
who walk not after the flesh, but after the Spirit.
For the law of the Spirit of life in Christ Jesus
hath made me free from the law of sin and death.
For what the law could not do,
in that it was weak through the flesh,
God sending his own Son in the likeness of sinful flesh,
and for sin, condemned sin in the flesh:
That the righteousness of the law might be fulfilled in us,
who walk not after the flesh, but after the Spirit."
(Rom 7:25-8:4 KJV)

While my friend's fleshly efforts had placed her in more bondage, the Truth set her soundly free. This thing is about God and faith in His Word and the declarations and promises it makes. We must believe in the ways and promises of God no matter what the circumstances. If we don't go here, we will go nowhere. Don't be afraid to wear it; when you become dead, death becomes you.

He hath showed strength with his arm;
*he hath scattered the **proud** in the imagination of their hearts.*
*He hath put down the **mighty** from their seats,*
and exalted them of low degree.
Luke 1:51 – 52

"Therefore thou art inexcusable, O man,
whosoever thou art that judgest..."
Romans 2:1

4

GUILTY OF JUDGMENT

In light of everything we have been studying, it seems almost unnecessary to broach the subject of judging. How is it possible for us to look down upon another after we have learned that, "within us dwelleth no good thing"?

Guilty of Judgment

Right Under our Nose

Those whom we look down upon are the number one enemies to our success in this Christian life. Paul taught us that we absolutely must reckon ourselves dead to sin even while we are sinning. We spent two entire chapters discussing this spiritual death. Through this knowledge, we afford ourselves the luxury of being dead to sin even while we yet sin, *"So then with the mind I myself serve the law of God; but with the flesh the law of sin."* Knowing this, should we now look at other believers and reckon them *alive* to sin when we see them sin? Paul said:

> *"Wherefore henceforth know we no man after the flesh...*
> *if any man be in Christ, he is a new creature:*
> *old things are passed away;*
> *behold, all things are become new."*
> *(2 Cor 5:16a & 17 KJV)*

Paul said he knew no man after the flesh, *"if any man be in Christ, he is a new creature."* Hence, if follows that if any man is not in Christ he is still the old man condemned to death. It is that simple. We are to look at ourselves according to who we are in Christ, we are to look at the brethren according to who they are in Christ, and we are to look at the unregenerate person according to who they are: Lost, without power, and in need of salvation.

Paul did not look at other believers according to their sin anymore than he looked at himself according to his sin. Anyone who is in Christ is a new creature. The old has passed away. That is another way of saying the old has died. The old has died and all things are become new because we have a new birth. That is how Paul saw himself and it is how he saw others who were born of God. Paul didn't judge himself according to his flesh and he wasn't going to judge the brethren according to their flesh.

As far as those who are not of the Christian fold, all is seen through the eyes of God. The wrath of God is already abiding on the unrepentant sinner. He is still operating according to a hell-bent flesh. He is in prison and needs to be set free. We do not dare judge him as we, at one point, were him! The unregenerate one we are tempted to judge is no different than every other person who is born of the flesh. In fact, he is no different than *our* old man who was born of the flesh. If God had not chosen to extend mercy to us and draw us to Him, we would be in their same boat. At all times we must keep these things in mind; we are never in a position to judge.

When we judge others, we are proving our ignorance. If we were really in touch with our inner sinner, it would cause us to see the offences of others in a much different light. I believe the main reason we judge others is because we don't fully comprehend the danger of this act. The act of judging others brings condemnation upon us. Condemnation is the worst possible scenario for anyone, but *especially* for the Christian.

The world does not understand the hell bent disposition; neither do they understand the grace that deals with it. The world judges one another because they don't know any better. We *do* know better, and where God is concerned, that makes all the difference.

Religion

Religion has always been more concerned about deeds than the heart behind the deeds. Our deeds are the only things that show on the outside; hence, our deeds are what get judged. And, no one knows the heart of a man except the man and his God, *"O LORD, thou hast searched me, and known me." (Psa 139:1 KJV)* So when we look at others, we see their deeds though we don't see their heart. This is why we are never in a position to judge. There is only One Who can judge.

It is very easy to hide a bad heart behind good behavior. As well, a good heart can hide behind bad behavior. When this happens, the one with a bad heart can be lulled into a false sense of security in his actions. As well, one with a good heart can be brought into condemnation by his behavior. We see this demonstrated in society. Those who are secure in their own righteous behavior fill our churches while many of a good heart are kept at arm's length because they are in bondage to their sin.

Jesus addressed this religious problem often and without mercy:

> *"And he spake this parable unto certain which trusted*
> *in themselves that they were righteous,*
> *and despised others:*
> *Two men went up into the temple to pray;*
> *the one a Pharisee, and the other a publican.*
> *The Pharisee stood and prayed thus with himself,*
> *God, I thank thee, that I am not as other men are,*
> *extortioners, unjust, adulterers,*

Guilty of Judgment

or even as this publican.
I fast twice in the week,
I give tithes of all that I possess.
And the publican, standing afar off,
would not lift up so much as his eyes unto heaven,
but smote upon his breast, saying,
God be merciful to me a sinner.
I tell you, this man went down to his house
justified rather than the other:
for every one that exalteth himself shall be abased;
and he that humbleth himself shall be exalted."
(Luke 18:9-14 KJV)

Jesus was addressing a group of people who despised others and trusted in themselves that they were righteous. We cannot miss this opportunity to put ourselves under this microscope. Have we ever felt comfortable in our level of righteousness? Do we feel less righteous when we fall into sin than we do when we withstand the temptation? If we do, then the opposite is true. If we feel *less* righteous when we sin, then we must feel *more* righteous when we behave well. And, if we feel more righteous when we behave well, we are trusting in ourselves that we are righteous. You should probably read this paragraph again.

The evidence of self-righteousness is the practice of despising others. That word "despised" is not the same word we are accustomed to using in the twenty-first century. This Greek word, exoutheneo, simply conveys the idea of looking down upon another. There is a significant difference between our idea of despising someone and the idea of simply looking down on someone. Hence, when we find ourselves looking down upon others, it is evidence of our self- righteousness. We, as Christians, rarely despise people; however, we are tempted *daily* to look down upon others due to their unseemly behavior. In this way we are no different than the Pharisee who compared himself to a sinner in this parable:

"The Pharisee stood and prayed...Thank God I am not as
other men – I don't cheat, I don't sin, I don't commit
adultery, and I don't steal like this publican. I fast twice a
week and give tithes of all I have."

The Sin within

The Pharisee

We tend to overlook this list. This Pharisee was a very righteous man! He even seemed to be thanking God and giving Him the credit for the way that he was living, *"I thank thee that I am not as other men are."* Jesus did not say this man was lying when he said that he didn't cheat, sin, commit adultery, and steal. Nor did He say that the Pharisee was exaggerating when he said that he fasted twice in the week and gave tithes of *all* he had. As a matter of fact, this wasn't even an actual man! This was a parable. If the man in question was lying or exaggerating, Jesus would have made that fact a part of His parable. So now we see that Jesus is depicting a man who is showing unparalleled godly behavior.

How many of us can say that we *never* lie, cheat, steal, commit adultery, or act unjustly in any way? Jesus said that if a man so much as looks at a woman to lust after her in his heart he is already guilty of adultery. Apparently this Pharisee had squeaky-clean actions and thoughts! How many of us fast twice in the week and pay tithes of *all* we have? Most Christians pale when compared with this Pharisee!

The Publican

Jesus says nothing either good or bad about the publican's behavior so we can assume this man was a typical publican. The Holman Bible Dictionary says, "The principal duty (of a publican) was extorting as much taxes as possible. It is believed, by some, that the publican was able to keep for himself any amount of monies collected beyond that levied by the government."

We complain about taxes in this day and age of accountability; imagine what it was like to not even have the ability to know exactly how much one actually owed and have to take the word of someone who had a reputation for exploiting the situation! These men were robbers who came to your door in the light of day in front of God and everyone and demanded your money; and there was nothing anyone could do. Publicans were deeply and universally despised in every sense of the word.

When we compare these two men, it is easy to see that one was living an exemplary life while the other was living a despicable life. We have to be honest about it; if these two men lived among us today, we as Christians, would tend to praise the just, fasting, and tithing Pharisee and look down upon the lying, cheating, and exploiting publican just as is depicted in the parable.

Guilty of Judgment

The Heart of the Pharisee

Jesus, being God, blasted right past the behavior of these men, saw the heart, and zeroed in on the matter at hand. You see the Pharisee was confident in his own ability to be righteous. Although he began his prayer by thanking God that he was not like the publican, his words were negated by his attitude of superiority. Had the Pharisee been sincere in his gratitude toward God, he would have put himself in the same category as the publican rather than exalting himself above him.

This attitude is at least as common today as it was in the days of Jesus. Many religious people give lip service to the idea that God is responsible for their righteousness while their attitudes positively ooze with arrogance and self-righteousness as they strut around judging the actions of others. Judging others absolutely exposes our self-righteousness. One cannot judge unless he sees himself as better: Self-righteousness.

Our Pharisee was comfortable enough in his behavior toward God to exalt himself above another. This action took him out of the game:

> *"For by grace are ye saved through faith; and that not of*
> *yourselves: it is the gift of God: Not of works,*
> *lest any man should boast." (Eph 2:8-9 KJV)*

The moment we lean upon ourselves, we are no longer under grace and we are out of the game. According to Jesus, this very righteous, upstanding Pharisee did not go down to his house justified. He had just as much sin going home as he had upon setting out.

The Heart of the Publican

While the Pharisee came to God with no apparent sin and an arrogant heart, the publican came to God laden with sin and a repentant heart, *"And the publican, standing afar off, would not lift up so much as his eyes unto heaven, but smote upon his breast, saying, God be merciful to me a sinner."* What we have is a picture of a man getting real with God.

The publican was well aware of the fact that he was no good and needed the mercy of God. Because of this, he went home justified. It is fabulous to think that Paul called himself a Pharisee of the Pharisees, yet he still did exactly what this publican did: He cried out for mercy showing us that there is hope for everyone.

We are *all* that wretched man. The only difference between one and the other is knowledge. One man knows he is wretched while the other still believes he should be praised a bit. In all fairness, it is much easier to become convinced of one's sin when one wears a lot of it on the outside. This publican had nowhere to hide; he was a walking epistle of sin. The Pharisee, on the other hand, found lots of places to hide. His sins were of an entirely different breed:

> *"Woe unto you, scribes and Pharisees, hypocrites!*
> *for ye pay tithe of mint and anise and cummin,*
> *and have omitted the weightier matters of the law,*
> *judgment, mercy, and faith: these ought ye to have done,*
> *and not to leave the other undone." (Matt 23:23 KJV)*

Jesus makes this so clear. The "church" people of that day were doing all the right things but they were remiss in attending the weightier matters of law, judgment, mercy, and faith. Before we begin to think of all the congregations that are failing in this manner, we must look first at ourselves. What do we really know about the law? Do we understand it the way we need to? Are we judging others? Do we extend mercy? How quick are we to give more attention to our behavior than to our faith? Where do we place our hope when we are manifesting sin? Have we ever been more concerned about how we look on the outside than how we really are on the inside? I believe there is a little Pharisee in each of us, just waiting to be discovered. Justification will be on the other side of this discovery.

A Pharisaical Mindset

As long as we at any time feel we are better than the least of all, we have a Pharisaical mindset. Paul shares with us his heart, *"This is a faithful saying, and worthy of all acceptation, that Christ Jesus came into the world to save sinners; of whom I am chief." (1 Tim 1:15 KJV)* Paul did not put himself in the chief sinner seat because he had sinned more than anyone else; he considered himself chief sinner because he knew he was *capable* of sinning at least as much as anyone else. Paul had a proper understanding of who he was in the flesh. Thankfully, he also had a proper understanding of who he was in the spirit.

When we focus on behavior instead of the more important

Guilty of Judgment

matters at hand we become blind guides to those who need us, *"Ye blind guides, which strain at a gnat, and swallow a camel."* If we were to take part in a murder, we would fall down on our knees and beg for mercy; how is it that we are so quick to judge our neighbor without so much as a second thought? The same God Who said, *"Thou shalt not murder"* also said, *"Judge not lest ye be judged."* This is the camel the Pharisees were swallowing. Rather than concern themselves with who they really were, the Pharisees concerned themselves with what they looked like; they strained at a gnat and swallowed a camel. We are guilty of the same thing.

In the following parable the Pharisees were doing all the right things on the outside while on the inside their hearts were far from God. Jesus says these guys looked clean and white on the outside while within they were full of death:

> *"Woe unto you, scribes and Pharisees, hypocrites!*
> *for ye make clean the outside of the cup...*
> *but within they are full of extortion and excess.*
> *Thou blind Pharisee, cleanse first that which is within the*
> *cup...that the outside of them may be clean also.*
> *Woe unto you, scribes and Pharisees, hypocrites!*
> *for ye are like unto whited sepulchres,*
> *which indeed appear beautiful outward, but are within full*
> *of dead men's bones, and of all uncleanness."*
> *(Matt 23:25-27 KJV)*

Here Jesus is instructing the Pharisees on how to get out of this mess, *"first clean that which is within the cup...that the outside of them may be clean also."* What this tells us is that when one first becomes clean on the *inside*, he will subsequently also become clean on the *outside*. Because we do not properly understand the Scriptures, we keep trying to make our outside clean while we ignore our inside. We care more about how we look to others than how we look to God. Just as Jesus said, we are missing the weightier matters of the law. This is precisely why we fail:

> *"Even so ye also outwardly appear righteous unto men,*
> *but within ye are full of hypocrisy and iniquity."*
> *(Matt 23:23-28 KJV)*

We are hypocrites as we look down upon others. We must find and eliminate the Pharisee in us because his end is not good. We must attend to the weightier matters of law, judgment, mercy, and faith.

The Warning

In the first chapter of the book of Romans, Paul deals with people who have "turned the Truth of God into a lie." He talks about the attitude of their heart, the way God sees them, how He deals with them, and how we should see them. Whenever we look at the Scriptures, we must look for ourselves and see what they are speaking to us. Paul wrote this letter to the Christians in Rome. He loved them and longed to be with them. Paul felt it necessary to relay to his beloved ones, the process by which men fall deeply into a reprobate mind. Evidently, Christians, (being Paul's audience), are in danger. Let us heed his words:

> *"For I am not ashamed of the gospel of Christ:*
> *for it is the power of God unto salvation*
> *to every one that believeth;*
> *to the Jew first, and also to the Greek.*
> *For therein is the righteousness of God*
> *revealed from faith to faith:*
> *as it is written, The just shall live by faith."*
> *(Rom 1:16-17 KJV)*

Paul begins by saying that he is not ashamed of the Truth concerning Christ because it is the power of God unto salvation to everyone who *believes*. The Truth concerning Christ is **not** the power of God unto salvation to everyone who *behaves well*. This is not a matter of doing; it is a matter of believing, *"For with the heart man believeth unto righteousness..." (Rom 10:10 KJV)*

The Just shall Live by Faith

Paul goes on to say that the righteousness of God is revealed from faith to faith and the just shall live by faith. Again, Paul does **not** say that the righteousness of God is revealed from one good act to another and the just shall live by good behavior.

When we stand back and look at our life, do we see a string of faith or a string of acts? According to Paul, we must find a way to live every moment of our lives by faith, *"The just shall live by faith."* A just person does not simply *have* faith, as all have faith, *"God hath dealt to every man the measure of faith."* A just man is ever endeavoring to find a way to live every moment of his life *by*

Guilty of Judgment

that faith. A "just" man is an innocent and holy man. If we are to be innocent and holy we must learn to live every moment of our lives by faith. Living outside of faith is not an option.

We have faith the way we have muscles. Everyone has muscles, but those who have exercised their muscles stand out and are considered "muscular". The more we use our muscles, the larger and stronger they will become. As well, everyone has faith, but those who have exercised their faith will stand out and be considered "men of faith".

All men have muscles and all men have faith. The just shall live by his faith the way a man lives by his muscles. A natural man cannot make a move without using his muscles. Even the heart is a muscle. As well, a spiritual man cannot make a move without faith; faith is the heart of our relationship with God. Faith is the only power that can defeat sin. We must exercise our faith in the face of our actions if we are to be successful. The more we use our faith, the more it will grow. We must receive our holiness as a gift from God, not labor to be holy in order to pay off a debt to God. Paul has begun our chapter by making a strong case for faith.

Meting Out

To judge a person does not mean that we wish them to hell; it simply means to measure another's behavior against our own. The Greek word means "to distinguish." When we distinguish one from another, we are judging. When we do this we are forcing God to judge us by our own measuring sticks:

> *"Judge not, that ye be not judged.*
> *For with what judgment ye judge, ye shall be judged:*
> *and with what measure ye mete,*
> *it shall be measured to you again."*
> *(Matt 7:1-2 KJV)*

We will be judged by how we judge and we will receive exactly what we have given out. This is a sobering thought. This does not mean that we cannot lead and restore others in a spirit of meekness:

> *"Brethren, if a man be overtaken in a fault, ye which are*
> *spiritual, restore such an one in the spirit of meekness;*
> *considering thyself, **lest thou also be tempted.**"*
> *(Gal 6:1 KJV)*

However, we are never in a position to *judge* others in comparison to ourselves. This is where the meekness comes in. We must go to this person in full knowledge that we are only grace away from being in his shoes. In the flesh we are guilty of all.

God wants someone spiritual (not someone who behaves well) to restore the man because someone spiritual will help the man conquer his fault by faith. We must always have in mind that we are capable of the same things we judge in others. This is a serious struggle for all Christians. We must see ourselves in the exact same light that we see others. We have no idea what we would have done given their set of circumstances; therefore we cannot say with any kind of assurance that we would have behaved differently. We have no idea what is in another's heart.

I was sitting in the passenger seat while my friend sat waiting to get onto the highway. She missed a couple of good opportunities to get out onto the road before she finally pulled out. The funny thing is that I had heard this same person make derogatory comments when others did that same thing. This is not unusual. We must get out of our heads the idea that we are better than others.

The Wrath of God

"For the wrath of God is revealed from heaven against all
ungodliness and unrighteousness of men,
who hold the truth in unrighteousness;"
(Rom 1:18 KJV)

Paul just finished telling us that a man is justified by faith. Having this knowledge, do we now hold this Truth in unrighteousness by judging others according to how they behave instead of how the Word sees them? Do we judge ourselves according to how we behave instead of how the Word sees us? Are we holding the Truth in unrighteousness? It is interesting that the following words are placed within this particular chapter of Romans:

"Because that which may be known of God is manifest in
them; for God hath showed it unto them.
For the invisible things of him from the creation of the
world are clearly seen, being understood by the things that
are made, even his eternal power and Godhead;
so that they are without excuse:" (Rom 1:19-20 KJV)

Guilty of Judgment

Paul tells us that God makes himself known to us in everything we see and experience on earth. We think this is a testimony to the unbelieving world, but Paul is not writing to the unbelieving world; they don't even have the ability to understand spiritual Truth (1Cor 2). Paul is warning *believers* that God put His fingerprint on everything in this life and we are responsible to learn from Him.

The entire world screams the message of faith. I have found it impossible to find something from which I could not learn a lesson of faith. That which may be known of God is manifest in mankind. The natural man does not even have the capacity to understand these marvels in their relation to God. However, the spiritual man has spiritual understanding and is responsible to take lessons about the spiritual realm from the natural world around him.

This world was designed in a very particular way. The invisible things of God from the creation of the world are clearly seen as they are understood by the things that are made. This is the way God chose to show Himself to us. God showed us how the invisible world works by examples of things that are visible. In this way mankind is without excuse. We cannot doubt God in any form; examples of His presence and His ways are everywhere.

Haaaave Mercy

We learned in <u>Hell Bent</u> that all mankind was born pre-disposed to sin. It matters not how much one manifests sin; we are guilty of all of it when we fail at any of it, *"For whosoever shall keep the whole law, and yet offend in one point, he is guilty of all." (James 2:10 KJV)* When it came to sin, God put us all in the same big pot.

We know that God is merciful and freely forgives each repentant sinner no matter how great his debt. This mercy and divine forgiveness is a spiritual thing. Paul said that the spiritual *"things of him from the creation of the world are clearly seen, being understood by the things that are made."*

God gave us the opportunity to learn about His spiritual mercy and divine forgiveness by allowing us to experience natural mercy and natural forgiveness. God created mercy and forgiveness in the spiritual realm, and then He brought mercy and forgiveness to the natural realm, and through this we learn to receive His mercy and forgiveness in the spiritual realm again: Spiritual, natural, spiritual.

If we really want to receive and embrace true merciful forgiveness, we are going to have to learn how that thing works right here in the natural realm. One of the reasons we struggle to walk in divine forgiveness is because we do not practice it enough to understand it. The tangible teaches us of the intangible.

Not Reasoning; Mercy

Through my willingness to welcome opportunities to forgive, I learned how God forgives. I used to, but no longer, forgive people only after I have reasoned out why they may have done whatever it was they did. Although I was being generous with those who had offended me, I was not practicing Godly forgiveness. Godly forgiveness is mercy. Mercy affords us luxuries we do not deserve. All reasoning is gone and one simply forgives as a gift to his offender in the exact same way God forgives us as a gift.

God does not measure our sins to see if we have a reasonable explanation for our behavior. The only thing God reasons with is His Word. God sees sin in one of two colors: Red or white, *"Come now, and let us reason together, saith the LORD: though your sins be as scarlet, they shall be as white as snow; though they be red like crimson, they shall be as wool." (Isa 1:18 KJV)* We must see sin in the same way; either it is still there and it is crimson red, or it has been cleansed and it is white as snow. There is no in-between.

Therefore, we must extend merciful forgiveness if we are to receive merciful forgiveness. This natural process will help us understand and receive God's mercy and forgiveness. The invisible things are clearly seen by things that are made.

Every Reason to Believe

A client came in to my office one day and said that she didn't believe in God. I started laughing spontaneously. The thought that there is no God is so ludicrous it amazes me that anyone is willing to admit this persuasion. It is not a matter of proving the existence of God; what unbelievers need to do is to prove there is no God. Someone needs to give any other explanation as to why we have a world full of miracles. If we think it takes faith to believe in God, try not believing in God! Now that takes some kind of faith! Where does one go when we take God out of the equation?

I was speaking to a man once who was considering the idea that God was not infinite, but rather that there was an end to Him. I asked him, "What is on the other side of the end of God? What is God the end of? We cannot understand nor escape an eternal God; we must stop trying.

Some argue that scientific phenomenon is responsible for the world around us. Again, that is funny. Where did we get scientific

Guilty of Judgment

phenomenon? Some say that two cells collided and caused all of this. So where did we get the two cells? Where did we get even one cell? Where did we get the space the cells occupied? What caused the cells to collide and cause the "Big Bang"? Are we really to suppose the beginning of all things was accidental? I don't know…is it just me? How stupid do we look?

What kind of intelligence could bring about everything around us in such a precise and orderly manner? Each species is full of infinite knowledge. We never come to the end of learning about a world that has sat in front of us for six thousand years. Where did this intelligence come from? To actually consider the idea that living objects just appeared out of nowhere (where is nowhere?) and began to interact with one another with mind-blowing intelligence and accuracy until they created a universe that defies human comprehension is insane.

I could go on, but my point is that anyone who has any spiritual understanding at all knows that there is a God, that He is amazingly powerful, and He is infinitely good. However, there is a valid reason why so many seem hell bent on ignoring the obvious presence of God. Paul, when speaking to these same people in Rome, quoted from Isaiah:

I See no Truth; I Hear no Truth

"Go and say to my people, You will hear my words,
but you will not understand; you will see what I do,
but you will not perceive its meaning.
For the hearts of these people are hardened, and their
ears cannot hear, and they have closed their eyes so their
eyes cannot see, and their ears cannot hear,
and their hearts cannot understand,
and they cannot turn to me and let me heal them. "
(Acts 28:26-27 NLT)

Due to the condition of their heart, people can become deaf and blind concerning the things of God. God will withhold from them the necessary ingredients to spiritual understanding if they resist His Truth. That is the only explanation for the absurd idea that there is no God. You may chose to worship a different god, but don't tell me that science, or even logic supports a Godless world lest I laugh you to scorn.

God constructed this universe in such a way that the very idea that there is no God is preposterous. As believers, we must accept the God of the universe and give Him credit for standing by what His Word. The physical universe speaks the Truth about God; we must not hold this Truth in unrighteousness.

When we doubt God at all, we are on a slippery slope. That is why it does us no good to measure ourselves against others, *"I thank thee that I am not as other men..."* Don't look now, but we are just as other men and we must not hold this Truth in unrighteousness. If the creative world screams God's message, then we are responsible to heed these lessons. Paul continues in the first chapter of Romans:

Glorified Him Not

"Because that, when they knew God,
they glorified him not as God, neither were thankful;
but became vain in their imaginations, and their foolish
heart was darkened." (Rom 1:21 KJV)

We see that Paul is referring to believers in this passage because he describes them by saying *"they knew God"*. We who know God must glorify Him as God. We must take Paul's words as a warning. We may think we are glorifying God as God, but many times we are not. To glorify God as God means to take Him at His Word. Not only are we guilty of neglect in this area, we act as though this behavior is permissible. It is not.

The same Christian who lives a life of worry and fear has no problem scoffing at those who lie, cheat, and steal. The same Bible that gives us a law, also tells us to cast our cares upon Him because He cares for us. Do we trust this God Who has promised to take care of us? Are we glorifying God with our worry and fear? We know this God; are we glorifying Him as God?

Paul described those who held the Truth in unrighteousness as unthankful, *"Neither were they thankful..."*. This same apostle encourages us from a prison cell, *"Rejoice in the Lord alway: and again I say, Rejoice." (Phil 4:4 KJV)* Are we thankful and rejoicing in the Lord always or do we begin to grumble when the going gets tough? My first instinct is to grumble when the going gets tough. I have to talk myself out of that thing. When we allow ourselves to grumble, we are holding the Truth in unrighteousness and we are without excuse.

Guilty of Judgment

It is in this way that even believers, *"...became vain in their imaginations, and their foolish heart was darkened."* To be "vain in our imaginations" means to have foolish, empty thoughts. As we think the foolish empty thoughts of the world, our foolish heart becomes darkened. Are we ever guilty of thinking foolish and empty thoughts? I know I am! Whenever our minds become focused on our problem instead of the Deliverer, we are thinking foolish and empty thoughts and we are not glorifying God as God.

Delusions of Grandeur

These worldly thoughts will have a persuading impact on our hearts. When this happens, we become delusional while we actually think we are being wise:

> *"Professing themselves to be wise, they became fools,*
> *And changed the glory of the uncorruptible God into an*
> *image made like to corruptible man, and to birds,*
> *and fourfooted beasts, and creeping things."*
> *(Rom 1:22-23 KJV)*

We are too quick to dismiss this. We see that thing about four-footed beasts and creeping things and we mistakenly take ourselves out of this equation. Surely we do not consider God as a bird, beast, or creeping thing! But that is not what the verse says. Those who thought they knew it all became fools and exchanged the glory of God for an image that *looked like* a regular man, or a bird, beast, or even a creeping thing.

Our Scripture says that when we do not glorify God as God, it is because we have convinced ourselves that our immortal God has no more power than a man, bird, beast, or any creeping thing. (I believe the "creeping thing" is a shot at the devil.) We are very quick to give credit to Satan and the power he exerts over our lives, but not so quick to give God the credit for having the ability and the desire to get that power back.

Giving Glory to Man

When we get into worry and fear and begin to look elsewhere for our provision, we are demonstrating our unbelief in the power of God. We easily trust the bank with our money but struggle to trust God with that same money. We easily trust and obey the doctor when he gives us his prescription for healing, but we wrestle with the doctrines concerning divine healing. We easily go to others for advice, but seldom seek God for wisdom. We look to our place of employment for our provision and expect that check at the end of the week, but we do not look to God as our Provider and expect Him to secure our provision.

The proof of this is in our actions. We trust ourselves to get out of bed in the morning and provide a service that is worthy of a paycheck, then we trust our employer to provide a salary, then we trust our spouse to run the check to the bank, then we trust the bank to take care of our money, but we do not trust our God to be true to His Word, *"But my God shall supply all your need according to his riches in glory by Christ Jesus." (Phil 4:19 KJV)*

We may try to convince ourselves that we are trusting God, but our words will betray us. Do we worry from day to day about whether we will get up in the morning and go to work? No. Do we worry from week to week about whether our employer will pay us? No. Do we worry about whether or not our spouse will bring the check to the bank? No. Do we worry about whether the bank will take care of our money? No. Do we worry about whether that check will be sufficient to meet our needs? Yes. The only beings we struggle to trust are our enemies and our God. That's just not right.

We have changed the glory of the incorruptible God into an image made like unto man. We do not see God as higher and more powerful than the world we see around us. God has become a nothing more than a neighborly chap who sometimes does us well rather than the Almighty God Who wants to do nothing but do us well. We do not see God the way the Bible portrays Him:

*"And God is able to make all grace abound toward you;
that ye, always having all sufficiency in all things,
may abound to every good work:"*
(2 Cor 9:8 KJV)

Changing Truth into Lies

The reason I bring all of this into light is because of the next few verses. There is no question that the Christian church struggles with pride, prejudice, and an acute lack of faith. We grapple with the very things Paul has been talking about while we judge those who are walking in the very manifestation of what this kind of behavior leads to:

Guilty of Judgment

"Wherefore God also gave them up
to uncleanness through the lusts of their own hearts,
to dishonour their own bodies between themselves:"
(Rom 1:24 KJV)

This is serious behavior and we see it evidenced profoundly in our world and in our churches. Sexual promiscuity and perversion is rampant everywhere we look. However, when we judge those who dishonor their own bodies between themselves we are judging ourselves because we are guilty of the very crimes that led to this dishonor. Paul summarizes these crimes: *"Who changed the truth of God into a lie, and worshipped and served the creature more than the Creator, who is blessed for ever. Amen." (Rom 1:25 KJV)*

These people changed the truth of God into a lie and worshipped and served the creature more than the Creator. Do we ever look at God's Word and think, "I tried that and it didn't work for me", or, "The Bible was written a long time ago and it is impossible to understand", or, "There are too many contradictions"? That kind of talk exposes the fact that we are changing the Truth of God into a lie. When dealing with the Bible, we must always work from the premise that it is true no matter what it says. All that is needed is study.

When we look to the world for answers, we will find ourselves serving this very world so that we can gain its reward. We try to placate our boss in order to get a promotion, we try to placate our spouse to get peace, and we try to placate our friends to have favor. However, God promoted Joseph while in a jail cell, Jesus gave us His peace, and God has given us His favor:

"For promotion cometh neither from the east, nor from the
west, nor from the south. But God is the judge: he putteth
down one, and setteth up another" (Psa 75:6-7 KJV)

Notice this verse does not mention the northern direction as a bad place to look for promotion; we must fix our eyes ever upward and we will find what we are looking for. When we do not, we have changed the Truth of God into a lie and now we are worshipping and serving the creature more than the Creator. Amazing. And again, what is the result of these kinds of crimes?

"And even as they did not like to retain God in their
knowledge, God gave them over to a reprobate mind, to do

Free to be Holy   89

those things which are not convenient;"
(Rom 1:28 KJV)

As the progression continues, we see that now they did not like to retain God in their knowledge. To retain God in our knowledge is to continually think upon God and keep what we know about Him in our hearts. Do we do this? Certainly we all think about God, but do we *retain* Him in our thoughts?

To retain is to keep. When we think at some times about God and at other times about the things of this life that concern us, we are not *retaining* God in our thoughts. Yes, it is possible to retain God in our knowledge. Everything we think and do must run through our knowledge of God.

But because they did not retain God in their knowledge, these people were given over to a reprobate mind. A reprobate mind is a mind that has been rejected and given over to complete and utter immorality. This is a serious end.

Guilty as Charged

I am going to back track so that we can find every negative attribute of those who have been given over to utter immorality:

1. They held the Truth in unrighteousness – not walking in what they know about God
2. They are without excuse because the manifest world proves the existence and ways of God
3. They knew God but did not glorify Him as God
4. They were ungrateful
5. They were full of empty and foolish thoughts
6. They had a darkened heart
7. They thought they were wise
8. They brought God down to the level of man
9. They changed the Truth of God into a lie
10. They served the creature more than the Creator
11. They did not retain God in their knowledge

If we have been honest, we have just admitted that, to some degree, we are guilty of the very things of which Paul is speaking. So let us go all the way with it: Is it possible that we are in danger of being given over to a reprobate mind?

Guilty of Judgment

If it is not of Faith, it is Sin

When we think of sins, we don't tend to think about this type of sin. We are too busy worrying about whether we are abstaining from alcohol, attending church, giving money, and being pleasant. However, the sins that Paul is bringing into light take great precedence over behavioral traits.

The Bible gives us a very easy definition for sin, *"for whatsoever is not of faith is sin."* In all we do, we must do it by faith. If our motivation is not faith, our works are sin, regardless of how pretty they look to the church. When we are more concerned about whether we sit in a pew once a week than we are about walking in the Truth of God's Word, we are faithless creatures. When we do not give God the glory He deserves and respect His Word for the ironclad Truth that it is, we are in danger of the following:

> *"Being filled with all unrighteousness,*
> *fornication, wickedness, covetousness, maliciousness;*
> *full of envy, murder, debate, deceit, malignity;*
> *whisperers, Backbiters, haters of God,*
> *despiteful, proud, boasters,*
> *inventors of evil things, disobedient to parents,*
> *Without understanding, covenantbreakers,*
> *without natural affection, implacable, unmerciful:*
> *Who knowing the judgment of God, that they which*
> *commit such things are worthy of death,*
> *not only do the same,*
> *but have pleasure in them that do them."*
> *(Rom 1:29-32 KJV)*

This is quite a list. I believe we have covered everything. When we look at this list, we cannot help to notice who it describes. Those who have been given over to reprobate minds are exhibiting the very behaviors we tend to judge. Yet, we also know how many of them came to have these reprobate minds. We made a list of their sins above. We have also admitted that we are guilty of these same crimes. Can we afford to judge?

Watch the Flow

Did immoral behavior cause apathy or did apathy cause immoral behavior? Seemingly innocent apathy actually *caused* this manifestation of evil. These people did not have a reprobate mind because of their evil actions; God gave them over to a reprobate mind and that is what *caused* the evil actions.

The progression is obvious: *Apathy -- reprobate mind -- evil.*

We must be honest and ask ourselves if Paul's description fits us. Do we neglect to glorify God in our circumstances as the miracle working God of the Bible? Do we respond to our situations the way the world responds, as though we have no God? Have we changed the Truth of God into a lie?

We know that God has promised to take care of us by the multitude of Scriptures that make this claim. Do all those Scriptures become as lies to us when we need them the most? Do we worship and serve our fellow man and ourselves more than God? In other words, do we look to others and ourselves for our protection, provision, and wisdom more than we look to God for these things?

Platitudes?

Several years ago a very upstanding Christian friend of mine discovered she had cancer. I hadn't seen her in awhile and when I did I was quick to encourage her with the Word of God. I was surprised when she basically just brushed me off.

A few months later this friend called me to apologize for her attitude on the day that we spoke. Her explanation was that everyone had been giving her Scriptures and at some point they just became platitudes to her. Platitudes? Hmmm...platitude: Banal statement: a pointless, unoriginal, or empty comment or statement made as though it was significant or helpful.

My friend thought I was giving her an empty comment to appear as though I was being helpful? I wondered if she found her chemo treatments pointless as well? Evidently not, as she attended each one religiously. Did my friend also brush off her doctor when he began to encourage her about all the things medical science could do to help her? Surely my friend had poured over any and all information she could get her hands on. Why didn't these things become platitudes as well?

My friend did good to apologize; she had been worshipping the creature by taking more solace in what he could do for her than in what her Creator had already done. In doing this she turned the Truth of God into a lie. If we cannot find solace in the Scriptures

Guilty of Judgment

when the worst things are happening, then they are of no value to us.

Thou art Inexcusable

Just so that we don't misunderstand the message, Paul furthers this thought even more emphatically in the following Chapter. This is an absolute continuation of the previous Chapter in that it begins by saying *"Therefore..."*

> *"Therefore thou art inexcusable, O man,*
> *whosoever thou art that judgest:*
> *for wherein thou judgest another,*
> *thou condemnest thyself;*
> *for thou that judgest doest the same things."*
> *(Rom 2:1 KJV)*

Paul, after going to great lengths to explain how one falls into reprehensible sin, turns his attention to those who judge even these, the worst offenders. The moment we judge another, judgment is turned on us and when we have broken the law in one place, we are guilty of all. In fact, when we judge someone, we are condemning ourselves of his very act.

These hellish creatures with reprobate minds are what they are because they misused what *we still have*. They began like us, which means that we can become like them if we follow their path. We must see these people through these eyes. We are inexcusable when we judge because when we judge another, we condemn ourselves for doing the same things. The moment we judge, we are guilty of the list we read from above! I have experienced this! I no sooner find myself judging someone than I find myself committing the same crime! O God, help us to receive this message.

Modern day Joseph

Shortly after my son Devon moved to Florida to live with his brother he got into trouble with the law, which resulted in a thirty-day jail sentence. As he relayed the story to me he said, "I don't know why I ended up with a sentence. The police were in the wrong. I prayed that justice would be served and while nothing happened to them, I am going to jail!"

Incredulous, I said, "You prayed for justice? You are lucky you didn't get the chair after such a self-righteous prayer!" I corrected my son by informing him that what the police did was between them and God while what he did was still wrong and the justice he prayed for was exactly what he got. Instead of judging the police and praying for justice, my son should have extended mercy and prayed for mercy. I encouraged Devon that it is never too late to win any spiritual war and that he must immediately ask God to forgive him of his self-righteous and judgmental attitude and ask God to have mercy on him and use this situation for good. I went on to spur him to expect great things...even in jail! Satan had stolen and now it was time for God to bless well beyond what he had to begin with.

Thankfully, Devon took my advice. Now his faith needed to be tried. My pre-planned visit with my sons happened to fall during the time that Devon was to go to jail. I had just completed the *Free to be Holy* series and had brought it with me so that Devon could have it while in jail. Unfortunately, this was not allowed. Although this upset me, Devon reminded me that we were going to walk this thing by faith and told me to mail it to him in sections as he could get mail.

We all went to the courthouse together to see him off to jail. Although we had a piece of paper at home, signed by the attorneys and the judge, that had previously given him a thirty-day sentence with a November 4th release date, for no apparent reason the judge pronounced a sixty-day sentence with a December release date! The public defender that had been assigned to Devon's case just shrugged his shoulders and that was the end of that. Now the thirty days had been doubled. Most importantly that meant two months without a paycheck instead of one.

I looked across the courtroom at Devon to see how he would respond. He turned to me and smiled. I knew what that smile meant: He was standing. As we watched him leave the courtroom in handcuffs, Nathan and I stood with him and believed God that somehow mercy would reign.

Immediately I began to mail the series and shortly thereafter I began getting letters. One would have expected to hear complaining about the judge, the attorney, the system, the jail, and so forth but that is not what I heard. Almost immediately my teen-age son began to mature before my eyes. I would like to share some excerpts from his letters in chronological order:

"Hello Mom and Dad...how ya doin?...me...oh...I'm ok...just going day by day. I have been reading a lot of the Bible. I went ahead and finished from Hebrews through Revelation then started from the beginning. Now I am at Joshua. I hope to read the entire Bible by the time I get out...I do need your book even with the

Guilty of Judgment

Bible...I know it will be uplifting...I can't wait to read it and really study it. I brag about it all the time to the guys...please get me Nick's address...I don't want to keep him in the dark...we are family and need to stick together...I love you very much and don't know what I would do without you...I'm doing everything possible in here to learn my lesson and never come back again...I just got my hair cut and it is just one step above bald...It looks pretty good! I hope Nate gets to see it before it grows out! Love Devon."

"Hello Mom and Dad...I was very happy to see some mail yesterday. I read what you sent that day and I plan on reading it a couple more times...it was pretty freaking good! I am able to understand it and take it in. (In the Bible) I've read up to Job...I'm really getting into the Old Testament...I'm trying to read as much as possible...I get interrupted a lot...Satan doesn't like me reading...I got moved into another room and that was good because I can read more (my roommate was getting annoying)...I work out every day and am up to 600 push-ups! The Lord has given me strength and peace...the time is flying by...I pray that this continues...He has answered my prayers concerning work because if I work I won't have any time to read...tell Nick and Jamie that I love them...you should send a chapter every three days...I want more...hope to hear from you soon...love you guys...Devon."

"Hey Mom and Dad...I just got your third envelope. I've read each chapter twice. I really do like it. I'm working on the last three chapters but I'm really getting tired of everyone being in my room...It's so hard to read...Satan is messing with me hard core when it comes to that...but when it comes to being at peace I am all over that...God has helped me tremendously...the time is flying...I got some ear plugs from my roommate that helped a lot but it's so funny...I'll be in my room by myself reading and someone will come in and start talking to me and I will take out my ear plugs and just look at them and they are like, 'O, I'm sorry...were you reading?' Yeah...it's crazy. I'm reading Isaiah now...I've read it all the way through but I'm re-reading a lot. I can't wait to see you at Christmas time...it's going to be awesome. And thank God I will be out by Thanksgiving. Well I'll let you go...I can't wait till your next chapters get here. I love you guys, Devon."

"Hey guys...How ya doin? I'm doing just fine. Most everyone that I know has left. Thank God He answered my prayers...I finally have time to myself to read. I also moved into the room across the hall...it has only one bed so I won't get a roommate and it has air conditioning which is awesome because my old room was hot. I have one more day of school left and that puts my release date at November 7th. Mom...your book is amazing...I got three chapters yesterday and finished them this morning...I just can't get enough. It all makes total sense...it's funny...when I read it reminds me of you so much I can picture you saying it right there in front of me. I have been praying for you concerning the book...as a matter of fact, I've been praying for all of you...especially our little guy in the family. He brings such joy to my heart when I think about him. He is so cute...Nick and Jamie...I love you guys and I cannot wait to see you and your son.

"Man let me tell you...if I wanted to get back into drugs this would have been the place to send me...I've met so many people who do and sell drugs it's not even funny. But when my friends that did drugs were leaving they always wanted to give me their numbers...I just said 'No thanks man...I'm clean and I want to stay that way.' I haven't gotten a number yet...thank you God for the power. I'm reading Jeremiah now...the next letter will be when I'm in the New Testament (God willing)...Love Devon."

Devon did not have to serve sixty days. As a matter of fact, he got released on the exact date (November 4th) that was originally written on that piece of paper that had been signed by the judge. The young man who left that jail was a completely different person than the one who had entered. Changing his judgmental attitude and leaning on the mercy of God blessed Devon beyond anything that may have happened outside of jail. Devon has since remained "clean".

The next time I visited Florida we ran into a man on the beach who recognized Devon from jail. This is what he said to me, his arm draped across Devon's shoulders, "Man...this guy was the top dog in the cell block...nobody could do anything without Devon's permission...he had made up all these games and we had to listen to him if we wanted to play." Devon got to live like Joseph because he dared to believe God. Mercy will get you everywhere.

"Do not be quick to judge, Froto,
the pity of Bilbo may well rule the fate of men."

Gandalf the Gray referring to the creature Gollum
as he spoke to Froto Baggins in
The Lord of the Rings, The Fellowship of the Ring

Part II

Real Getting

Blessed are the poor in spirit:
for theirs is the kingdom of heaven.

Blessed are they that mourn:
for they shall be comforted.

Blessed are the meek:
for they shall inherit the earth.

Blessed are they which do hunger and thirst
after righteousness: for they shall be filled.

Blessed are the merciful:
for they shall obtain mercy.

Blessed are the pure in heart:
for they shall see God.

Blessed are the peacemakers:
for they shall be called the children of God.

Matt 5:3 - 9

A new spirit will I put within you: and I will take away the stony heart out of your flesh, and will give an heart of flesh. (Ezekiel 11:19)
What a wonderful promise! And it is yea and amen in Christ Jesus to the glory of God by us. Let us lay hold of it; accept it as true, and appropriate it to ourselves. Then shall it be fulfilled in us, and we shall have, in after days and years, to sing of that wondrous change which the sovereign grace of God has wrought in us.
Charles Spurgeon, All of Grace

5

THE HEART
OF THE MATTER

We are about to step into an arena I deeply enjoy. There is a way to be holy in our behavior in spite of the fact that we contend with a hell-bent flesh. All that is required is that we get real with God and just deal with Him on the premise of what we know.

The first thing we must do is find out more about this thing called "behavior".

The Same, yet Different

It was my friend's anniversary and her husband had forgotten. While at another friend's home, the husband noticed a rose in a vase and was reminded of what day it was. He ended up taking that rose and giving it to his wife. Upon receiving the rose my friend sensed something was up and her husband confessed. She was no longer interested in the rose.

Several years ago my eight-year-old son, Nathan, was eating his breakfast when he discovered it was Mother's Day. He snuck out of the house, walked a mile to a store on a blustery morning and bought me flowers. By the time those flowers got to me they were sorely wind-whipped.

The act of good behavior was present in both; however, the joy of the behavior was only present in Nathan. Although my friend's rose was beautiful, it was rejected while my wind-whipped flowers were warmly received. The act was the same while the heart and the responses were different. The heart carries the key as to whether the behavior will be received.

So is it enough to be merely obedient? When a child is told to do something and he gives a dirty look and a snide answer before doing it, are we satisfied? Don't the dirty look and snide answer speak volumes about the heart within the child? And isn't the attitude within the child even *more* important than what the child does?

Let's go back to the Andy Griffith Show once again. Andy's sidekick, Barney was always screwing up. Andy put up with his constant blundering for one and only one reason: He meant well. His heart was in the right place. Andy, with a warm smile, was commonly heard saying (in his southern drawl) things like, "Aw, he means well...he's just a little spirited."

So what we learn about behavior is that it does not have any personal substantiation; it cannot stand on its own merit. For behavior to be truly good, it must issue from a right heart. Why even bad behavior can be seen as good when it issues from a right heart.

The Condition of the Heart

God has always been very interested in the heart behind the act. As a matter of fact, the heart is the center of God's attention:

> *"But the LORD said unto Samuel, Look not on his*
> *countenance, or on the height of his stature; because I*

The Heart of the Matter

have refused him: for the LORD seeth not as man seeth;
for man looketh on the outward appearance, but the LORD
looketh on the heart." (1 Sam 16:7 KJV)

Here Samuel was looking over the sons of Jesse to find which one God wanted him to anoint as King of Israel. No one expected God's choice to be David, the youngest boy out tending sheep.

God makes it very plain that He moves directly past everything else and zeroes in on the condition of the heart. God referred to David as a man after His own heart. It was the heart aspect of David that appealed to God. This is a sobering thought. We can pretend on the outside with all of our good acts, but our hearts cannot pretend; they lay naked before God.

The Good of the Land

We all want to prosper and be blessed. Well, there is a way to do that. As God peers at our naked hearts, He is looking for one thing:

"If ye be willing and obedient,
ye shall eat the good of the land:"
(Isa 1:19 KJV).

Willingness. Notice that we must be *willing* and obedient. It's not enough to just obey; we must be willing about it. If we are willing and obedient, we will eat the **good of the land**. We will eat in the finest restaurants, live in the biggest houses, stay in the nicest hotels, shop in the best stores, drive the fanciest cars, enjoy the best health, raise the finest families within the best marriages, and be a part of the best possible relationship with God. That is what it means to eat the good of the land.

We know that we are not always going to *look* like we are eating the good of the land; however, that does not mean that we aren't. When we become willing, even the tough times turn into the "good of the land". If a king were to invite us to his country and give us the "good of the land" it would mean that we could have our pick of anything. In the Old Testament, the good of the land was very literally the *good of the land*; the Israelites were being offered a land flowing with milk and honey. The prophet Isaiah is telling us that if we can get our heart into this thing, we will eat the good of the land.

A Bad Attitude

How many times do we find ourselves doing things with a bad

attitude? We don't want to go to that family reunion, we don't want to go grocery shopping, we don't want to rake the yard, we don't want to have that talk with our child, we don't want to fire that employee, we don't want to give money to the church, we don't want to put mom in a nursing home, we don't want to share our home with the homeless, we don't *want* to be inconvenienced in any way. It is our preference to have everything go our way.

Realistically, we know that we must do things that we do not want to do, but how do we get to the place where we become willing about it? The only way our deeds are going to merit any sort of a reward is if we get to the place where we *want* to do them.

Willing in the Day of Thy Power

> *"The LORD said unto my Lord,*
> *Sit thou at my right hand,*
> *until I make thine enemies thy footstool.*
> *The LORD shall send the rod of thy strength out of Zion:*
> *rule thou in the midst of thine enemies.*
> ***Thy people shall be willing in the day of thy power,***
> *in the beauties of holiness from the womb of the morning:*
> *thou hast the dew of thy youth."*
> *(Psa 110:1-3 KJV emphasis mine)*

This Psalm, written by David, is a prophecy about Jesus that is commonly quoted in the New Testament. We know that after Jesus was raised from the dead:

> *"But this man, after he had offered one sacrifice for sins*
> *for ever, sat down on the right hand of God;*
> *From henceforth expecting*
> *till his enemies be made his footstool."*
> *(Heb 10:12-13 KJV)*

If this is what happened after Jesus died, then the *"day of thy power"* from above must be now.

According to our verse, *"Thy people shall be **willing** in the day of thy power..."* King David prophesied that when the Messiah sat down at the right hand of God it would be "the day of His power" and God's people would be a willing people. Well, Jesus is sitting at the right hand of God as we speak; therefore, the day of God's power is today.

The Heart of the Matter

This is good news. If it has been prophesied that we would be "willing" in this, the day of God's power, then the grace to be willing is Biblically available to us right now. Paul speaks of this very grace in his letter to the Philippians:

> *"For it is God which worketh in you*
> *both to will and to do of his good pleasure.*
> *Do all things without murmurings and disputings:"*
> *(Phil 2:13-14 KJV)*

It is God that works in us both to *will* and to *do* of His good pleasure. In this day, God's power will work in us in such a way that not only will we become *capable* of being obedient; we will become willing, or wholehearted about it. The Bible is telling us that God will work in us concerning our behavior, *and* concerning our heart behind the behavior. This is what it means when it says God *"works in us both to will and to do of his good pleasure."*

Hence, it follows that if we do a thing wholeheartedly, we will do it without murmuring and disputing. Why would we complain about doing something we *want* to do? God has promised to give us the power to be obedient, and the heart to enjoy it. When we are willing and obedient, we will eat the good of the land.

So we see that the Bible has taught us two things: We must be willing and obedient if we are going to benefit, and God has provided the grace for both.

King Asa and the Perfect Heart

Now I would like to show you that not only is a willing heart necessary to every act of obedience, it is even *more important* than the act itself. We may be doing our services correctly or incorrectly, but, most importantly, we must be doing them wholeheartedly. This is what God is interested in.

We are going to look at two kings, first King Asa and then King Amaziah. King Asa had a willing heart and King Amaziah had an unwilling heart.

Asa was king during an interesting time in Israel, *"Now for a long season Israel hath been without the true God, and without a teaching priest, and without law." (2 Chr 15:3 KJV)* But, *"...when they in their trouble did turn unto the LORD God of Israel, and sought him, he was found of them." (2 Chr 15:4 KJV)* Israel had been separated from God for a long spell before they finally called out to Him and He showed up.

Now Azariah, the prophet on staff, was prophesying to King Asa concerning the nation's present status with God and what they could expect from Him, *"Be ye strong therefore, and let not your hands be weak: for your work shall be rewarded."* *(2 Chr 15:7 KJV)* This was excellent news. God was on their side again. The story goes on to say that when Asa heard this prophecy he was encouraged and he, *"put away the abominable idols out of all the land."*

Zealously Affected

So zealous was he that:

> *"King Asa even deposed his grandmother Maacah from her position as queen mother because she had made an obscene Asherah pole. He cut down the pole, broke it up, and burned it in the Kidron Valley."* *(2 Chr 15:16 NLT)*

King Asa removed his own grandmother from the throne! He was serious about this thing; King Asa had a willing heart. We see this evidenced in his passion.

Afterwards there was a huge offering made to the Lord:

> *"And they entered into a covenant to seek the LORD God of their fathers with all their heart and with all their soul;"* *(2 Chr 15:12 KJV)*.

This entire people were so wholehearted about following God that they willingly entered into a covenant made by their own terms.

A Serious Covenant

What could possibly make God happier than a people who sought Him with all their heart and soul? Evidently, King Asa's enthusiasm was contagious. Consider the terms of this covenant into which these people willingly entered:

> *"That whosoever would not seek the LORD God of Israel should be put to death, whether small or great, whether man or woman."* *(2 Chr 15:13 KJV)*

Terms of the covenant: Seek the God of Israel or die. These people were on fire about this:

The Heart of the Matter

"And all Judah rejoiced at the oath:
for they had sworn with all their heart,
and sought him with their whole desire;
and he was found of them:
and the LORD gave them rest round about."
(2 Chr 15:15 KJV emphasis mine)

Rest Round About

The Lord gave the Israelites rest round about because they sought Him with their whole desire. The Israelites already had the good of the land; to have rest round about meant they could relax for a bit and enjoy it. When we get willing, God gets generous; God gave them rest until the *thirty-fifth* year of King Asa. That is a long time.

To have rest "round about" was a big deal for these people who had been in warfare for as long as they could remember. The world has been cursed and the default setting in the life of every man is warfare of some sort. To say that God gave these people rest round about is to say that God reversed the curse in the lives of these people. Are we interested in having rest "round about"? I know I am. If a willing heart moves the hand of God then I want to be willing.

Perfect?

King Asa was not a perfect king, *"But the high places were not taken away out of Israel..."* or was he? *"...nevertheless the heart of Asa was perfect all his days."* (2 Chr 15:17 KJV) These two thoughts are summed up in a single verse. King Asa did not remove all the high places; *nevertheless*, the heart of Asa was **perfect all his days**...yes, even all the days he refused to remove the high places.

King Asa failed behaviorally in not removing the high places; nevertheless, his heart was perfect all his days. Imperfection and perfection ran side by side, yet God considered the heart of Asa rather than his actions. So is it possible to be imperfect in our actions while we remain perfect in our hearts? Evidently it is.

King Amaziah and the Imperfect Heart

We must take the emphasis off of our actions and put it on the heart behind our actions. We are really straining at a gnat while we swallow a camel in this place. Consider the commentary on our second king, Amaziah:

The Sin within

*"Amaziah was twenty and five years old when he began to
reign, and he reigned twenty and nine years in Jerusalem.
And his mother's name was Jehoaddan of Jerusalem.
And he did that which was right in the sight of the LORD,
but not with a perfect heart."*
(2 Chr 25:1-2 KJV)

Now we see where the opposite scenario is played out in King
Amaziah's life. Again, all in one sentence, Amaziah did that which
was right in the sight of the Lord but not with a perfect heart.
Perfection and imperfection ran side by side, yet God considered the
heart. So is it possible to do right things but with a wrong heart?
Evidently it is.

Self Reliance

We watched what happened to King Asa with his imperfect actions
and his perfect heart, now let us watch to see what happens to King
Amaziah with his perfect actions and his imperfect heart. When we
do the right things with the wrong heart, we are running on our own
steam and it is just a matter of time before we run out. The
following from the New Living Testament is an example of King
Amaziah's good works:

*"When Amaziah was well established as king,
he executed the men who had assassinated his father.
However, he did not kill the children of the assassins,
for **he obeyed the command of the LORD
written in the Book of the Law of Moses:***
*"Parents must not be put to death for the sins of their
children, nor the children for the sins of their parents.
Those worthy of death
must be executed for their own crimes."*
(2 Chr 25:3-4 NLT emphasis mine)

The Bible gives us an example of Amaziah's good works. Since we
were told that King Amaziah did what was right in the sight of the
Lord but not with a perfect heart, we see that he is doing his acts in
his own power; that is what it means to have an imperfect heart.
King Amaziah is not relying on the Lord in faith, and this is
evidenced by how he begins to prepare for battle without seeking the
Lord's direction. Again, from the New Living Translation:

The Heart of the Matter

"Another thing Amaziah did was to organize the army,
assigning leaders to each clan from Judah and Benjamin.
Then he took a census and found that he had an army of
300,000 men twenty years old and older,
all trained in the use of spear and shield.
He also paid about 7,500 pounds of silver to hire
100,000 experienced fighting men from Israel."
(2 Chr 25:5-6 NLT)

He must be Stopped!

Amaziah, king over Judah, was going to battle all by himself. He organized an army, took a census of fighting men, and hired 100,000 fighting men from Israel. All was set in order to defeat the Edomites. However, God sent a prophet to King Amaziah to stop him:

"But a man of God came to the king and said,
"O king, do not hire troops from Israel,
for the LORD is not with Israel.
He will not help those people of Ephraim!
If you let them go with your troops into battle,
you will be defeated no matter how well you fight.
God will overthrow you,
for he has the power to help or to frustrate."
(2 Chr 25:7-8 NLT)

This is proof that Amaziah was running on his own steam; he had to be stopped before he brought disaster upon his kingdom. Had Amaziah sought the counsel of the Lord, he would have been directed differently. So, after hearing this, Amaziah did the right thing and took the advice from the prophet:

"So Amaziah discharged the hired troops and sent them
back to Ephraim. This made them angry with Judah and
they returned home in a great rage."
(2 Chr 25:10 NLT)

Pay Back is Not Sweet

However, God only gives "rest round about" to those who are of a willing heart, such as was King Asa. Although King Amaziah was gruesomely successful in his battle against the Edomites,

> *"Then Amaziah summoned his courage*
> *and led his army to the Valley of Salt where*
> *they killed ten thousand Edomite troops from Seir.*
> *They captured another ten thousand and took them to the*
> *top of a cliff and threw them off,*
> *dashing them to pieces on the rocks below."*
> *(2 Chr 25:11-12 NLT),*

King Amaziah was far from rest "round about":

> *"Meanwhile, the hired troops that Amaziah had sent home*
> *raided several of the towns of Judah between Samaria and*
> *Beth-horon, killing three thousand people and carrying off*
> *great quantities of plunder." (2 Chr 25:13 NLT)*

Because King Amaziah did not have God in his heart when he prepared his troops for battle, he ignorantly hired those who were presently distanced from God's favor. This action had its price and Amaziah's Judah lost three thousand people and much plunder. This was mistake number one under the mighty reign of Amaziah. Mistake number two seemed to come at Amaziah sideways:

So Bad

> *"When King Amaziah returned from defeating the*
> *Edomites, he brought with him idols taken from the people*
> *of Seir. He set them up as his own gods, bowed down in*
> *front of them, and presented sacrifices to them!"*
> *(2 Chr 25:14 NLT)*

Why would a king who had a penchant for "doing the right thing", do something that was so obviously wrong? Because Amaziah was working in his own power; his heart was not right with the Lord. When we work in our own power, we are destined for complete failure. It matters not how much we *want* to do the right thing, the harder we try to do it, the more utterly we fail at it. I have heard testimony from high school guys who have said that the more religious a girl is, the easier it is to get her into bed. Religious girls try with all of their hearts to be good, but the flesh profits nothing.

The Heart of the Matter

Self Reliance...always Self Reliance

We must get over our self-reliance. The only problem with the king's heart was that it was self-reliant. If Amaziah was doing what was right in the sight of the Lord, he obviously had respect for God's Law. His fault was not in the Law written in stone; Amaziah's fault was in thinking he had the wherewithal to satisfy that Law in his own power.

We saw where he worked under his own steam as he prepared for battle. That is a ridiculous thing for the king of Judah to do. All previous victories were determined by whether or not God was with the king. Although Amaziah was doing right things, he was still in control of his life; he had not surrendered to God.

King Amaziah proved he was self-reliant when he did not seek the Lord's wisdom for battle. How many times have we gone to battle on our own steam and by our own counsel?

Evil is Present in this Place

Paul told us that when he purposed to do good, evil was present with him. Obviously, King Amaziah purposed to do good since that is what he was doing. However, Amaziah, in all his good works was waking the evil that was inside of him. When this evil unleashed itself upon him, he found himself doing things he never dreamed he would do. That is what self-reliance will get us, *"King Amaziah returned...brought idols...set them up as his own gods, bowed down in front of them, and presented sacrifices to them!"*

King Amaziah and all of his efforts fell hard. One must never think he is above even the basest behaviors. We are talking about the chosen King of Judah! Jesus is the Lion of Judah. Amaziah is a man of whom it can be said, "He did what was right in the sight of the Lord." _This man_ set up pagan idols as his own gods and bowed down to them and presented sacrifices to them. Oh my. This is the eventual end to all who labor in the flesh. At some point, we will bow to what is not God.

The End of an Imperfect Heart

We watched how King Asa failed to remove the high places, yet he had a perfect heart and he was blessed according to that heart. Now let us see what happens when one fails with an imperfect heart:

> *"This made the LORD very angry, and he sent a prophet to ask, "Why have you worshiped gods who could not even*

save their own people from you?"
(2 Chr 25:15 NLT)

Although God is angry with Amaziah, in His mercy, He sends him a prophet to try to shake him into reality. It doesn't work:

"But the king interrupted him and said,
"Since when have I asked your advice?
Be quiet now before I have you killed!"
(2 Chr 25:16a NLT)

Now we have rejected a prophet of God and thus sealed our fate:

"So the prophet left with this warning: "I know that God
has determined to destroy you because you have done this
and have not accepted my counsel."
(2 Chr 25:16b NLT)

The prophet is the voice of God. When His voice comes, we must listen. This was Amaziah's chance to get right with God and begin as a new man. In the end, his sin was in rejecting God's counsel.

Avenging Judah from Israel

In the meantime, Amaziah still had the matter of Israel killing three thousand Judeans and taking much plunder. Therefore, still running in his own steam, King Amaziah met with his counselors and decided to send a challenge to Jehoash, King of Israel in his response to their attack on Judah while he was defeating the Edomites. However, Jehoash knew the score and he sent back a warning:

"You may be very proud of your conquest of Edom, but my
advice is to stay home. Why stir up trouble that will bring
disaster on you and the people of Judah?"
"But Amaziah would not listen, for God was arranging to
destroy him for worshiping the gods of Edom."
(2 Chr 25:19-20 NLT)

Amaziah would not listen. However, what neither of them knew was that God was behind this challenge. God still had a score to settle with Amaziah concerning his idol worship.

The Heart of the Matter

King Asa's sin was covered because of the condition of his heart. King Amaziah had to pay for his sin because of the condition of his heart:

"After Amaziah turned away from the LORD,
there was a conspiracy against his life in Jerusalem, and
he fled to Lachish. But his enemies sent assassins after him,
and they killed him there."

In a very sad ending we see that:

"They brought him back to Jerusalem on a horse,
and he was buried with his ancestors
in the City of David."
(2 Chr 25:27-28 NLT)

This is the final commentary on the life of a man who did what was right in the sight of the Lord, but not with a perfect heart. Let's go back and reread what was said of *King Asa* during the time that he had a perfect heart:

"But the high places were not taken away out of Israel:
nevertheless the heart of Asa was perfect all his days. And
he brought into the house of God the things that his father
had dedicated, and that he himself had dedicated, silver,
and gold, and vessels. And there was no more war unto the
five and thirtieth year of the reign of Asa."
(2 Chr 15:17-19 KJV)

Side by Side

Let's put the verses together describing King Asa and King Amaziah and see what we have:

"But the high places were not taken away out of Israel:
nevertheless the heart of Asa was perfect all his days...
And he (Amaziah) did that which was right
in the sight of the LORD, but not with a perfect heart."

The Bible is telling us we can do wrong things with a right heart and right things with a wrong heart. The heart is the central issue. We are going to spend the balance of this book series dealing with doing the wrong things with the right heart, but we are first going to deal with doing the right things with the wrong heart.

God shows Himself Strong

When we think about God, we tend to think of Him as though He were Santa Claus making a list and checking it twice to see if we are naughty or nice. We have our eyes so focused on our behavior that we are neglecting the more important issue at hand:

> *"For the eyes of the LORD run to and fro throughout the whole earth, to show himself strong in the behalf of them whose heart is perfect toward him..."*
> *(2 Chr 16:9a KJV)*

God said this to our King Asa from above at the thirty-five year mark when his heart began to slip away from the Lord. The peace was about to end and God was trying to remind Asa of how much he was blessed when he had a willing heart. God tells Asa that his eyes are forever scanning the whole earth, in search of one with a perfect heart so that He can show Himself strong in that person.

The eyes of God are not running to and fro throughout the earth to show Himself strong on behalf of those who, like Amaziah, were *behaving* well.

Why is God so concerned about a willing heart? God looks for a willing heart because a willing heart is what is necessary in order for works to be authentic. God is not interested in what we can do when we try really hard. Empty works are as filthy rags to God. There are all kinds of people who are doing good things, but if they are not doing those things with a perfect heart their works are worthless and in vain. God is not interested in our second-hand rose.

In the Old Days

Throughout the Old Testament we can see that the condition of the heart trumped all else. For God, this thing has never been about behavior. Although God uses the children of Israel as an example to believers of what not to do, His beef with them centered on their evil hearts of unbelief; not their behavior per se. Now we are going to pull passages from Second Chronicles to see how the heart of the king moved God concerning the children of Israel:

The Heart of the Matter

Heart Prosperity

*"And God said to Solomon, **Because this was in thine heart**, and thou hast not asked riches, wealth, or honour, nor the life of thine enemies, neither yet hast asked long life; but hast asked wisdom and knowledge for thyself, that thou mayest judge my people, over whom I have made thee king: Wisdom and knowledge is granted unto thee; and I will give thee riches, and wealth, and honour, such as none of the kings have had that have been before thee, neither shall there any after thee have the like."*
(2 Chr 1:11-12 KJV)

Solomon did not ask for wisdom and knowledge because it was the "right" thing to do. Solomon could have asked for riches, but it wasn't in his *heart* to ask for riches, *"Because this was in thine heart, and thou hast not asked riches"*. Solomon's heart wanted wisdom and knowledge to lead God's people and that is what his heart asked for. Now we have willingness and obedience. King Solomon is about to eat the good of the land.

God was so well pleased with the condition of Solomon's heart that He gave Solomon what he asked for *plus* riches, wealth, and honor such as no other king had ever had before, and more than any king will ever have! King Solomon had a willing heart and he ate the good of the land and then some!

Heart Obedience

*"But the LORD said to David my father, Forasmuch as it was in thine heart to build an house for my name, **thou didst well in that it was in thine heart:**"*
(2 Chr 6:8 KJV)

David did not build a house for God, but it was imputed to him as though he had because it was in his heart to do it, *"Even as David also describeth the blessedness of the man, unto whom God imputeth righteousness without works,"* (Rom 4:6 KJV). Absolutely no action had to take place for David to do well. David did well only and entirely in his heart. A huge faith notch was added to David's belt simply because he desired in his heart to build a house for God. What do our hearts desire for God?

Abraham did not have to kill his son, Isaac, but it was accounted to him as though he did because he was *willing* to do it. This non-act is listed with the heroes of faith in the book of Hebrews. The entire salvation package was symbolized by something that never even happened; Abraham only needed to be *willing* to kill his beloved son to pave the road for God to sacrifice *His* Son. The death of Isaac was real in the spiritual realm the moment Abraham made the decision to obey. The condition of his heart is what was counted for that righteous act in Abraham's life. This is precisely how we must be children of Abraham: Willing and obedient. Whether or not our acts are good or bad, they must at all times issue forth from a true heart. God knows full well when people try to exploit this Truth. God alone knows the hearts of men.

God Knows our Heart

"Then hear thou from heaven thy dwelling place, and forgive, and render unto every man according unto all his ways, whose heart thou knowest; (for thou only knowest the hearts of the children of men:)"
(2 Chr 6:30 KJV)

This verse starts out by asking God to render to every man according to his *ways* and then says, *"whose heart thou knowest."* God will judge us, not according to our *works* but according to our *ways*.

It is not *what* we do but the *way* we do it. The world can see our works, but God knows our *ways*. In what *way* did we help our neighbor? Did we do it sighing and wishing we didn't have to? Did we do it for brownie points with God? Did we do it to get the world's praise? Or, did we do it with a perfect, trusting heart? We will be judged, not according to *what* we did but rather the *way* we did it, *"(for God only knows the hearts of the children of men.)"*

Willingness Comes from God

"Also in Judah the hand of God was to give them one heart to do the commandment of the king and of the princes, by the word of the LORD." (2 Chr 30:12 KJV)

The power of God's hand moved on the hearts of the people and gave them a *willingness* to do the commandment of the king. God holds the power to move upon the hearts of men, *"For it is God which worketh in you both to will and to do of his good pleasure."*

The Heart of the Matter

Heart Trumps All

"Since many of the people there
had not purified themselves,
the Levites had to slaughter their Passover lambs
for them, to set them apart for the LORD.
Most of those who came from Ephraim, Manasseh,
Issachar, and Zebulun had not purified themselves.
But Hezekiah prayed for them, saying,
The good LORD pardon every one
That prepareth his heart to seek God,
the LORD God of his fathers, though he be not cleansed
according to the purification of the sanctuary.
And the LORD hearkened to Hezekiah,
and healed the people. "
(2 Chr 30:17-20 NLT&KJV)

In this instance King Hezekiah asked God to pardon the fact that some of the people had not purified themselves for the Passover according to the Mosaic Law. However, he did not ask the Lord to pardon *everyone*, but rather he asked God to pardon those who, *"preparest his heart to seek God...".* God obliged. God looks at the heart. It did not matter that they broke the Mosaic Law; they were justified, or made holy, by the condition of their heart. The heart trumps all.

The Best of the Land

"And thus did Hezekiah throughout all Judah, and
wrought that which was good and right and truth before
the LORD his God. And in every work that he began in the
service of the house of God, and in the law, and in the
commandments, to seek his God,
he did it with all his heart, and prospered. "
(2 Chr 31:20-21 KJV)

We have to ask ourselves if King Hezekiah was blessed by what he did or by the way he did it. Our Scriptures say that King Hezekiah did what he did with *"all his heart".* That is what caused him to prosper.

We saw where it was said in one verse that King Asa neglected to take away the high places, *"...nevertheless the heart of Asa was perfect all his days."* And then we read a single verse that stated how King Amaziah did what was right in the sight of the Lord, *"...but not with a perfect heart."* From this we know that the condition of the heart is what matters. So although the beginning of our verses concerning King Hezekiah gave us a list of right things that Hezekiah *did*, we know that the closing remark of *"...he did it with all his heart..."* is what caused him to prosper. God prospered King Hezekiah according to his heart.

Pride

As with many Israelite kings, Hezekiah fell into a trap. At some point, blessings can be seen as things for which to be proud, as though we had somehow earned them. I have seen this happen with many men and ministries. What started out as faith ended with good works and the praise of men:

> *"About that time, Hezekiah became deathly ill.*
> *He prayed to the LORD, who healed him*
> *and gave him a miraculous sign.*
> *But Hezekiah did not respond appropriately*
> *to the kindness shown him, and he became **proud**.*
> *So the LORD'S anger came against him*
> *and against Judah and Jerusalem.*
> *Then Hezekiah repented of his **pride**,*
> *and the people of Jerusalem humbled themselves.*
> *So the LORD'S anger did not come against them*
> *during Hezekiah's lifetime."*
> *(2 Chr 32:24-26 NLT)*

Pride is a condition of the heart. Look at how the condition of King Hezekiah's heart moved God and affected the people of the kingdom, *"he became proud...then the LORD'S anger came against him and against Judah and Jerusalem...Then Hezekiah repented of his pride...so the LORD'S anger did not come against them."* We cannot overstate the importance of the condition of our heart. If we are not willing and wholehearted about what we do, we cannot expect to be blessed in our deed.

We see where King Hezekiah slipped in his heart and brought down Judah and Jerusalem and then turned from his pride and saved Judah and Jerusalem. That is a lot of power. The heart is the only essential component to success. When his heart failed, he kindled the anger of the Lord. When Hezekiah's heart regained the lead, he quelled the anger of the Lord.

Riches beyond the Imagination

"Hezekiah was very wealthy and held in high esteem.
He had to build special treasury buildings
for his silver, gold, precious stones, and spices,
and for his shields and other valuable items.
He also constructed many storehouses for his grain,
new wine, and olive oil; and he made many stalls for his
cattle and folds for his flocks of sheep and goats.
He built many towns and acquired vast flocks and herds,
for God had given him great wealth...
And so he succeeded in everything he did."
(2 Chr 32:27-30 NLT)

Although King Hezekiah had just angered the Lord, the minute he got his heart in the right place he was back in business. King Hezekiah became so wealthy that he had to construct buildings to hold all his wealth, *"if you are willing and obedient you shall eat the good of the land."* Special treasury buildings held his silver, gold, and precious stones and Hezekiah built many storehouses for his foods, many stalls for his herds, and he built many towns. King Hezekiah was the Bill Gates of Israel.

The Test

"However, when ambassadors arrived from Babylon to ask
about the remarkable events that had taken place in the
land, God withdrew from Hezekiah in order to test him and
to see what was really in his heart."
(2 Chr 32:31 NLT)

God wanted to sit back and watch to see how King Hezekiah would act in front of these ambassadors. Would King Hezekiah get back into pride and brag about all his wealth, or would he give God the glory from a willing heart? The story doesn't tell us, but I assume Hezekiah gave God the glory from a willing heart because this is where the story ends, and I've not known God to end on a bad note.

A tender Heart quells Wrath

Josiah became king at a time when the Word of God had been lost for long enough that no one even had a copy. Clearly the people were no longer even considering the Mosaic Law, let alone obeying it. As it happened, *"Hilkiah the priest found a book of the law of the LORD given by Moses"* and brought this book to the king.

What King Josiah learned from reading the Mosaic Law is that they were in T-R-O-U-B-L-E. Josiah was deeply moved by the words that were written and *"And it came to pass, when the king had heard the words of the law, that he rent his clothes."*

Evidently, that was the right thing to do:

"Because thine heart was tender
and you humbled yourself before God when you heard
what I said against this city and its people.
You humbled yourself and tore your clothing
in despair and wept before me in repentance.
So I have indeed heard you, says the LORD.
I will not send the promised disaster
against this city and its people...
until after you have died and been buried in peace."
(2 Chr 34:27-28 KJV & NLT)

God reversed the curse of an entire city because the heart of the king was tender and he humbled himself and repented. God brought the promised disaster, but not until this tenderhearted king had died and been buried in peace.

God is moved by the condition of the heart of man. God is looking for a tender, willing, and whole heart. When He finds this, He will show Himself strong. When we are willing and obedient we will eat the good of the land.

Now we must learn how to get willing.

Because thou servedst not the LORD thy God with joyfulness, and with gladness of heart, for the abundance of all things...
Deuteronomy 28:47

6

THE EXPEDIENCE OF OBEDIENCE

All Christians would agree that it is a good idea to obey God's laws. We know that God would agree with this and Jesus would agree with this and the Holy Ghost would agree with this. We all want to be holy and we are all angling for that end. Since all parties involved agree on this thing, surely we can make something happen.

A New and Better Way

There is a better way to obey. We tried to obey by the power of the flesh and we failed. The flesh profits nothing. Even if we seem to be having some success, our balloon deflates when we hear God say, *"all our righteousnesses are as filthy rags"*, because we did not do what we did with a perfect heart of faith. There is no getting around it; we must find a way to be obedient that actually pleases God, and stifles our flesh. Seems like a tall order, but it is not.

I have heard much teaching about the whys and wherefores of obedience to God. Some teach that we must be obedient no matter how we feel about it. Others teach that we must be obedient simply because it is the right thing to do. Still others teach that we must be good in order to protect God's reputation. In all, the consensus is that much toiling is required. Many are the *wrong* reasons to obey God and all of them require human effort.

A Pat on the Back

To say that our good works require laborious human effort is to say that our works are of the flesh and we know that, *"no good thing can come from the flesh."* The first thing we must ask ourselves in all we do is this: Who deserves to get the glory for this act? Regardless of whether or not I want to be, am I in a position to receive praise? Have I exerted my own personal effort in accomplishing this task? If God were handing out bozo buttons, would I be in line for one? If so, we are acting according to the flesh and our works are filthy rags to God. I once watched a preacher actually reach around and pat himself on the back for loving his enemy through gritted teeth: Filthy rags.

We are going to learn how to Biblically obey God with a perfect heart by the power of the Holy Spirit. This is a new and better way:

"For the law made nothing perfect,
but the bringing in of a better hope did;
by the which we draw nigh unto God."
(Heb 7:19 KJV)

The law has never rehabilitated anyone, but a new way entered the scene and now we have hope for something better! Through this new way we will draw near to God. We must leave the law behind and get about the "better hope" that brings us into God's presence.

The Expedience of Obedience

Right Thing -- Wrong Way

Most of us obey God with incorrect motives. Overall, Christians are generally motivated to obey God in three ways: Because we love Him, because we fear Him, or because we feel a sense of duty toward God. Although these are very honorable reasons to obey God, they are virtually ineffective in accomplishing this task.

Why? Because we Like You!

We do like God and we want very much to obey Him. And, as long as everything goes all right, we will do just fine. However, what is going to happen when we feel threatened? Do we continue to tithe when the electricity has been turned off? Do we continue to love a neighbor who is taking us to court? Do we continue to honor a father who is abusing us?

Although we love God, it is easy to step into our fall back position of forgiveness with this loving God. "I'm sorry God. The lights went out and I am afraid so I cannot tithe. Please forgive me." And so we go through our lives obeying God because we love Him and when the going gets tough, we back out. Our love for God is not enough motivation to keep us on the straight and narrow through thick and thin. When I was first married, I was a Christian and I loved God. I wanted to obey Him but my situation became unbearable. Unfortunately, my love for God was not enough motivation to keep me in line. I stayed on the hamster wheel of failure and forgiveness for years.

Why? Because we Fear You!

I had a friend who attended a fear-based church. Fire and brimstone sermons were the pastor's specialties. Those who sinned were in line for the wrath of God. Unfortunately, my friend was trying to shake a colored past and these sermons were not helping the situation. She would leave church in terror of the wrath of God and a strong resolution to try harder. Paul taught us that when he tried to do well, evil was present with him. My friend returned home only to fail again and again. She felt doomed and forsaken Monday through Saturday, and condemned on Sunday. My friend died...never receiving the freedom she so desperately sought.

The reason my friend did not receive her deliverance is because her church convinced her that she was under the wrath of God. That is not true. The unsaved world *is* under this threat, *"...he that believeth not the Son shall not see life; but the wrath of God abideth on him." (John 3:36 KJV)* The wrath of God abides on those who do not believe Jesus. However the born-again Christian should not fear the wrath of God, *"...even Jesus, which delivered us from the wrath to come...For God hath not appointed us to wrath, but to obtain salvation by our Lord Jesus Christ," (1 Thess 1:10&5:9 KJV).* Fear of the wrath of God must never be what motivates a believer. Fear is the very thing that attaches us to wrath! The fearful and unbelieving will have their part in the lake of fire! (Rev 21:8) It is through faith, not fear, that we obtain salvation from wrath.

When we try to be good in order to fend off the wrath of God, we are proving that we are ignorant concerning what has already been accomplished through Jesus! The moment we become born of God, His wrath is turned away from us. We are not appointed to wrath; wrath abides on those who *don't* believe on the Son. That does not describe us.

When we obey God in order to escape His wrath, we are beginning with false doctrine and we cannot expect to get anywhere like this. Fire and brimstone speeches have their place, but not for the believing Christian. Fear is not a good motivator.

Why? Because we Owe it to You

I know of a particular family who does what they do simply because they believe they owe it to God. The thinking is that since God has gone out of His way for us, so we should go out of our way for Him. Again, we have a great sentiment that is void of power. Outwardly, this family looks like a beautiful, God-fearing Christian family. However, behind closed doors, it is not so.

Hostility, fits of anger, abusive language, sexual perversion, and numerous acts of deception positively rule this household. Although everyone is trying with great earnest to do their duty toward God, each one of them is failing miserably. This has been going on for decades in this Christian family. Every Sunday they sit like little soldiers, singing their hearts out in the neighborhood church. We are not sufficiently motivated to be good out of a sense of duty.

It is only logical that we would *feel* we owe a debt to God for saving us and making us His children. However, if the invisible things of the creation of the world are clearly seen being understood by things that are made, we must look at our natural example to see if a sense of duty is proper motivation for good behavior.

As a child, I never felt that I owed my parents good behavior because they had given me life and loved me. Neither did I know

The Expedience of Obedience

anyone who had this conviction. I did what I did because of what was in it for me and I'm pretty sure that is how all children act. I grew up and had three sons. Never did I feel that they *owed* me good behavior because I birthed them and loved them. I cannot even imagine my children doing dishes, studying their schoolwork and getting along with one another because they felt they owed me. It would actually make me feel terrible if it were the case! What kind of a mom am I if my children feel forever indebted to me?

I did not do my children a favor by giving birth to them and nurturing them through their lives. I chose to give life and love to my children just as God chose to give life and love to us:

> *"Ye have not chosen me, but I have chosen you,*
> *and ordained you, that ye should go and bring forth fruit,*
> *and that your fruit should remain: that whatsoever ye shall*
> *ask of the Father in my name, he may give it you."*
> *(John 15:16 KJV)*

Look at this loving Father! God chose to give us life, love us, and bless us exceedingly, *"whatsoever ye shall ask of the Father in my name he may give it you."* God offers this to us from a loving heart and is not impressed when we try to pay Him back.

The covenant God made with Abraham was a one-way covenant. Abraham was not indebted to the covenant; God was. We, as Christians, are called to live and walk in the Abrahamic Covenant. As we believe God it will be counted unto us as righteousness. We are not indebted to this covenant and we are not indebted to God. We are on the receiving end of this covenant. God gives while we believe and receive. We owe God nothing but our complete heart allegiance; all else is received.

So we can see that love, fear, and a sense of duty do not properly motivate us to behave properly. These are all well intended, nonetheless, they are also futile. This is not what God had in mind.

All Things are Lawful

Paul says something amazing to the church at Corinth:

> *"All things are lawful unto me,*
> *but all things are not expedient:*
> *all things are lawful for me,*
> *but I will not be brought under the power of any."*
> *(1 Cor 6:12 KJV)*

What does Paul mean by this? How can all things be lawful to him? All things are lawful to Paul because he knows that he has been delivered from the law:

"But now we have been released from the law, for we died with Christ, and we are no longer captive to its power. Now we can really serve God, not in the old way by obeying the letter of the law, but in the new way, by the Spirit." (Rom 7:6 NLT)

We have been delivered from the letter of the law so that we can be free to serve in the newness of the spirit. Rather than serving God to earn brownie points, we serve with a trusting, and therefore, *willing* heart and this is the "newness of our spirit".

Not all are Expedient

This is why, although all things were lawful to Paul, not all were expedient. To say something is expedient is to say that it is advisable, useful, practical, and that it will achieve the desired end. So although all things are indeed lawful to Paul, not all things are advisable, practical, or useful in achieving his desired end.

Under the Power

In addition, Paul says that he will not be brought under the power of any. For example, it is perfectly permissible to eat a piece of cake, however, if one *must* have a piece of cake, we have a problem. It is fine to take a day to relax, but when a slothful spirit takes over, we have a problem.

Smith Wigglesworth, one of the most prominent men in Christian history, was commonly seen smoking a pipe. Because he lived many years ago, this was a relatively harmless act. The nicotine in tobacco today is much higher than it was back then. A person could smoke an occasional cigarette, cigar, or pipe without acquiring an addiction. We saw this evidenced in early television programming. Characters occasionally smoked cigarettes but most were not addicted to them.

Smoking like a chimney and eating like a pig may be lawful because we are no longer under the law, but they are not expedient. It's not the *consumption* of food and nicotine that is harmful, it is the *addiction* to food and nicotine that is harmful. It is lawful to have a cigarette or a piece of pie, however, the cigarettes and pie must not have us, *"All things are lawful unto me but I will not be brought*

The Expedience of Obedience

under the power of any. "

Recently I spoke with a girl about this very thing. I had been explaining how one could expose [himself] to foul spirits through obsession. I used the example of fad toys such as Care Bears. I had no idea I had hit a hot button. She immediately blurted out, "I won't give up my Care Bears." I asked her a series of questions to which she answered with the exact same words, "I won't give up my Care Bears." Hmmm…it is one thing to *have* a Care Bear; it is another when the Care Bear *has* you, *"Thou shalt have no other gods before Me."*

So what Paul is saying is that although he is free from the law, he sees obeying the law as profitable to him. Paul doesn't say, "All things are lawful, however, I love God and don't want to hurt Him." Nor does he say, "All things are lawful to me but I fear the wrath of God if I disobey His law." Nor does Paul say, "All things are lawful unto me but God did so much for me that I owe Him at least that much." As well, Paul does not say, "All things are lawful to me but obeying it is the right thing to do." This final one is a true contradiction, and Paul does not contradict himself.

No, Paul had numero uno in mind when he made this statement. In using the word *expedient* Paul said that it was profitable for *him*, not God, to act in a particular fashion. Decisions concerning the law of God should only be motivated in one way:

Why? Because we NEED Him

We have thoroughly discussed the idea that we are hell-bent creatures who cannot be held responsible for any good thing. We have acknowledged our need to embrace our death to sin by faith. So how does one incorporate these thoughts into obedience to God?

We remember the mountain of self and the mountain of God. The mountain of self was not a *selfish* mountain, but rather a *self-reliant* mountain. Christians absolutely are *selfish* people. This is not a bad thing. We are selfish the way a baby is selfish. We know that we have needs that must be met or we will die. We need salvation, peace, joy, love, health, prosperity, wisdom, guidance, and the air we breathe. We have no problem asking for these things because we are selfish and we want things to go well with us. There is nothing wrong with that.

A baby is born with a great deal of need. He needs to be fed and kept warm and clean. There is no shame in that. We are perfectly fine with responding to that cry for help. We understand that the baby is brand new and does not have the faintest idea about anything.

Taking the Fun Out

What if we birthed a child and his immediate reaction to us was, "I'm sorry Mother, that must have been horrible for you. You go rest, I'll grab a bite in the cafeteria." Talk about taking the fun out of a thing. I know that when my babies were born, I heard them cry and wanted nothing more than to take them into my arms and comfort them. I enjoyed the fact that my babies needed me and weren't inhibited from admitting it through their cries. That is what I was there for and that is what God is here for, *"Let the children come to me. Don't stop them! For the Kingdom of Heaven belongs to such as these."*

The Bible is full of verses that promise to meet mankind's every need. God knows all about our co-dependence on Him. If we have no needs to be met, we have no need of God. God is here with us on earth in order to meet the needs of a helpless people. You see, it will either be we attempting to meet God's needs through our works, or God satisfying our needs through His power. The flow of this thing must never be from earth to heaven; it must always be from heaven to earth, *"Thy will be done on earth as it is in Heaven."*

There is no disgrace in being selfish through our trial of faith on earth. We learn to honor, trust, and love our parents through our selfishness and we will learn to honor, trust, and love our Father in heaven in the same way, *"The invisible things from the creation of the world are clearly seen being understood by things that are made."* And so we stop hiding from our selfishness; we embrace it and work with it.

Death Appropriated

So how do we walk in our "death" in all of this? That is easy. The creature that is dead is not a selfish creature; he is a self-reliant creature. This is the one who thought he could do anything if only he tried hard enough. He did not need a God.

When we got to the end of ourselves and realized we were dead in sin, we turned to God and a new creature was born. Now, as newborn babes, we do not rely upon our own goodness, rather we lean hard upon God's goodness. This is how our flesh dies. Whenever we find ourselves trying hard to do something, we know our flesh is alive and well.

As we learn to obey God by the Spirit, we will not be using carnal effort -- or, we will not be using the old man's power. In this

The Expedience of Obedience

way we are appropriating our death. The moment that nasty "can-do" spirit wells up, this thing will become a struggle and the old man will be back on that mountain of self-reliance beating his chest with his fists like King Kong on the Empire State Building.

True Christians are selfish, not self-reliant. We must allow ourselves the privilege of being the apple of God's eye. We should be relishing this moment as God takes his precious children into His loving arms and satisfies their every need. The Scriptures have promised it; we must believe it. So, rather than trying to beat ourselves into submission we must allow our Father to do His creative work in us in His way and by His timing. When we can say that we are a peculiar people who are, not *responsible for*, but rather *zealous of* good works, we are on the mountain of God and our new man is enjoying the view.

The Low Place

Let me show you what this looks like in practical matters. Everyone knows that Christians are supposed to be humble. The question is not *whether* we are to be humble, but *how* we are to be humble. This is a sorely misapplied precept. To be humble is not to put on a show to let everyone know we are humble. It is not our job to make the world think we are degenerate beings who are ashamed of ourselves.

James clearly tells us, *"Humble yourselves in the sight of the Lord, and he shall lift you up." (James 4:10 KJV)* Peter adds to this thought, *"Humble yourselves therefore under the mighty hand of God, that he may exalt you in due time:" (1 Pet 5:6 KJV)*. We are not to humble ourselves because it is the "right thing to do"; we humble ourselves *before God* so that He will lift us up and exalt us. We are not angling for the "best in show" ribbon for humility; we are selfish beings who want to be exalted and God is instructing us to use this selfishness to show Him that we trust Him. This is not self-reliance; this is God-reliance.

Jesus used a parable to get this thought across to His disciples:

> *"...and he put forth a parable to those which were bidden,*
> *when he marked how they chose out the chief rooms...*
> *"When thou art bidden of any man to a wedding,*
> *sit not down in the highest room;*
> *lest a more honourable man than thou be bidden of him;*
> *And he that bade thee and him come and say to thee,*
> *Give this man place;*

and thou begin with shame to take the lowest room.
But when thou art bidden, go and sit down in the lowest
room; that when he that bade thee cometh,
he may say unto thee, Friend, go up higher:
then shalt thou have worship
in the presence of them that sit at meat with thee.
For whosoever exalteth himself shall be abased;
and he that humbleth himself shall be exalted."
(Luke 14:7-11 KJV)

In this parable, Jesus taught His disciples how to be blessed by behavior. His lesson is spelled out in the last verse, *"For whosoever exalteth himself shall be abased; and he that humbleth himself shall be exalted."* Those who lift themselves up will be brought low and those who choose to go low will be raised up.

Sitting at the Foot of the Office

This concept works every time. When my children were thirteen, nine, and seven, God told me to begin home schooling them. I agreed and through many miracles, we accomplished this task. I wasn't home schooling because it was the "right thing to do", neither did I have an axe to grind with the school system; I was simply obeying God expecting His reward.

In August of the first home school year, I went to speak with the superintendent of the school system. I explained what I was going to do and why. I made it a point to let him know that I was not doing this because I was in any way disappointed in the school system, and I let him know that I respected him and his leadership.

The Superintendent's response to me was very caring and helpful. He offered to look into ways that the boys could be involved in band, student leaders, driver's education, and other such things. I assured him that I would understand if that was not possible and that I was submitted to his authority in the school system.

At one point the superintendent told me that he had seen this before and he predicted that I would probably have the boys back in school by the next year. Instead of standing on my laurels, I said, "Well, last year at this time I didn't know I was going to be home schooling, so who knows what God will lead me to do a year from now!"

Before I left his office, the superintendent told me to feel free to borrow any of the school's textbooks that I may need. He stated that

The Expedience of Obedience

the school and its possessions were at my disposal. He even said that he would look into the possibility of allowing us to use the lab when it was free.

Exalted

From that year forward my children were welcomed at band, student leader events, and driver's education. I was even able to help with band camp and be one of the "crew moms" when we went to state with the marching band. We honestly never had a problem with the school system.

I had taken the low place and God exalted me. Now I didn't take the low place so that God would see me and say, "Oh, now isn't she wonderful? Look at that humility! She loves (fears, feels a sense of duty) so much that she is obeying me. Now I won't have to punish her." We must stop attributing godless actions and attitudes to our God. This is not how we respond with our children. When we see our children trust us enough to follow us, we smile and bless them. God is no different. If His love so far outdistances ours, then shouldn't the actions of His love do the same?

I took the low place with the school system for one and only one reason: I wanted to be exalted. I wanted the high seat. Jesus told me to take the low seat so that He could reposition me to the high seat so that is exactly what I did and that was the exact result. I use this practice daily and get daily results. I am a selfish person. I want my needs met. I look to God to meet these needs and my "good deed" is now the result of a willing heart, *"If you be willing and obedient you shall eat the good of the land."*

The Other Side of the Story

We belonged to a home school group that met monthly. It was not uncommon for different ones to talk about the struggles they had with their school systems. At first I chalked it up to the fact that they were dealing with different systems, but then I met "Beatrice" (not her real name).

Beatrice was from my own hometown. One day she was talking to me about a struggle she was having with our school system. She shared with me that she had gone into their offices and let them know her "rights" as a home schooler and they had soundly turned her away. She took the high seat and she was brought low just as the parable spoke.

Although it was lawful for Beatrice to take the high seat, it was not expedient. Beatrice had all her facts straight, and the law was on her side, however the attitude of her heart was exalted and that is exactly why she was brought low. The same people who rolled out the red carpet for me slammed the door in her face. Beatrice was so shocked by the relationship I had with the school system that she asked me to speak in her behalf! I could not speak in her behalf; she had already spoken herself into the place she had.

Give and it will be Given

Let us look at another example. In the sixth chapter of Luke Jesus speaks about the expedience of obeying and the correct motivation for doing it. He begins by setting the standard:

"But I say unto you which hear, Love your enemies,
do good to them which hate you,
Bless them that curse you,
and pray for them which despitefully use you.
And unto him that smiteth thee on the one cheek
offer also the other;
and him that taketh away thy cloak
forbid not to take thy coat also.
Give to every man that asketh of thee;
and of him that taketh away thy goods
ask them not again.
And as ye would that men should do to you,
do ye also to them likewise. "
(Luke 6:27-31 KJV)

We are to love our enemies, do good to those who hate us, bless those who curse us, pray for those who use us, turn the other cheek, offer more to those who take, give to all who ask, let others take what they wish, and generally treat others the way we would like them to treat us. Here we have our very stringent marching orders.

However, marching orders are not enough. When one attempts to obey these edicts because they love, fear, or feel a sense of duty toward God, or simply because it is the "right thing to do", he is looking at a monumental task. The words of Jesus become a very difficult commission when our only motivation is the knowledge that we are doing the "right thing."

Read through that list. Do we really have the wherewithal to obey these words simply because it is the "right thing to do"? I don't. If we are to adhere to the words of Jesus, we must have the

The Expedience of Obedience

proper motivation, which is precisely why He goes on to give it to us:

> *"For if ye love them which love you,*
> *what thank have ye?*
> *for sinners also love those that love them.*
> *And if ye do good to them which do good to you,*
> *what thank have ye?*
> *for sinners also do even the same.*
> *And if ye lend to them of whom ye hope to receive,*
> *what thank have ye?*
> *for sinners also lend to sinners,*
> *to receive as much again. "*
> *(Luke 6:32-34 KJV)*

No Grace

Our Scriptures tell us that when we do things expecting the world's reward, we have no "thank". That word *thank* is *charis* and is the exact same word that is translated *grace* in the following verse, *"For by **grace** are ye saved through faith; and that not of yourselves: it is the gift of God:" (Eph 2:8 KJV)*. If you remember from earlier, the Greek word charis is *"the divine influence upon the heart, and its reflection in the life."* This same word was translated "reward" in the fifth chapter of Matthew when referring to the same words of Jesus.

When we do things with the improper motive of receiving from the world, we have no grace, *charis*, for the situation. In order to function in a holy manner, my heart must be divinely influenced to a point where it is reflected in my life. If I have no grace, I have no power to be holy.

The World's Reward

You may argue, "I don't do things expecting a reward!" What we must realize is that we are all looking for a reward. We need "reward" in order to survive. We need that job, we need that home, we need that healing, and we need that peace of mind. In all that we do, we are looking for some sort of a reward. Just try to think of one thing you do that you do not seek some sort of a reward, no matter how small.

I am rewarded when I take a walk, get the mail, do the shopping, rake the lawn, go to work, take a shower, talk to a friend, eat, sit, lay down, think thoughts, breathe, sleep…I think you get the picture. My rewards are the joy of walking, receiving my mail, having food, enjoying a raked lawn, receiving a paycheck, becoming clean, enjoying fellowship, nourishment, rest, repose, meditation, vitality, health and precious slumber. In all that we do there is a reward.

Our default setting has us looking to the world for the world's reward. This law is as old as man himself. We work hard for our boss to get his reward. We treat our neighbor well and expect him to reciprocate. We obey our doctors expecting their reward of health. We obey our taste buds and trust food to reward our palette.

I could go on, but God would have us working hard at our jobs for *Him* and expecting *His* reward. God would have us to love our neighbors for God and His reward, not theirs. God would even have us to follow the doctor's orders, not for the doctor's reward, but for God's reward. As well, when we eat, we must look to God, not our food, to reward us by satisfying our palettes. God is the only One Who is capable of true reward, *"And whatsoever ye do, do it heartily, as to the Lord, and not unto men; Knowing that of the Lord ye shall receive the reward of the inheritance: for ye serve the Lord Christ."* *(Col 3:23-24 KJV)*

The Rewarder

The question is not whether there will be a reward; the question is who will be the rewarder? The actions are all the same, however, the heart behind the actions will reveal the true rewarder. If I do what I do looking for the world's reward, I have no grace for the situation and I am destined to fail. If I do what I do looking for God's reward, I am given the grace for the task, *"God's people will be willing in the day of His power."* This is a promise God is ready to keep. He gives us both to will and to do of His good pleasure when we look to Him as our Rewarder.

I need grace to be able to accomplish my marching orders. If my heart is not pinned on God as my Rewarder, I am destined to failure. There is no such grace to help when we do our works expecting from men instead of God, *"what thank have ye?"*

The world operates in this fashion, however the Christian should not. The sinner looks to the world as its provider and deliverer; the Christian has a God Who is the Deliverer and Who provides all things according to His riches in glory in Christ Jesus. This seems like it should be a relatively easy task, however in real life our tendency is to put expectations on just about everyone with whom

The Expedience of Obedience

we come in contact. We need a tremendous transfer of trust. What grace have ye when you seek and gain the world's reward?

Your Reward shall be Great

If we can expect no grace (a divine influence upon our heart with its reflection in our life) and only a man's shaky reward from the world, what can we expect from trusting God? Jesus continues His speech to us:

> *"But love ye your enemies, and do good, and lend, hoping for nothing again; and your reward shall be great, and ye shall be the children of the Highest: for he is kind unto the unthankful and to the evil. Be ye therefore merciful, as your Father also is merciful." (Luke 6:35-36 KJV)*

Jesus doesn't just leave us wanting; He promises us that when we look to God as our Provider, not only will we have the grace to carry out our deeds effortlessly, but also our reward will be *great* and we will be the children of the Highest.

I don't love others because it is the "right" thing for a Christian to do; I love others so that God will respond back to me with love. According to the Bible, that is how that works. I lend hoping for nothing in return so that my reward can come from God. I am a selfish child and I want to be rewarded heartily.

I want the best and the most. Therefore, it is with a willing and glad heart that I love my enemies, and do good and lend, hoping for nothing in return because my generous God will greatly reward me! God uses me to be kind to the unthankful and to the evil and then He rewards me from His heavenly storehouse! That is why I obey, and why I obey heartily.

Attitude

Because of this my attitude is superb. I am not looking to the other person for anything, and because I am expecting a great reward, I am happy to oblige my neighbor and meet his needs. I am free to obey God because this is expedient for me. I cannot possibly out-give God.

I am dead to sin in that I am not exerting great effort in forcing my old man to be good; rather I am happy to do these things as I know what is in it for me. I am not obeying a law written in stone; I am obeying the longing of my heart. I am completely in this thing with God because He has made it very profitable for me to be so.

Judge Not

Continuing His talk, Jesus says:

> *"Judge not, and ye shall not be judged:*
> *condemn not, and ye shall not be condemned:*
> *forgive, and ye shall be forgiven:"*
> *(Luke 6:37 KJV)*

I don't know about you, but I certainly do not want to be judged, nor do I want to be condemned. What I *do* want is to be forgiven. So how do I walk before God in complete forgiveness without judgment or condemnation? I just give these things freely to others.

I will not do it because they deserve it, because I love God, because I fear God, or because I feel that I owe it to Him. I will judge not, condemn not and I will show forgiveness because of what is in it for me. One cannot be unhappy about these acts under these circumstances.

This is how we become willing to obey God. When we can take ourselves out from under the penalty of the law and begin to look for God's reward, we will become willing and obedient and we will eat the good of the land. I will extend mercy in order to receive mercy, and I will forgive so that I can be forgiven. I must do these things because I selfishly need mercy and forgiveness and I'm not afraid to admit it. If we do not practice divine forgiveness in our life, we will not have the capacity to receive divine forgiveness in our death.

Overflow

Jesus goes on to tell us what we can expect when we extend mercy and forgiveness to others:

> *"Give, and it shall be given unto you; good measure,*
> *pressed down, and shaken together, and running over,*
> *shall men give into your bosom. For with the same*
> *measure that ye mete withal*
> *it shall be measured to you again."*
> *(Luke 6:27-38 KJV)*

Give and it will be given. It is that simple. Just so that we understand what kind of compensation we can expect, Jesus spells it out, *"it shall be given unto you; good measure, pressed down, and shaken together, and running over"*. God fills our reward bin all the

The Expedience of Obedience

way to the top, gets His foot in there and presses it down, shakes it back and forth to get rid of all the air holes, and then adds more to the point that it overflows.

According to the Scriptures, when we give with the motive of receiving from God, we end up with so much that it will flow from us. We will not be able to contain it. This should be our one and only motivation for giving all that we are asked to give.

Measure carefully

"For with the same measure that ye mete withal it shall be measured to you again." When it comes to judgment, condemnation, and mercy, God will use our own standard of measurement when He metes these things out to us. Whatever standard of measurement we use will be used against us.

When we are racist, God has to judge us according to our race, and we better be Jewish. When we judge someone according to how they look, we will be judged according to how we look. When we judge someone for how they responded to a situation, we will be judged according to how we respond to our situations. When we condemn someone according to their actions, we will be condemned according to our actions.

On the other side of this coin, when we extend mercy to all and reserve judgment and condemnation, we will receive mercy and we will not be judged or condemned. This is a wonderful blessing. It should be our good pleasure to extend mercy to those who have offended us. This is a perfect opportunity to fill up our bins with mercy. We need mercy.

David's Judgment

David is a good example of this concept. King David lived an exemplary life from the time he was a youth until one fateful day when he stayed home from war:

"And it came to pass, after the year was expired,
at the time when kings go forth to battle,
that David sent Joab...
but David tarried still at Jerusalem."
(2 Sam 11:1 KJV)

We all know the story of how David then spied Bathsheba taking a bath and the next thing we know Bathsheba is pregnant and David is in a state of panic. We know that David was panicking because what ensued was the exact opposite of the rest of David's life. David became a different man for the space of a few short months.

When two attempts to get Bathsheba's husband to sleep with her failed, David did the unthinkable and ordered the man's death. God was not pleased and He sent an inquiry to David in the form of a story through Nathan the prophet:

"And the LORD sent Nathan unto David.
And he came unto him, and said unto him,
There were two men in one city;
the one rich, and the other poor.
The rich man had exceeding many flocks and herds:
But the poor man had nothing, save one little ewe lamb,
which he had bought and nourished up:
and it grew up together with him, and with his children;
it did eat of his own meat, and drank of his own cup,
and lay in his bosom, and was unto him as a daughter.
And there came a traveller unto the rich man,
and he spared to take of his own flock and of his own herd,
to dress for the wayfaring man that was come unto him;
but took the poor man's lamb, and dressed it for the man
that was come to him." (2 Sam 12:1-4 KJV)

This was clearly a test. God needs a measuring rod from David's own hand because He is about to measure David. With what measure we mete will be measured back to us. So what was David going to do? Would he have mercy on the one who did this dastardly deed, or would he judge? David was the King and he held the power of judgment! This sinner's fate was in David's hands. David gives his verdict:

"And David's anger was greatly kindled against the man;
and he said to Nathan, As the LORD liveth,
the man that hath done this thing shall surely die:
And he shall restore the lamb fourfold,
because he did this thing, and because he had no pity."
(2 Sam 12:5-6 KJV)

I guess we know what is going to happen. David judged this man harshly; he showed no mercy. God has to use *this* measuring rod to now measure David. Interestingly, David judged this man for

The Expedience of Obedience

showing no pity. It is true the man showed no pity, however, neither did David show pity to the man, *"for thou that judgest doest the same things."* Therefore, according to David's measuring rod, both men must be judged without mercy. Indeed both men were; you see, both men were David:

> *"And Nathan said to David, Thou art the man."*
> *(2 Sam 12:7a KJV)*

Nathan the prophet brought David a story about his own situation to see how he would react. God's judgment reflected David's judgment of the man. In judging the man, David judged himself:

> *"...Therefore the sword shall never depart from thine*
> *house...I will raise up evil against thee out of thine own*
> *house, and I will take thy wives before thine eyes,*
> *and give them unto thy neighbour...*
> *the child also that is born unto thee shall surely die..."*
> *(2 Sam 12:10a,11&14 KJV)*

David's sin wasn't his problem. David's problem was his lack of faith. Consider what God said to him concerning his actions:

> *"...Thus saith the LORD God of Israel,*
> *I anointed thee king over Israel,*
> *and I delivered thee out of the hand of Saul;*
> *And I gave thee thy master's house,*
> *and thy master's wives into thy bosom,*
> *and gave thee the house of Israel and of Judah;*
> *and **if that had been too little,***
> ***I would moreover have given unto thee***
> ***such and such things."***
> *(2 Sam 12:7-8 KJV)*

God is reminding David how He has been on His side from the beginning and if that had not been enough, He surely would have done more if that were what David wanted. But David took things into his own hands leaving God out of the matter. That was his sin.

Although David's judgmental and self-reliant attitude brought this immediate judgment to his life, David did not lose his salvation as he repented of his faithless behavior:

The Sin within

*"And David said unto Nathan, I have sinned
against the LORD. And Nathan said unto David,
The LORD also hath put away thy sin; thou shalt not die."
(2 Sam 12:13 KJV)*

Had David extended mercy to this fabled sinner, God would have
had to have mercy on David, otherwise our New Testament Scripture
is incorrect. But because David gave a harsh judgment and ordered
the man to die and restore fourfold, God had to give a harsh
judgment. David would suffer the death of three children and his
wives were going to be stolen from him.

Nice, Full Mercy Bin

God honors His Word. We must do the same. We don't ever have
to wonder how God is judging us; all we have to do is look at how
we are judging others. I can honestly say that I do not look at people
to judge them. Not because I am a good Christian, but because I
trust God to honor His Word and not judge me. I purpose to see
every person as an opportunity to fill my mercy bin. In this way I
am not grumbling my way through my fleshly acts in an attempt to
show God how much I love, fear, and feel that I owe Him, rather I
am a peculiar person zealous of good works because my reward is
great. As I trust God, He blesses me and I fall more deeply in love
with Him. What could possibly be wrong with that?

In this way I am obeying the law, not by the letter, but by the
Spirit, for the letter kills, but the Spirit gives life. Jesus did not come
to abolish the law but to fulfill it. It is not that we have no law; it is
that we have no *written* law. Our obedience will issue from a willing
heart that is inscribed with the law and it will produce everything
that willing heart could desire. We do not obey a commandment;
we trust a Commandeer.

Peculiarly Zealous

The Bible says that Jesus:

*"...gave himself for us, that he might redeem us from all
iniquity, and purify unto himself a peculiar people,
zealous of good works." (Titus 2:14 KJV)*

I am peculiarly zealous of good works. Why wouldn't I be? I have a
sure and great reward coming! I can influence the way God looks at
me by the way I look at others. And I can influence the way God

The Expedience of Obedience

treats me by the way I treat others. That is why Jesus said to do unto others, as we would have them do unto us. God is going to do unto us what we have done unto others. What kind of a crazy power is this?

Disney World

I want you to picture a family going about their business in a very normal way. The children are squabbling, there are toys on the floor, the phone is ringing, Mom is scrubbing the sink and Dad is at work. At five fifteen Dad comes bursting in the front door waving tickets in his hand, "We're going to Disney World! Get the house in order and pack your bags because we are leaving in the morning!"

How will the environment change? The children will stop squabbling and, with a toy under each arm, begin to talk with great enthusiasm about the upcoming "reward" at the end of their cleaning and packing. Mom will continue her chores at a quicker pace, but with a smile on her face and a song in her mouth. Everyone will not only do what needs to be done under normal circumstances, but they will also add the strenuous chore of packing for a vacation.

Adrenaline pumping through their bodies they scurry around yelling things to one another and working together like a fine tuned watch. This family, who just moments before had been trudging their way through their day, is now flying through that same day and doing those same chores with the joy of anticipation permeating their every effort. Now we have a peculiar people who are zealous of good works. The reward was the key that turned the lock.

We are the same way; if we could ever become convinced that the promises of the Bible are true we would go about our deeds with great enthusiasm. God broke into the front door of our heart, waving His promises in His hand and said, *"Your reward will be great!"* This should light a fire under us just as a fire was lit under that family.

Can you imagine what it would be like for God to look down at His people and see them scurrying about spreading love around with a smile on their face and a song in their heart in great anticipation of the reward of a loving and generous Father? All of them working together and helping one another to meet the common goal of letting their Father bless them and show the world what a wonderful God He is. Oh what delight this would be for Him. Oh, Lord God, let it be seen in us.

That is motivation that will get us through the tough stuff. When

I am in dire straights, I may not have enough love, fear or obligation to get me through, but I *will* need a God Who has promised to give above and beyond my needs. I will trust this God, serve Him in faith expecting a reward, and see this thing through. I am peculiar from the world in this way.

Wrong Expectations

The world is doing unto others expecting the world system to deal with them fairly. Well, there is nothing fair about a cursed system. Unfortunately, the Christian commonly falls into this same trap. That is why we have a world that is well rehearsed in complaining and a church that looks a whole lot like the world.

When we obey God with wrong motives such as love, fear, and a sense of duty, our expectation is not on God but on man. After all, we are not doing our good deeds *for God's reward*; we are doing them *for God*. This changes the flow of output. When we do our deeds *for God's reward*, the flow runs from God to us through the reward. When we do our deeds *for* God, the flow runs from us to God. Is God then rewarded as He watches us do our deeds laboriously because we love, fear, or feel a sense of duty toward Him? Hardly, *"...all our righteousnesses are as filthy rags"*

And when it is all said and done, even though our motive for obeying God is to satisfy our own need for all things pertaining to life and godliness, we are actually satisfying the other motives at the same time. How can we not love a God Who is showering us with His rewards? It is obvious we have reverential fear because we are extending mercy so that we will receive mercy. And as far as a sense of duty, this is our duty. Our duty is to trust God enough to obey His Word in faith and expect a reward just as Jesus taught.

The Curse of Improper Motivation

Right before Moses went up to Mount Sinai to forever be with the Lord, he went over the entire Mosaic Law with the children of Israel in preparation for their entrance to the Promised Land. It is here that he relayed the infamous words of God:

> *"I call heaven and earth to record this day against*
> *you, that I have set before you life and death,*
> *blessing and cursing: therefore choose life,*
> *that both thou and thy seed may live:"*
> *(Deut 30:19 KJV)*

The Expedience of Obedience

Obey the Mosaic Law and be blessed, or disobey it and be cursed. However, Moses had previously placed a clause on this obedience. We have been remiss in heeding his words. Moses had warned the Israelites:

> *"But it shall come to pass, if thou wilt not hearken unto the voice of the LORD thy God, to observe to do all his commandments and statutes which I command thee this day;that all these curses shall come upon thee, and overtake thee:" (Deut 28:15 KJV)*

If we do not do all God's commandments and statutes, all the curses will come upon us and overtake us. Following these words we find a very lengthy list of consequences to disobedience. I strongly recommend reading through this list in Deuteronomy. When we look at the world, we can see these curses playing out. Unfortunately, we also see them played out in the lives of many Christians. God's final word concerning those who disobey:

> *"Moreover all these curses shall come upon thee, and shall pursue thee, and overtake thee, till thou be destroyed; because thou hearkenedst not unto the voice of the LORD thy God, to keep his commandments and his statutes which he commanded thee: And they shall be upon thee for a sign and for a wonder, and upon thy seed for ever."*
> *(Deut 28:45-46 KJV)*

It is obvious God is quite emphatic about obedience to His commandments. It is important that we understand the finality of God's statements concerning those who are disobedient. You see, we are about to come to the important clause I referred to earlier. It is not enough to be merely obedient to the Law; one has to be happy about it:

For the Abundance of all Things

> *"Because thou servedst not the LORD thy God with joyfulness, and with gladness of heart, for the abundance of all things..."*
> *(Deuteronomy 28:47 KJV)*

Moses did not say that the curse came only upon men who were disobedient; he said that the curse also existed in the lives of those who *were* obedient, but with wrong motives. There are three ways in which we have been admonished to be obedient: *Joyfully, with gladness of heart, and for the abundance of all things.* God is not interested in rote obedience; however, He is very interested in the heart behind the obedience.

We are told by Moses to serve the Lord *for the abundance of all things.* It is easy to serve the Lord joyfully when we are doing it for the abundance of all things. Who does not want the abundance of all things?

The problem comes in when we serve the Lord with the wrong motives of love, fear, or a sense of duty. We cannot obey God for these reasons while at the same time obey Him for the abundance of all things. We will either obey God because we feel we owe this to Him, or we will obey Him for the abundance of all things. We cannot have it both ways. It is time to ask ourselves some serious questions about where we are placing our trust.

We cannot expect to have a glad heart when we are doing what we do simply because it is the "right thing to do." However, we cannot help but to have a glad heart when we are looking to God to bless us with the abundance of all things. Moses said that all these curses came on those who did not obey God with a glad heart.

We notice from the words of Moses that if we obey without joyfulness and gladness of heart for the abundance of all things:

> *"Therefore shalt thou serve thine enemies*
> *which the LORD shall send against thee,*
> *in hunger, and in thirst, and in nakedness,*
> *and in want of all things:*
> *and he shall put a yoke of iron upon thy neck,*
> *until he have destroyed thee."*
> *(Deuteronomy 28:48 KJV)*

When we don't obey God for the abundance of all things, we will serve our enemies in want of all things. This is precisely how most Christians live their lives. Our dead service is a yoke of iron upon our necks and we are being destroyed as a result.

Come Unto Me

Everyone talks as though this thing is supposed to be difficult and

The Expedience of Obedience

how we are to labor heavily to obey God's laws. I have heard many a clergy make great claims about how difficult it is to be truly obedient to God. But consider the words of Jesus:

> *"Come unto me, all ye that labour and are heavy laden,*
> *and I will give you rest. Take my yoke upon you, and learn*
> *of me; for I am meek and lowly in heart: and ye shall find*
> *rest unto your souls. For my yoke is easy,*
> *and my burden is light." (Matt 11:28-30 KJV)*

What is it that causes us to labor and be heavy laden? Trying to obey the law by the power of the flesh! Adam couldn't do it, Paul couldn't do it and we can't do it. It is not that we don't want to; it is that we simply are not able to.

We are instructed to unburden ourselves from the yoke we are carrying so that we can take up His yoke. Jesus promises that this is an easier way, *"I will give you rest."* Rather than carry the yoke of the burden of the law, we are instructed to take the yoke of Jesus and learn from Him. What is it we must learn? To be meek and lowly in heart.

I am Meek and Lowly in Heart

We are not supposed to go into this thing all cocky, ready to conquer the world; we are to be meek and lowly in heart. Jesus said we are to learn from Him by being meek and lowly in heart. To be meek simply means to be gentle and humble. We must take ourselves down a peg or two. To be lowly in heart means to be humiliated or consider oneself of low degree. We are to learn of Jesus by humbling ourselves and considering ourselves of low degree.

What this tells us is amazing: Jesus humbled Himself and considered Himself of low degree. When we read the New Testament, it sure doesn't look like Jesus considered Himself of low degree. Jesus conducted Himself with utmost confidence; He was very bold in all He did. How is it that one can be both humble and meek, *and* bold and confident?

Meekness is not something we wear on the outside like a badge; meekness is something we *know* on the inside. Jesus knew where His goodness came from, *"And Jesus said unto him, Why callest thou me good? there is none good but one, that is, God." (Mark 10:18 KJV)* Jesus was meek and lowly in heart because He knew that in and of Himself, He was not good, *"When ye have lifted up the Son of* man, then shall ye know that I am he, and that I do nothing of myself". In all He did, Jesus worked upon this premise. This is how Jesus was meek and lowly of heart.

And I will Give You Rest

If we will learn of Jesus, we will embrace the fact that we are hell-bent. This will cause us to be properly motivated to obey God in meekness, expecting a great reward. We do not go into this thing all fired up expecting to be successful. We go into this thing meekly, expecting *God* to be successful, because we know that we are nothing outside of Him.

We will find our proper motivation when we obey God out of a sense of trust and complete reliance upon Him as our Savior and Deliverer. One who has learned to give himself over to God in this way will soon find that He takes very good care of His beloved children. Look how He took care of Jesus.

In the end, we must unburden ourselves from the obligation of the law and begin to embrace the God of the Law. God provided everything we could possibly need, wrote a list of these provisions in His Word, showed us how to tap into these provisions through a joyful heart, and now He is asking us to trust Him enough to obey.

For this is the love of God, that we keep his commandments: and his commandments are not grievous.

1 John 5:3

7

THE TEN COMMANDMENTS

Love God and do as you please.

-- St. Augustine

We have been talking an awful lot about the spiritual realm and its inerrant Truths and the natural realm and its temporary facts. We saw in Genesis how God began His interaction with mankind on this very premise. We watched Elohim create everything in the spiritual realm and then we watched Jehovah Elohim birth these same things into the natural.

In addition to this, we have learned that God set things up in such a way that the natural world would be a constant visual aid in understanding this spiritual world:

> *"For the invisible things of him*
> *from the creation of the world are clearly seen,*
> *being understood by the things that are made..."*
> *(Rom 1:20a KJV)*

The Mosaic Law is no exception to this rule. Each of these laws shows us an aspect of the spiritual realm and teaches us about the heart of God. I brought this to light in *Hell Bent* when I showed how the natural marriage was a symbolic picture of the marriage that is to take place between God and man.

Women are to honor men as an example of how mankind is to honor God. Men are to take care of women as an example of how God takes care of us. This is why our marriage relationships will cease when we enter eternity; they will have already fulfilled their purpose on earth, *"For in the resurrection they neither marry, nor are given in marriage, but are as the angels of God in heaven."* *(Matt 22:30 KJV)*

It is my personal belief that the reason polygamy was tolerated in the Old Testament and banned in the New is because it had already served its purpose. In the Old Testament, a man could take more than one wife, but a woman could not take more than one husband. This natural "law" was symbolic of the fact that God can be the Husband of many wives while we, the "wife" must not have more than one God/Husband. But, that is just my thought on the subject.

We must look at everything in the Old Testament as a natural example of a spiritual concept. When we take this method into the Ten Commandments we find the same holds true.

We have also learned that we are selfish beings who are dead to self-reliance. We do not look to our own power to obey God; we look to His promised reward to motivate our behavior. In this way we become a peculiar people who are zealous of good works. The whole world is trying by their own effort to "do the right thing", how are we peculiar when we do the same?

It is when we do things joyfully and with a glad heart, for the abundance of all things, that we are given the grace for the task and are enthusiastic about it. This is what is peculiar, *"He gives us both to will and to do of His good pleasure."* The world grumbles through its tasks trusting a faulty system. If the Christian knew and understood what was in it for him, he would be singing as he breezed through his tasks.

The Big Ten

Many separate the Ten Commandments from the rest of the Mosaic Law because we sense this is what Jesus did in the Gospels as we see in this example from the book of Matthew:

> *"...if thou wilt enter into life, keep the*
> *commandments...Thou shalt do no murder, Thou shalt not*
> *commit adultery, Thou shalt not steal, Thou shalt not bear*
> *false witness, Honour thy father and thy mother: and,*
> *Thou shalt love thy neighbour as thyself."*
> *(Matt 19:17-19 KJV)*

This understanding releases us from the hundreds of meticulous rituals and mandates that were placed on the Jewish nation, but still holds us to the main "Ten." However, if we are to hold to these ten, we must do so with proper motivation: For the abundance of all things. The full list of the Ten Commandments is taken from the fifth chapter of the book of Deuteronomy:

1. We are to have no other gods before God
2. We shall not make, serve, nor bow down to any graven images
3. We must not take the Lord's name in vain
4. We are to keep the Sabbath day holy
5. We are to honor our mother and our father
6. We are not to kill
7. We are not to commit adultery
8. We are not to steal
9. We are not to lie
10. We are not to covet, or desire what another has

Let's take a closer look at these commandments.

No gods Before Me

Laws are not given to bring people into bondage; laws are given to set people free! Moses was speaking to a people who had a *real* God. All other nations of the world had fake gods such as Dagon, Baal, and Diana. In essence, God was saying to these people, "Hey…you, unlike the rest of the world, have a real God. You don't need additional fake gods. Don't look to them." Because we have been invited to enter into the blessing of the children of Israel, *we also* have a real God. Since there is no other true God, it is senseless to extend our worship to any other but the One True God.

When I want to go somewhere, I will take my car, not because it is the "right thing to do", but because I know that my car will get me to my destination. I will not sit on my couch and expect it to behave like a car. If I want the benefits of a car, I must use a car.

As well, when I want to go somewhere spiritually, I will worship the real God, not because it is the "right thing to do" but because I know that the real God will get me to my destination. It is not expedient for me to worship any other but the One True God. Therefore, I will worship the One True God joyfully and with a glad heart, for the abundance of all things. Therefore, I will live in the blessing.

The spiritual parallel is in the fact that the gods of the Old Testament were gods of stone; they were tangible in this natural realm. The gentiles worshipped their gods because they thought they had the power to deliver blessings.

In the same way, anything that we look to for any type of blessing is a god in our life whether it is a spouse, boss, child, friend, church, or any other thing. When we need a blessing, we must worship the One True God and look to Him to meet our needs. God may use any one of these people to bring us blessing, but they will never be more than a vessel of God.

I will have no other gods, not because it is the "right thing to do", but because of what is in it for me. My God is real and He delivers. I will not look elsewhere.

Everyone Will Bow

At one point, the Ark of the Covenant fell into the hands of the Philistines. God shows the Philistines and us, just how ridiculous was the practice of worshipping any but the One True God:

"And the Philistines took the ark of God,
and brought it from Ebenezer unto Ashdod.
When the Philistines took the ark of God,
they brought it into the house of Dagon,
and set it by Dagon.
And when they of Ashdod arose early on the morrow,
behold, Dagon was fallen upon his face to the earth

The Ten Commandments

before the ark of the LORD.
And they took Dagon, and set him in his place again.
And when they arose early on the morrow morning,
behold, Dagon was fallen upon his face to the ground
before the ark of the LORD;
and the head of Dagon and both the palms of his hands
were cut off upon the threshold;
only the stump of Dagon was left to him."
(1 Sam 5:1-4 KJV)

In this life, we find many things that are just as dangerous as the god "Dagon". It is not uncommon for us to look to money, a career, a marriage, a home, a child, or a friend to fill our empty places. These things can be loved, but they cannot be the thing we look to for blessing, reward, and fulfillment. We cannot look to these things to meet our needs. These relationships only exist to show us how to relate to God. The Bible says specifically that we are not to bow down and serve any but God. We will be rewarded, whether good or bad, by the one we serve.

We will know when we have crossed that line when we begin to expect certain things from money (the abundance of all things), a career (exaltation), a marriage (love and provision), a home (shelter from the world), a child (respect and honor), or a friend (companionship).

God is the only One Who can provide these things. God is the One Who provides the abundance of all things, He has promised to exalt us, He has promised to love and provide for us, He has promised us to shelter and protect us, He will cause our children to rise up and call us blessed, and God will be our constant Companion. All expectation needs to be taken from the world and placed on God. Anything else is the act of having other gods.

Relationship of Blessing

God has invited us into a very intimate relationship with Him. He is intent on us and calls us to be intent on Him. We are purposed and equipped to be in a marriage with God. He is to be our very best Friend, our faithful Brother, our dutiful and loving Spouse, and the only One Who can meet our needs. God wants to assume these roles because He loves us and He set things up so that He would be the only One capable of meeting those needs.

The Sin within

This is why God tells us to not serve the idols of this world. They are empty and vain. We serve a God Who comes through for us in ways the world can only try. The world fails. Our money, jobs, marriages, homes, children, and friends are all apt to fail while God remains true. The Bible says that when we serve the idols of this world, we, at the same time, hate God. We must serve the One and Only, God.

I worship the One True God; not because it is the "right thing" to do, but because He is the only One Who is worthy of my worship in that He is the only One Who has the power to do anything worthy of worship! I worship God joyfully and with a glad heart for the abundance of all things.

Taking His Name in vain

We who are under the New Covenant have reduced this commandment to nothingness with our religious ways. We have convinced the world that this commandment means that we cannot say, "Oh my God!" without breaking this commandment. All I have to say is, "Oh my God." How ridiculous. Only the devil could possibly be responsible for this rendering of the Scriptures.

We studied some of the names of God in _Hell Bent_. God is Who He says He is. God gave Himself many names because He assumes many roles. God does not tell us what He will do; He tells us Who He is because Who He is, is exactly what He does.

All through the Old Testament God presents Himself to people by introducing Himself with one of His names. When God blessed Abraham through Melchizedek He announced Himself by proclaiming He is El, the God of strength. When God came to Hagar in the wilderness and ministered to her, she did not take His name in vain but called Him Jehovah Roi, the One Who Sees. God's names are very important to Him because they are the essence of Who He is. When we take God's name in vain, we take God in vain.

To take God's name in vain is to live our lives in such a way that we do not look to Him as our Healer, our Deliverer, our Peace, our Security, our Provider, and our Savior. We have taken His name as we call ourselves the children of God and then we conduct ourselves as though we have no God! This is what it means to take His name in vain: We take it for nothing. We may as well have not taken it at all. All of our despondent phone conversations about our problems add up to nothing but taking the Lord's name in vain. Where is our God in our thoughts, worries, and conversations?

The Ten Commandments

We must ask ourselves this question: Do those who watch us know of our God of deliverance? Or do they rather hear our 'woe is me' speech, "I guess all I can do is pray about it." Does our Christianity speak of many laws and a shaky, unreliable Deliverer? Does all of our religious hype boil down to vanity?

All for nothing

To take the Lord's name in vain is to call ourselves the people of God and have it mean essentially nothing. We have the same problems as the world and the same responses to them. Vanity. The world says, "What am I going to do?" and we say, "What am I going to do?" The world worries about sickness, we worry about sickness. The world is afraid of gas prices and interest rates and we worry about gas prices and interest rates. Where is our God? Are we taking His name in vain? We call ourselves Christians while our lives mimic the world. This is what God meant by, *"Do not take My name in vain."*

I purpose to not take God's name in vain. When circumstances bring me to a place where I have a need, I call on the God of all circumstances. When I speak of my situations, I make known the name and deliverance of the Lord. My God is real to me and His names are precious to me.

I do not watch my language to make sure I do not say His name out of context because it is the "right thing to do"; I joyfully and with a glad heart, for the abundance of all things that God is and all He calls Himself, watch my language to make sure I am giving God's name the glory it deserves. I do not take the Lord's name in vain.

Keeping the Sabbath

This is another place where we miss the blessing of obedience. I was visiting an adult Sunday school one time when the Sabbath was the subject at hand. The entire forty-five minutes was spent picking apart the blessing of the Sabbath in an attempt to get at all the laws. Should a person work on the Sabbath? Should a person shop on the Sabbath? Should a person do household chores on the Sabbath? What about cooking? Is television okay? Can I visit friends? Should I spend that time in prayer? Do I have to go to church? Would I be an accomplice to breaking someone else's Sabbath if I dine in a restaurant or shop at a store? What about doctors and nurses?

This went on and on until I wanted to blow my brains out. What do we not understand about rest? Jesus did His level best to show us the blessing of the Sabbath and we continue to try to turn it into something that God is using to hold us down.

Elohim Rested First, We Rest Last

The very first *idea* of the Sabbath was given to us in Genesis. The book of Hebrews mentions God's Sabbath at the end of creation, *"For he spake in a certain place of the seventh day on this wise, And God did rest the seventh day from all his works." (Heb 4:4 KJV)* God entered a Sabbath rest at the end of creation, then He went on to provide the blessing of the Sabbath to the Israelites through the manna, and finally, He gave the Israelites a law concerning the Sabbath.

The spiritual parallel is stunning. We, in these times, have been invited into God's rest permanently, *"if you will enter into his rest."* God gave us the law of the Sabbath as a natural example so that we could better understand what it means to rest spiritually. One day a week, throughout our whole Christian lives, we are reminded what it means to rest, *"thou shalt do no work."* The Sabbath was very specific and difficult to get around, which is why the Pharisees were ever watching Jesus to see what He would do on the Sabbath.

When God calls us into His eternal rest, He is not messing around. The same rules apply. If we are to truly enter His rest, we are to cease all human effort and do absolutely nothing by the power of the flesh. In this way we are free to obey the Sabbath, but not because it is the *right thing to do.* When we observe the Sabbath because we are fine, responsible, upstanding Christians, (like the Pharisee), we must exert human effort to accomplish this task, as we have no grace for the situation. And we are dishonoring the eternal Sabbath rest of God by working so hard to obey the natural rest!

When I look to the reward, God will move upon my heart and cause me to be zealous of the Sabbath. I am motivated because I am a selfish human being and I can see what is in it for me: A day of rest and the abundance of all things! Truly honoring the Sabbath requires no effort at all.

To rest is to cease work. We are not to *labor* into our blessings; we are to *rest* into them. In addition to being a natural lesson concerning a spiritual Truth, the Sabbath has always been intended to be a blessing to be enjoyed, not a burden to be borne.

Manna for the Week

The very first time any kind of a human Sabbath was observed in the Bible was in connection with the Manna. When God first instituted

The Ten Commandments

this Sabbath observance with the children of Israel He made all the necessary arrangements. Every day enough Manna fell to feed everyone for exactly one day. In addition, the manna had a short expiration date: One day. If the Israelites tried to keep the manna overnight they would wake up to the stench of maggots.

God told the Israelites that on the sixth day He was going to provide them with enough Manna for two days so that they could rest on the seventh day. This is a miracle. The very same manna that had a one-day expiration date suddenly morphed into manna with a two-day expiration date. Evidently, God added a special preservative to every sixth batch of manna. This was a very thoughtful gift from God. God wanted His children to have a day where they could put up their feet and just rest, so He provided a miracle.

Imagine if we had a boss who came up to us one day and said, "I'm going to pay your wages for Friday on Thursday so that you can take Friday off and just relax for a day. You seem to need a day to catch your breath and regroup. However, I still own you for that day and I insist that you take advantage of this rest." Would we go home and feel bound by this rest? Would this rest be burdensome for us? I imagine I would thank my boss and go home and rest. After all, if my very generous boss thinks I need rest, I must need rest.

God gave us the blessing of the Sabbath because He created us as creatures that benefit from a day of rest. Because God's laws are not to be grievous, there must be a way to take advantage of this blessing without it being burdensome. There is! Just as God gave the Israelites enough manna to get them through the Sabbath, He will give us what we need to get through our Sabbaths. We must believe and look for the extra provision on our sixth days to get us through our seventh days. If God provided it for the Israelites, He will provide it for us as we have been grafted into their branch!

We can believe God to orchestrate our lives in such a way that we can take a whole day off every single week. God showed us how to do this, "Expect enough on the sixth day to get you through the seventh day." If God did it for the Israelites, He will do it for us.

Awww, Do we Have to?

Do we have to spend time with God? Gosh, I don't know. The Bible doesn't expressly say. I can't imagine *not* spending it with Him; He is Lord of the Sabbath. Jesus was always with His disciples on the Sabbath. It is a glorious time of rest, how could leaving God out of it make it better? God loves to spend time in our presence while He is blessing us.

So how is work defined? Work is defined by a single thought: Do nothing that you do not feel compelled to do. We cease works by obeying this one edict. Rest is defined by another thought: We are to enter, not just rest, but *His* rest. God rested from *all* His works; He did nothing. We are to join God and share our day of doing nothing we do not want to do. God did not burden us with a law about the Sabbath; He blessed us with a day of rest. No guilt, no worry; just rest.

Sabbath was Made for Man

In particular, healing on the Sabbath was one of the main complaints the Pharisees had against Jesus, *"And they watched him, whether he would heal him on the sabbath day; that they might accuse him."* *(Mark 3:2 KJV)* Jesus obliged them by healing a man with the palsy and then threw in a bonus by telling the healed man to take up his bed and walk. Well, you may be able to get around the healing part, but toting a bed is in clear opposition to the Mosaic Law, *"Thou shalt do no work..."* Jesus was redefining the idea of a Sabbath rest.

The accusations were as predicted and a murderous spirit ensued, *"And therefore did the Jews persecute Jesus, and sought to slay him, because he had done these things on the sabbath day."* *(John 5:16 KJV)* The mob wanted to kill Jesus because He had healed a man and instructed him to pick up his bed and walk. A miracle working God is ignored while the Law is observed. These Pharisees were bound to a law, but not to a God.

Jesus clears everything up, *"And he said unto them, The sabbath was made for man, and not man for the sabbath: Therefore the Son of man is Lord also of the sabbath."* *(Mark 2:27-28 KJV)* Jesus did not explain how it was perfectly legal to heal a man on the Sabbath or for a man to pick up a bed and carry it home on the Sabbath. Neither did Jesus defend Himself with the particulars of the Mosaic Law concerning the Sabbath.

Rather, Jesus said that man was not made so that a law concerning the Sabbath could be observed; the Sabbath was made *for* man. The Sabbath is a gift from God to man. The moment it becomes a law, the blessing is lost. The Sabbath was made for the sole purpose of giving man a day to rest. It is that simple.

If it is your good pleasure to heal others on this blessed day of rest, then it is not a work and it still falls under the heading of rest. If

The Ten Commandments

it gives one pleasurable rest to pick up and carry a bed -- something that had been an impossible task for thirty-eight years -- then one must joyfully, and with a glad heart, for the abundance of all things pick up that bed with a willing heart and enjoy the rest of divine healing, *"...Wherefore it is lawful to do well on the sabbath days." (Matt 12:1b2 KJV)*

God has given us a day of rest and it is a privilege to receive this weekly rest. If I normally walk five miles a day, I should rest from this habit one day a week. Any physical therapist would agree with this logic. However, if I am not a regular walker, it may feel very nice and end up being very relaxing to go out and take a walk.

As well, if I have cooked every day for six days, I should rest from this job on the Sabbath day. However, if my life is so busy that it does not afford me the time to cook, I may find preparing a meal to be a relaxing task. So we see that it is not that we should make laws about what it means to observe the Sabbath. The only requirement is rest and the definition of rest will vary from one person to another. We know if we are resting or not, and we know that God looks at our heart. There is no hiding from God.

Seventh – First – It's All the Same

What does one do when their occupation requires them to work on the Sabbath? Observe the Sabbath on another day. Do we really think God is going to nit pick this thing? He wants us to rest one day a week. And He wants us to take that rest as a lesson about spiritually resting in Him. That is all.

The Sabbath was observed on the seventh day in the Old Testament. Over the years, the church has come to observe the Sabbath on the first day. The early church gathered together on the first day, broke bread together on the first day, took up an offering on the first day, and Jesus appeared to them after His resurrection on the first day and blew on them so that they would receive the Holy Ghost. As well, Jesus rose on the first day, which was a Sunday. His rising was the beginning of a rest to end all rests. And so the church observes the Sabbath on Sundays, or first days while the Israelites, then and now, observe the Sabbath on Saturdays, or seventh days.

Saturday...Sunday...Tuesday...the day of the week does not matter as much as the heart behind the obedience. We are to simply receive rest as a gift from a loving God, enjoy it, and learn from it how to enter into His eternal rest. We are to trust God to provide a way for us to rest one day a week and, according to His Word, He will.

No matter what, our motivation for observing the Sabbath must not be because we love God, fear God, or feel a sense of duty toward God. These are not Biblical motivators. As a matter of fact, we do not *have* to obey the Sabbath at all, *"All things are lawful to me..."*, however, only an ignoramus would refuse to allow God to teach him and minister to him through His blessing of the Sabbath, *"...not all things are expedient."*

I observe the Sabbath joyfully and with a glad heart, for the abundance of all things. The Sabbath is not a law to me; it is a blessing. I do not worry about the particulars of it; I simply enjoy it.

Honor Thy Mother and Thy Father

I think everyone has struggled at one time or another with the fifth commandment, *"Honour thy father and thy mother, as the LORD thy God hath commanded thee..."*. However, if we keep the entire instruction of this commandment, we will have the proper motivation for obeying it, *"...that thy days may be prolonged, and that it may go well with thee, in the land which the LORD thy God giveth thee."*

We are not told to keep this commandment because we love, fear, or feel a sense of duty toward God; rather we are encouraged to keep this commandment so that our days will be prolonged and it will go well with us wherever God takes us. Wow. That is your great reward.

This is About Us

Obedience to this command is clearly in relation to the person being obedient and not in relation to God. God does not stand to benefit from this obedience. God did not say, "Honor thy mother and thy father so that I will be pleased with how much you love, fear, or feel a sense of duty toward Me." No, He said *"Honor thy father and thy mother that **your** days may be prolonged and that it may go well with **thee**, in the land which the LORD thy God giveth **thee.**"*

God made this about us, not about Him. We stand to gain everything when we trust God. He has promised us the world in this one Scripture: Long life and all around goodness the entire time no matter where we go. Although this is about us, God is not left empty-handed. God's greatest delight is in watching His children walk by faith. This is the predominant message of the Bible.

What job position could offer this kind of compensation? How could anyone or anything in this world compete with, "I will prolong

The Ten Commandments

your life and cause it to be well with you no matter where you go or what you do"? All I have to do is honor my parents and my life will be prolonged and it will go well with me. That is amazing.

We are no longer under the law as, *"all things are lawful unto me"*; however, it is expedient to honor one's parents. Dishonoring our parents will only produce shortened days where things will not go well with us. How can that possibly be good for us? All things are lawful but not all are expedient.

Our Daddy, Who art in Heaven

And, just as with the other commandments, this law shows us a spiritual picture of how God functions as our "Parent". The reason God wants us to honor our natural parents is because our spiritual Parent, God is worthy of honor. We are to learn the blessing of honoring and obeying God by honoring and obeying our natural parents.

The invisible things from the creation of the world are clearly seen, being understood by things that are made, even His eternal power and Godhead. To honor and obey our natural father and mother is to honor and obey God our Father Who is in heaven. I do not honor my parents because they are worthy of honor; I honor them because God is worthy of honor and I utilize this natural example to embrace a spiritual Truth. We miss it when we see this thing as a law to be obeyed because it is the "right thing to do."

It's Neither Here nor There

When dealing with my children I remind them that it matters not whether my advice or my actions are good or bad, what matters is that I am the vessel of their long life and prosperity when they honor me. As a human I will fail, but faith doesn't fail. When we honor our parents, looking to the reward, they will become vessels of God's blessing in this life.

Although God often uses parents as vessels of blessing, He is just as good at getting around natural parents to fulfill His end of the deal by blessing us according to our honor. When we honor our parents while they are unworthy of honor, we, by faith, honor God and, *"our days will be prolonged and it will go well with us."* Whenever the world fails us, it should be seen as a perfect opportunity to exercise our faith and move the hand of God.

The New Testament goes further with this thought when it says, *"Children, obey your parents."* Even as an adult, I see this admonition as an opportunity to be led of the Lord. I do not look to my parents for direction because I believe they have all the answers; I look to them because God has all the answers and He promised to guide me through my parents.

Default Settings

The world has a default setting: Cursed. God has a default setting: Blessed. We are the x-factor in this equation. It is not what the world does that matters; it is how we respond to what the world does in relation to what we know about God. This is what matters.

One time I asked my father which television set I should buy. I trusted that God would tell me which television I should buy through my father. If I had gone to my father in his own merit, I may not have gotten Godly direction, but because I went to him in faith, I was led in the right direction.

And so I do not honor my parents because I love, fear, or feel a sense of duty toward God. Neither do I honor my parents because they have somehow earned this honor. I honor because of what is in it for me: I will have a prolonged life and it will go well with me. I can't turn that down. That is the kind of motivation that gets us through when our parents do not act worthy of honor.

I honor my parents joyfully and with a glad heart, for the abundance of all things, and I am blessed in this honoring.

Thou Shalt Not Kill

This particular commandment is worthy of a chapter all by itself, but alas, we are here in the middle of the Ten Commandments and so we must address it, however long it takes to sufficiently do that.

How many times have we wanted to kill someone? Come on…be honest. People can be exasperating. Each one of us has enemies that we would just as soon see removed from the earth, or at least taken out of the way. However, we do not have to kill anyone:

"Who can snatch the plunder of war
from the hands of a warrior?
Who can demand that a tyrant let his captives go?
But the LORD says, "The captives of warriors will be
released, and the plunder of tyrants will be retrieved.
For I will fight those who fight you,
and I will save your children.
I will feed your enemies with their own flesh.
They will be drunk with rivers of their own blood.
All the world will know that I, the LORD,

The Ten Commandments

am your Savior and Redeemer, the Mighty One of Israel."
(Isa 49:24-26 NLT)

Who can retrieve our blessings from the grasp of the sin nature? Who can demand that the devil let his captives go? But the Lord says, *"The captives will be released and the plunder will be retrieved. For I will fight those who fight you so that the world will know that I, the Lord, am your Savior and Redeemer, the Mighty One of Israel."* God will fight those who fight you.

The commandment, *"Thou shalt not kill"* does not just speak of murdering a person; it speaks of a murderous spirit that goes about killing:

> *"From whence come wars and fightings among you?*
> *come they not hence, even of your lusts that war in your*
> *members? Ye lust, and have not: ye kill, and desire to*
> *have, and cannot obtain: ye fight and war, yet ye have not,*
> *because ye ask not. Ye ask, and receive not, because ye*
> *ask amiss, that ye may consume it upon your lusts."*
> *(James 4:1-3 KJV)*

Yes, we have enemies, but we are not to go through this life struggling and trying to bully our blessings out of these people. We are to leave the murderous spirit behind and learn to trust God concerning our enemies, or those who bring out a murderous spirit in us. When we look to God as our Provider and ask for what we need, we will have no need to look for these blessings from another; hence we will have no reason to have a murderous spirit:

> *"Ye have heard that it was said by them of old time, Thou*
> *shalt not kill; and whosoever shall kill shall be in danger of*
> *the judgment: But I say unto you, That whosoever is angry*
> *with his brother without a cause shall be in danger of the*
> *judgment..." (Matt 5:21-22 KJV)*

It is all the same with God. If we are angry without a cause, given the right circumstances we could murder. We think that this takes us out of the equation because we feel that we *do* have a "cause" to be angry. That is a lie that exposes our misplaced trust.

If we have cause to be angry with our brother it is because we have placed our expectations on him and he fell short of these expectations. If we expect nothing from our brother, he cannot possibly disappoint us and we have no reason to ever be angry with him. Therefore, we really have no "cause" to be angry. So we see that our anger speaks more about us than our brother. We have a murderous spirit because we have misplaced trust. However, there is a sure way to quell a murderous spirit when he arises from his sleep.

Vengeance is Sweet

The Book of Psalms teems with examples of Godly vengeance. These worshippers had no problem calling down the fire of God on their enemies. Forgive me for the length, but notice this smattering of verses from the book of Psalms:

"Arise, O LORD; save me, O my God:
for thou hast smitten all mine enemies upon the
cheek bone; thou hast broken the teeth of the ungodly
...Arise, O LORD, in thine anger,
lift up thyself because of the rage of mine enemies...
When mine enemies are turned back,
they shall fall and perish at thy presence...
I will call upon the LORD, who is worthy to be praised:
so shall I be saved from mine enemies.
When the wicked, even mine enemies and my foes,
came upon me to eat up my flesh,
they stumbled and fell...
My times are in thy hand:
deliver me from the hand of mine enemies,
and from them that persecute me...
Through thee will we push down our enemies:
through thy name will we tread them under
that rise up against us...
For I will not trust in my bow,
neither shall my sword save me.
But thou hast saved us from our enemies,
and hast put them to shame that hated us...
He shall reward evil unto mine enemies:
cut them off in thy truth...
When I cry unto thee, then shall mine enemies turn back:
this I know; for God is for me...
Through God we shall do valiantly:
for he it is that shall tread down our enemies...

The Ten Commandments

Though I walk in the midst of trouble, thou wilt revive me:
thou shalt stretch forth thine hand against the wrath of
mine enemies, and thy right hand shall save me. "

God will avenge us of our enemies. Whether they are without, within, or part of the legions of Satan, God will contend with whatever dares to contend with us. I have witnessed this many times. God has avenged me of many enemies both seen, and unseen.

"But Jesus Said. .".

You may say, "But we are now under the New Covenant; Jesus said to love our enemies." That is true, however, we are to love them in the proper way and with the proper motive. We are free to love our enemies because we trust God to deal with them. We have nothing to lose in the situation. God is going to avenge us and this frees us to just love our enemies while we wait for justice to be served. The very act of loving our enemies is living proof that we believe God is on task.

Yes, right in the New Testament, God shows that He is still interested in avenging us of our enemies; Jesus came for this very purpose as was prophesied by Zacharias, the father of John the Baptist:

"As he spake by the mouth of his holy prophets,
which have been since the world began:
That we should be saved from our enemies,
and from the hand of all that hate us;"
(Luke 1:70-71 KJV)

The entire reason why we are to love our enemies is because God has promised to save us from our enemies and from the hand of all who hate us. If we trust Him to be good to His promises, we will joyfully and with a glad heart, for the abundance of all things, put down our murderous spirit and love our enemies:

"Dearly beloved, avenge not yourselves,
*but rather **give place unto wrath**:*
for it is written, Vengeance is mine;
I will repay, saith the Lord.
Therefore if thine enemy hunger, feed him;
if he thirst, give him drink:

> *for in so doing thou shalt heap coals of fire on his head.*
> *Be not overcome of evil,*
> *but overcome evil with good.*"
> *(Rom 12:19-21 KJV)*

Right here in the New Testament, Paul says not to avenge ourselves, but rather we are specifically to *back off and make room* for the wrath of God because, as it is written, *"Vengeance is mine, I will repay saith the Lord."* And so we see that although we have been told to love our enemies in deed, we have been told to do it in order to give God the opportunity to wreak vengeance upon them. That is an amazing thought. Can we pull out of our emotions long enough to allow God to perform His Word? How easy it would become to love our enemies if we could only believe that justice *would be* served. This would change the direction of our heart entirely.

Praying Sincerely

We have been going at it all wrong. We have been begrudgingly loving our enemies because it is the "right thing to do" and we have been heartlessly praying for our enemies by calling down blessings into their lives simply because we think it is the "right thing to do": "Lord bless so and so...even though he's my enemy, Lord bless him." That makes no sense. Why would it be a good idea to pray blessings into a life that we believe is detached from God?

We must get genuine about this thing. It is when we are willing and obedient that we will eat the good of the land. It is easy to be willing to love our enemy when we know God has promised to avenge us. In this way our works are genuine before God. Those who are heirs of salvation will warmly receive our genuine love; however, this same love will be coals of fire upon the head of those who are not yet heirs. Either way, we win by loving our enemy.

If we truly love our enemy, we will correctly pray that the Holy Spirit will bring deep conviction upon his soul. We should pray that the pseudo peace of the world be taken from him so that he is left empty and void. We should pray that he be plunged into the fiery furnace for a reality check. We should pray that the wind will blow and his house of straw will come to complete ruin.

This is what will cause a man to fall to his knees. If we pray blessings into his life, how will he know he has a need? Do we want to help him or not? If we love him, we will help him and give him what everyone in the world needs: A kick to the spiritual groin. We

The Ten Commandments

must all fall to our knees before this God. If I should ever find myself distanced from God, I would hope those who loved me would pray this way for me.

We will love our enemy in deed, knowing that God is at work in the situation and we are on the winning side. We will pray in earnest about our enemy's soul. What a wonderful set up. We are showering our enemy's life with love from a pure and zealous heart while God messes with his godless life. When this man does fall to his knees, he will have a comrade to help him back up a different way.

Movies upon movies have moved us to tears as they told stories similar to this. God outdoes the movies. If we ever start playing this thing right, we will absolutely be walking exactly the way the apostles did in the book of Acts.

It's Nothing Personal

This thing that exists between Christians and their enemies should not be personal. Our enemies should not move us to anger and rage. We need to see things the way they really are. The world is never the x-factor in our equation. It is silly to take offence against a carnal world that is powerless against the sin nature. They don't know God; how else are they expected to act? All goodness comes from a God they don't even know. The world is doing to us exactly what God purposed the world to do to us.

For the Israelites every battle was an opportunity to seize more of the Promised Land. Every one of our battles is an opportunity to seize more of our Promised Land. Our enemies are really our best friends. So when we get all emotionally involved in what our enemies are doing to us, we are missing the opportunity at hand.

If we can see our enemies for what they are, our emotions will change from hatred and murder, to the expectation of the abundance of all things. When we get all emotional, it shows we are not walking in faith. God has promised to work in our favor against our enemies. We are responsible to respond to our enemies as though this were true. The world is going to let us down every time. We are the x-factor. If there is a true enemy, it is we.

Second Hand Emotions

In the Old Testament, the Israelites were sent into the land of Canaan for the specific purpose of destroying its inhabitants and forcefully taking over their land. The Israelites did not go into these lands and do this because they were angry at the Canaanites. This was not personal for them. The Canaanites simply inhabited a land that had been promised to Abraham. Therefore, when someone inhabits a land that has been promised to us, we are to simply go in and take it by faith – minus all the drama.

The Canaanites knew about God; that is the reason Rahab and her family were saved. Everyone has equal access to God and can get on the winning side any time they want to. And so it is not a personal thing. When my boss is making my life miserable, I will trust God to avenge me of him and I will prove my trust in God by showing love to my boss and praying sincerely for him.

Through this process one of two things is going to happen in addition to my personal success: Either my boss will be moved to salvation through my love or he will be the target of the wrath of God. But that is none of my business. My business is to do one thing: Trust God to do as He has promised and obey Him joyfully and with a glad heart for the abundance of all things.

The Battle is the Lord's

Never was a single section of the Promised Land seized or kept by human effort or emotion. Whenever either of these two was involved, failure was sure. The reason for this is that man can never be victorious over man. When God fights, there are winners and there are losers. When man fights, there are two losers. In all victorious Israelite battles, God was the One doing battle and God doesn't lose. David spoke of this:

"And all this assembly shall know that the LORD saveth
not with sword and spear: for the battle is the LORD'S,
and he will give you into our hands." (1 Sam 17:47 KJV)

At one particular time when Jehoshaphat was king of Israel, several armies came against the Israelites in battle. In his supplication to God, King Jehoshaphat prayed the following:

"O our God, wilt thou not judge them? for we have no
might against this great company that cometh against us;
neither know we what to do: but our eyes are upon thee."
(2 Chr 20:12 KJV)

At that point, the Spirit of the Lord came upon a man named Jahaziel and he spoke:

The Ten Commandments

"And he said, Hearken ye, all Judah, and ye inhabitants of
Jerusalem, and thou king Jehoshaphat,
Thus saith the LORD unto you,
Be not afraid nor dismayed
by reason of this great multitude;
for the battle is not yours, but God's."
(2 Chr 20:15 KJV)

It matters not how many people may be against us, when we turn to
the Lord and say, "Our eyes are upon Thee", the battle will transfer
from us to God:

"Ye shall not need to fight in this battle:
set yourselves, stand ye still,
and see the salvation of the LORD with you,
O Judah and Jerusalem: fear not, nor be dismayed;
to morrow go out against them:
for the LORD will be with you."
(2 Chr 20:17 KJV)

When our enemies come against us, we must not attempt to fight this
battle. Rather, we must stand still and see the salvation of the
Lord…God will be with us. Jehoshaphat knew what it meant to trust
God and he instructed his troops likewise:

"And they rose early in the morning,
and went forth into the wilderness of Tekoa:
and as they went forth, Jehoshaphat stood and said,
Hear me, O Judah, and ye inhabitants of Jerusalem;
Believe in the LORD your God, so shall ye be established;
believe his prophets, so shall ye prosper.
And when he had consulted with the people,
he appointed singers unto the LORD,
and that should praise the beauty of holiness,
as they went out before the army, and to say,
Praise the LORD; for his mercy endureth for ever."
(2 Chr 20:20-21 KJV)

Believe in the Lord your God and you will be established. Sing a
song of praise to the beauty of holiness and praise the Lord for His
mercy endures forever. When we are in battle, we must believe in

the Lord enough to begin praising Him before the battle is ever won. Only pure confidence in God can do such a thing, however, the results are impressive:

"And when they began to sing and to praise,
the LORD set ambushments
against the children of Ammon, Moab, and mount Seir,
which were come against Judah; and they were smitten.
For the children of Ammon and Moab
stood up against the inhabitants of mount Seir,
utterly to slay and destroy them:
and when they had made an end of the inhabitants of Seir,
every one helped to destroy another.
And when Judah came toward the watch tower in the
wilderness, they looked unto the multitude, and, behold,
they were dead bodies fallen to the earth,
and none escaped."
(2 Chr 20:22-24 KJV)

The Israelites won this battle, not by lifting a single finger, but by lifting their voices in praise. Their enemies ended up destroying one another. When we take God at His Word and praise Him prematurely for His reward, our enemies will destroy one another.

God was not finished showing the Israelites what it meant to trust the One True God:

"And when Jehoshaphat and his people came to take away
the spoil of them, they found among them in abundance
both riches with the dead bodies, and precious jewels,
which they stripped off for themselves, more than they
could carry away: and they were three days
in gathering of the spoil, it was so much."
(2 Chr 20:25 KJV)

Three days of gathering riches and precious jewels? That is a lot of wealth. The Israelites were so overwhelmed with the abundance of the spoil that they named this place Berachah, which means "prosperity". Good name. This is what happens when we expect God to avenge us of our enemies and proceed as though it was done.

The Ten Commandments

When all things are considered, it is easy to obey the command to not kill. We have no reason to kill. We have no reason to kill. God is on our side and promises to contend with those who contend with us (Isa 49:25) and prosper us while doing so. Joyfully and with a glad heart, for the abundance of all things, I will love my enemy and withhold from taking my own revenge because I trust God to deal with him:

"I will freely sacrifice unto thee:
I will praise thy name, O LORD; for it is good.
For he hath delivered me out of all trouble:
and mine eye hath seen his desire upon mine enemies."
(Psa 54:6-7 KJV)

Thou Shalt Not Commit Adultery

Adultery is commonplace in today's culture. There are a lot of reasons for this. The carnal world has been pushing this regime for close to a century to get it where it is. Another indication that Christians are not ciphering the Bible correctly: Statistics say the church is not much different than the world when it comes to sexual promiscuity. The spirit is willing; the flesh is weak.

It seems we are all running around looking for happiness. We are living in a world where true happiness is rare. And like fish among baited hooks, we are drawn to that one who promises everything but seldom delivers anything.

Christians are not called to avoid trials; they are called to withstand them. We will keep getting the same test until we pass. When we stop running from it and learn to withstand it we will be ready to move on. If we find ourselves in a bad marriage, we must find the place of faith and overcome the situation. It is there for us.

Paul tells us, *"For the unbelieving husband is sanctified by the wife, and the unbelieving wife is sanctified by the husband: else were your children unclean; but now are they holy." (1 Cor 7:14 KJV)* What this tells us is that God purifies and makes holy the spouse of a believer. In this way God is able to work with the unbeliever in a way He otherwise wouldn't. God and His wealth of power are on our side in our marriages.

And so we do not obey this commandment because it is the "right thing to do"; we obey it because we trust our God Who has promised to work victoriously with us in the midst of the battle that is presently being waged against marriage. My marriage is proof positive that God will work miracles if only we will let Him. There aren't too many people who really faith it through a tough marriage. Those who do are in for a ride. If our motivation for obeying this commandment is love, fear, or a sense of duty toward God we are not in faith and we can expect no grace to perform what can be a very tall order. When we have wrong motives we lack power. We are to obey joyfully and with a glad heart, looking to God. If we do not, we can expect the cursed end of the commandments:

> *"Because thou servedst not the LORD thy God with joyfulness, and with gladness of heart, for the abundance of all things; Therefore shalt thou serve thine enemies which the LORD shall send against thee, in hunger, and in thirst, and in nakedness, and in want of all things: and he shall put a yoke of iron upon thy neck, until he have destroyed thee."*
> *(Deut 28:47-48 KJV)*

And, just as with all the commandments, "Thou shalt not commit adultery" holds a spiritual lesson for us. There will be times when we become discouraged in our "marriage" with God. There will be times when it seems as though He is not being the "Husband" we need. At these times it is easy to be seduced by the world and its promises of happiness. We are in covenant with God just like we are in covenant with our marriage partners. God wants us to learn how to stick it out with a spouse so that we will understand how God sticks it out with us and how we should stick it out with Him. We are not to give up on Him and look to see how the world can meet our needs. When we do, we are being an adulterer:

> *"Ye adulterers and adulteresses, know ye not that the friendship of the world is enmity with God? whosoever therefore will be a friend of the world is the enemy of God." (James 4:4 KJV)*

We cannot act and believe as the world acts and believes without adulterating our relationship with God. If the invisible things from the creation of the world are clearly seen being understood by things that are made, then we must see this commandment in its truest form: "Thou shalt not commit adultery against God by being a friend of the

The Ten Commandments

world." God loves us with a jealous love, *"...the LORD, whose name is Jealous, is a jealous God:" (Ex 34:14 KJV).* If we understand the pain of adultery, we understand what upsets God.

We are motivated to stay true to our marriages, not because it is *the right thing to do,* but because we trust God to be working in our situation for His ultimate good. When we wait on God in faith, we will see miracles happen. We are motivated to stick it out with God and not start looking to the world to meet our needs, not because it is the right thing to do, but because we trust Him to meet our needs. When we wait on God in faith, we will see miracles happen. I think miracles are all God knows how to do. We must simply let Him work His magic in our lives. He is amazing.

Thou Shalt not Steal, Lie, nor Covet

It is probably becoming clear to you how this works and you probably don't even need me to do these last three. Why would we steal when we serve a God Who owns the cattle on a thousand hills? Why would we trust in a lie when all that matters or counts is Truth in the inward part? What reason would we have to covet when God promises to satisfy the desires of our heart?

So we do not abstain from stealing, lying, and coveting because these are the *right things to do,* we abstain from these because we no longer need them to meet our needs. I will not steal, I will not lie, and I will not covet…joyfully and with a glad heart, for the abundance of all things. That takes me out from under the curse and because I have a willing heart, I will eat the good of the land.

Stealing

When we steal, we are saying in essence, "Hey, I don't trust God to meet my needs. I have to steal from the IRS because God is not enough." If we trusted in our God, our needs would be met and we would not have to steal. I do not abstain from stealing because "Christians ought not to steal"; I abstain from stealing because I have no need to steal. When I steal I may get a temporary reward that may or may not meet my needs, however, when I trust God and deal honestly with my fellow man, I get God's great reward. God wins…hands down.

The spiritual parallels are interesting. How do we steal from God? By not giving Him the only thing for which He asks: Trust. God has only asked man to trust Him from the moment He met him. When God tells us to not steal, He is telling us to trust Him. And so

I do not steal from Him the one thing He asks of me and I will have my reward. Thou shalt not steal. It is very simple.

Lying

Lying is the single most satanic of sins. Satan owns deception the way God owns Truth. God moves at the sound of His Truth and the devil moves at the sound of a lie. If we want to take God completely out of the equation, all we must do is trust in a lie. If we want to step soundly into the will and domain of Satan, trusting in a lie will get us there.

The lie, in and of itself, is not the culprit. Rahab the Harlot was instructed to lie. As well, the Holocaust teems with testimonies of believers who lied to save lives. I am convinced those lies were Spirit led just as Rahab's lie was Spirit led. Rahab received life eternal because of her lie. God was at work.

It is the *trusting* in a lie that is the true enemy of God. Rahab lied, although she was trusting in God when she did it. When we trust in a lie, we are working against the Truth.

Eternal Truth

Our spiritual parallel tells us that God wants us to walk in His eternal Truth. Everything outside of His Truth is an abomination to Him. He gave us His Truth in black, white, and red and we are without excuse. We are living in the day of complete revealed Truth. Owning Truth is a privilege the carnal world is not afforded. We are responsible for these Truths. Thou shalt not lie.

We know that it is the truth that sets us free; however, there are two "truths" in this world: The facts that lay naked before us, and the Truths of the spiritual realm that we cannot yet see. It is not enough to speak the truths we can see; one must speak the higher Truths of the Spirit realm. Many times we must speak the higher Truths of the spiritual realm right in the face of the "truths" of the natural realm. We must be beings of *God's* Truth. This is the essence of what it means to live in the spiritual realm.

I speak and walk in the Truth, not because it is the "right thing to do", but because I believe that Truth and respect it for being the very Person of Jesus Christ. I know that God's Word, alive and thriving in the spiritual realm, will manifest in this natural realm all in good time. I live by the Truth and do so joyfully and with a glad heart, for the abundance of all things. The Truth of God's Word sets me free.

The Ten Commandments

Coveting

To covet what our neighbors have is to accuse God of not taking care of us sufficiently. If God were doing His job of meeting our needs, we would not be longing for what we do not have. When we get a longing for what we do not have, we must ask ourselves why our longing has not been met. The Word of God has said that He will satisfy the desires of our heart and provide all we need according to His riches in glory. Since the Word of God is absolute Truth in the spiritual realm, our deficiency is only of the natural realm, which makes it temporary. More time is needed; the baby is not ready.

When that feeling of looking over the fence comes, all one must do is thank God that He will satisfy our needs and desires. The longer we believe, the more mature in our faith we become until our blessing is ready to be birthed into the natural realm.

Heavenly Places

We must not covet what our neighbor has; we must rather covet what the spiritual realm holds in store for us:

"Blessed be the God and Father of our Lord Jesus Christ, who hath blessed us with all spiritual blessings in heavenly places in Christ:" (Eph 1:3 KJV)

Our eyes should be lovingly and longingly looking over the "fence" toward the spiritual realm with all of its blessings. This is what we should be drooling over. All of our blessings are at a residence called "Heavenly Places". Where is this place? This is the residence of God and His Son, Jesus:

"Which he wrought in Christ, when he raised him from the dead, and set him at his own right hand in the heavenly places," (Eph 1:20 KJV)

This heavenly place is the only place where Truth resides on the Throne of God. Every single word of the Bible is manifest in this heavenly place. This is God's Truth. He does not see us except through this Truth. We are invited into God's Truth, to live with Him amid all that is really true about us:

"And hath raised us up together, and made us sit together in heavenly places in Christ Jesus:" (Eph 2:6 KJV).

This is a tremendous blessing. Absolutely the only way to enter this realm is by respecting the Truth of this realm.

This is why it is ridiculous for a blood bought Christian to covet something his neighbor has. We have everything we can possibly need in the one place where it cannot be destroyed or taken away, *"But lay up for yourselves treasures in heaven, where neither moth nor rust doth corrupt, and where thieves do not break through nor steal:" (Matt 6:20 KJV)*. If the price tag for having all my needs met is patience, so be it. I will have patience.

I covet my blessings in heavenly places, not because that is the "right thing to do", but because I trust God to be true to His Word and satisfy all my needs and desires. I abstain from coveting, joyfully and with a glad heart, for the abundance of all things. In doing this I have a willing heart and I will eat the good of the land.

> *"But covet earnestly the best gifts…"*
> *(1 Cor 12:31a KJV)*

And so we come to the end of the Ten Commandments. We are living in the age of a new and better way. God has written His laws upon our hearts, given us the grace to perform the requirements of these laws, *and* promised to reward us for being vessels of His goodness! This is how it is that God's laws are not burdensome to us. This is how we shine forth as a peculiar people who are zealous of good works. We are not under the burden of the law; we are under the blessing of the law! It really is all good.

O How I love Thy Law

For ever, O LORD, thy word is settled in heaven.
Thy faithfulness is unto all generations:
thou hast established the earth, and it abideth.
They continue this day according to thine ordinances:
for all are thy servants.
Unless thy law had been my delights,
I should then have perished in mine affliction.
I will never forget thy precepts:
for with them thou hast quickened me.
I am thine, save me; for I have sought thy precepts.
The wicked have waited for me to destroy me:
but I will consider thy testimonies.
I have seen an end of all perfection:
but thy commandment is exceeding broad.
Psalm 119:89 – 96

8

O HOW I LOVE THY LAW

"O how I love thy law! it is my meditation all the day."
Psalm 119:97

The Sin within

Can you stand one more chapter designed to teach and motivate you to obey God in the correct manner and for the right reasons? If not, skip ahead. But for those of you who are interested in seeing this thing played out a bit more, stick around; you will enjoy.

All of these things that seem like they are holding us down...our authorities, our enemies, our trials...actually hold the keys to our blessings. We are on the winning side. We cannot lose. The only thing that separates the winners from the losers is faith. God has shown us in His Word how to exercise our faith and then provided opportunities for this faith to be used. Faith is what pleases God.

We should be leaving no stone unturned in our quest for submitting to authorities, loving our enemies, and enduring our trials. These are the very things God has placed in our path for the sole purpose of blessing us!

Submission

There is so much squabbling about submission and there really is no need. Paul gives us very simple advice concerning submission:

"Submitting yourselves one to another in the fear of God.
Wives, submit yourselves unto your own husbands,
as unto the Lord. For the husband is the head of the wife,
even as Christ is the head of the church:
and he is the saviour of the body.
Therefore as the church is subject unto Christ,
so let the wives be to their own husbands in every thing.
Husbands, love your wives, even as Christ
also loved the church, and gave himself for it;
That he might sanctify and cleanse it
with the washing of water by the word,
That he might present it to himself a glorious church,
not having spot, or wrinkle, or any such thing;
but that it should be holy and without blemish...
Children, obey your parents in the Lord: for this is right.
Honour thy father and mother;
(which is the first commandment with promise;)
That it may be well with thee,
and thou mayest live long on the earth.
And, ye fathers, provoke not your children to wrath:
but bring them up in the nurture

O How I love Thy Law

and admonition of the Lord.
Servants, be obedient to them that are your masters
according to the flesh, with fear and trembling,
in singleness of your heart, as unto Christ;
Not with eyeservice, as menpleasers;
but as the servants of Christ,
doing the will of God from the heart;
With good will doing service,
as to the Lord, and not to men:
Knowing that whatsoever good thing any man doeth,
the same shall he receive of the Lord,
whether he be bond or free."
(Eph 5:21–29& 6:1-8 KJV)

How do we submit one to another? By recognizing that lines of authority are *blessings from God,* *"Knowing that whatsoever good thing any man doeth, the same shall he receive of the Lord, whether he be bond or free."* God will reward us according to what we do by faith. So long as we have faith, we do not have to look to authorities to provide what we need in the home, the work place, and in the world.

Paul is telling everyone to find their authorities and submit to them, *"Submit one to another."* After telling everyone to find their authority and submit to it, Paul gives us the motivation behind this submission through the examples found in a family, *"The invisible things from the creation of the world are clearly seen being understood by things that are made."*

The Example

I am only going to use the instructions to a wife from these verses because I already feel I am belaboring the subject and I don't want to go into all the different authorities. However, the same advice pertains to all authority figures in our lives. Whatever authority is in your face right now is the one you should be thinking about as we continue.

Wives, submit to your husbands as unto the Lord. Why? Because the husband is the head of the household in the exact same way that Christ is the Head of the church. A wife running contrary to her husband is tantamount to the church running contrary to Christ. This will not do.

Without Spot or Wrinkle

Wives must not submit to their husbands because they feel a sense of duty to it; rather wives should submit to their husbands because of what is in it for them. According to our verses, the same way that Christ is equipped to present the church to God without spot or wrinkle, so our husbands are equipped to present us in like manner *when we submit to them.* When we get out from under their authority, we are no longer under the anointing, and our authority is no longer a minister of good to us.

Submitting as Unto the Lord

Wives are to submit to their husbands *as unto the Lord.* This does not mean that they are to submit to their husbands *in the same way* that they submit to the Lord. What this verse means is that wives are to submit to their husbands *as though* they are submitting to the Lord. Wives have an opportunity to show God how much they trust Him by submitting to their husbands as though they are submitting to the perfect God Almighty. To obey a husband is to obey God.

Women are to submit to their husbands, not as men pleasers who are looking for attention, but as servants, not of men, but of Christ. In this way women do the will of God from their heart. It is much easier to submit to a perfect God than it is to submit to an imperfect husband. It is with good cheer that women submit to their husbands because they know they are submitting to the Lord and not to men. They do this because, *"Knowing that whatsoever good thing any man doeth, the same* **shall he receive of the Lord,** *whether he be bond or free."* No matter what the wife's situation, the Lord will reward whatever submissive thing she does. A wife submits to God by submitting to her husband.

The great thing about God is that His blessings are always vertical. A woman need not have a cooperative husband in order to take part in the blessing of submission. God did not need cooperative jailors to promote Joseph to second in command over all of Egypt. I was married and submitted to an unbeliever for several years. God used my husband to bless me in direct relation to how I submitted in spite of how he behaved. Our authorities can be nothing more than vessels of God when we believe the Scriptures and submit to them as though we are submitting to God, regardless of how they are conducting themselves.

O How I love Thy Law

Take this Job and. . .

There is much contention in the work place. I am absolutely positive God placed contrary bosses in our lives on purpose. It is very difficult to get under a boss who is clearly in the wrong. Well, what I say by saying this is that it takes faith. One cannot submit to a contrary boss unless he is sure there is something in it for him. It takes faith to be able to submit to someone who is making your life miserable. That is a good thing; faith is what pleases God.

I'm sorry, but I do not know of a single person who has the wherewithal to submit joyfully to an unfair boss simply because it is the "right thing to do". So we keep in mind that our bosses cannot help but to be ministers to us for good as long as we are submitted to them. When this submission is in place, it is only a matter of time. The good must come. We must stand.

Trust and authority

Let's take a look at exactly how authority works to bless us. After all, everything in life is set up in lines of authority. From government to families to churches to businesses, everything runs by governing authorities and everyone falls somewhere in line.

God is the head of Jesus. Jesus is the Head of the church. The church is the head of men. Men are the head of the wife. The wife is head of the children. The firstborn is the head of the heirs. The heirs are heads of the servants. Servants are heads of their wives, and so on. Everyone deals with authority of some kind every day of his life.

And this is probably why we can always be caught bucking authority at one level or another. Whether it's our bank, our boss, our dry-cleaner, our congressman, our husband, our pastor, our parents, or whatever authority is in our face every day, it is easy to become frustrated with those who are in authority. However, this is one of the most powerful ways to get sure guidance from God.

Rather than submitting to our God ordained authorities because we love, fear, or feel a sense of duty toward God, we submit to them because in so doing they become a pipeline of God's anointing:

> "Behold, how good and how pleasant it is for brethren to
> dwell together in unity! It is like the precious ointment
> upon the head, that ran down upon the beard, even Aaron's
> beard: that went down to the skirts of his garments;"
> (Psa 133:1-2 KJV)

From God, to authorities, and then to us, the anointing flows down. The brethren dwell together in unity when everyone submits to their governing authorities! The anointing of God flows down from authorities to those under them just as it flowed over Aaron's beard down to his skirts. As we dwell together all lined up in this way, we all get under the anointing. It is when we come out from under our authorities that we come out from under the anointing. God places authorities in our lives to bless us and protect us.

Ordained by God

God ordains, or appoints all lines of authority for the purpose of blessing those who submit to authority, and punishing those who do not:

> *"Let every soul be subject to the governing authorities.*
> *For there is no authority except from God,*
> *and **the authorities that exist are appointed by God.***
> *Therefore whoever resists the authority*
> *resists the ordinance of God,*
> *and those who resist will bring judgment on themselves.*
> *For rulers are not a terror to good works, but to evil.*
> *Do you want to be unafraid of the authority?*
> *Do what is good, and you will have praise from the same.*
> ***For he is God's minister to you for good.***
> *But if you do evil, be afraid;*
> *for he does not bear the sword in vain;*
> *for he is God's minister,*
> *an avenger to execute wrath on him who practices evil.*
> *Therefore you must be subject, not only because of wrath*
> *but also for conscience' sake."*
> *(Rom 13:1-5 NKJV emphasis mine)*

A Minister of Good

We are to be subject to our governing authorities because they have been appointed by God to reward us. When we resist them we bring judgment upon ourselves. So while we are trying to evade *their* judgment, we are in fact bringing upon ourselves *God's* judgment. No wonder we are such a mess.

We are to look to our authority for a reward, *"For he is God's minister to you for good"*, but we are to see this authority as nothing more than a vessel of God to us. In this way we do not trust the authority; we trust the God behind the authority.

If we have a boss who is acting very unjustly toward us, our first instinct is to take the high place and try to bring our boss under subjection to how *we* feel about the situation. That is a reversal of flow. Suddenly, because we are no longer under our boss, he can no longer be a minister of good to us. As a matter of fact, he will become the opposite:

> *"But if you do evil, be afraid;*
> *for he does not bear the sword in vain;*
> *for he is God's minister,*
> *an avenger to execute wrath on him who practices evil."*

We do evil when we set aside our faith and come out from under our authorities. The authority, in and of himself, can execute neither good nor evil to us; he is at the mercy of how we are responding to him. If we respond by trying to gain power over him, he will become an avenger of wrath; if we respond in faith and stay under his authority, he will become a minister of good. The authority, himself, has no choice in the matter.

I can't even tell you how many times I have put this to the test. This was one of the first spiritual lessons I learned as a believer. I was taught the proper motivation for submitting to my husband and then I carried this to all the authorities in my life. I looked for authorities under every rock. From my parents, to my husband's boss, to a loan officer at the bank, to spiritually older women, I embraced any and all authorities as potential ministers of good. I looked for ways that I could get under them so that God's anointing would flow down on me. These do not sound like the ramblings of someone who is obeying the law because it is the right thing to do. I am a peculiar person who is zealous of good works.

Submitting to an Ungodly Authority

My biggest tests always involved my husband, Roger. We ran into problems early in the game. To say that our marriage was in trouble would be a gross understatement. However, after coming close to a nervous breakdown, I sought the advice of a true sage and learned how to submit to my husband by faith and receive the blessing of the anointing.

Roger was not an easy man to submit to. The entire time I did it, I had to do it by faith. But that is a good thing. Whenever we are forced to practice our faith we are building it inside of us. I honed my submission skills on my husband. I didn't submit to my husband because it was the proper thing for a Christian wife to do; I submitted to my husband because of what was in it for me.

Can You Spare a Twenty?

Just a month or so into this newfound portal of blessing, I experienced a good example of how authority functions as a vessel of God. Roger and I were living at his parent's house do to financial problems, so money was scarce. God eventually worked it all for a multitude of blessings, but at this particular time we had no money to spare.

I was this brand-new, born again Christian while Roger had no interest at all. As a matter of fact, I had to keep my Christianity under wraps around him. I had just completed a simple version of the Bible, so I visited a Christian bookstore to look for a new one. I don't know what I was thinking since I only had five dollars and no hope of getting more.

While shopping I found the Bible that I *needed* and at the same time I also found a leather Bible cover that I really *wanted*. Together these added up to twenty-five dollars. I wasn't sure what to do when an employee came up behind me and told me that they had a one-week lay away plan. I asked her how much I would have to put down. She said, "Five dollars." Okay. I gave her my five dollars and told her I would be back the next week.

I didn't know what I was going to do. I couldn't ask Roger for twenty dollars for a *Bible*, I couldn't put faith in a lie, and I had no way of earning money. So, because I was submitted to my husband, I told God that I expected Him to work through Roger to give me the twenty dollars I needed. You see I did not just assume my authority would bless me; I actively involved my faith in God's Word and made a demand on it. That is what God wants us to do.

The week went by with no money in sight. I was not discouraged. On the night before my balance was due I was standing in the kitchen while my husband and his mother stood talking nearby. They were deep in conversation when Roger reached into his back pocket, removed his wallet, pulled out a twenty-dollar bill and thrust it toward me without breaking his gaze or his concentration on his conversation with his mother.

O How I love Thy Law

Not once did he look in my direction so I ignored what he was doing. I was not going to rush God. Roger held that money out there for a while before he finally looked at me with frustrated bewilderment and shook the bill until I took it from his hand. He then turned and resumed his conversation with his mother who seemed unaware of my existence in the room.

I raised my eyebrows and looked for my purse. Although I have moved on to another Bible, I have used that Bible cover for twenty-four years. For years I was not able to tell this story to my husband because it would have been lost on him. But, when I finally was able to tell him, he had no memory of the incident. Although Roger was far from the Lord at the time, God still used this, my authority, as a minister for my good.

Good Housekeeping

The following is another example of what happens when we keep our eyes open for authorities.

Twenty-one years ago Roger decided that we needed to buy a home. Our credit was terrible, but we live in a small town that deals a lot with contracts so he was hoping to be able to work with someone. My husband's parents had given us money for a down payment; hence, between Roger and his folks I already had three authorities involved. I paid attention to whatever they had to say on the subject. Now we just needed to see where the Lord would take us.

We looked at house after house and it seemed we just couldn't find anything decent for the amount of money we could borrow. We had two children and one on the way so we couldn't move into anything that needed a lot of work; we didn't have the money or the time. Our search went on for several weeks with no natural answers in sight. I didn't give up and I didn't complain. I do not say this to brag...I just knew God would somehow find us a house and this knowledge carried me through.

The Light at the End of the Tunnel

Finally one day Roger said that his *boss* had a house he wanted us to look at. Immediately my eyes lit up. *A fourth authority.* As long as I am under him I will be blessed by his direction. I had made it a point to submit to my husband's boss, so I couldn't wait to see the house. From the moment we pulled in front of it I knew this would be our home.

The Test of Faith

The house was perfect inside and out and we were soon ready to get through the authorities in order to secure it. Roger and I sat across from the owner who was offering to sell the home to us on contract as long as we had a co-signer. This was the test. Not too many people are financially capable of co-signing a mortgage. I asked the only person in our family who was even close and he was not willing. I didn't blame him. I reminded myself that God is going to bless me through these authorities no matter what it looked like.

I went to see the owner, and submitting to his authority, I said this, "We do not have a co-signer but I believe God wants us to have this home and I give you my word that by the grace of God, we will fulfill our end of the contract. So it is up to you. I will honor whatever decision you make."

"A" Plus!

He looked at me for a moment and then said, "Well how can I turn down a good Christian girl?" And that was the end of that. I passed the test of faith. I did not get into worry and fear and try to work it out on my own. God was free to work in my situation all by Himself. We got the home and we have been nothing but blessed by it.

We have continued to live in that home for over two decades and have loved every minute of it. This home has been blessed more than any other home I know. Although it is a modest home, I really cannot imagine ever leaving it. I absolutely love living here.

It aint Over till it's Over

A couple of years before we had gotten this home, we had lost our first home when we broke the contract by getting behind in payments. That seemed like a bad thing at the time. We had to move in with Roger's parents. That seemed like a bad thing at the time. But I knew it wasn't over.

Through all of this, God kept me in a good attitude. I believed Him and knew that He would take care of us. I didn't complain and worry. I just lived and knew it was being worked out. I was very young in the Lord so this attitude did not come after years of laboring for it. It is into a simple faith that we must enter.

The house we had lost two years earlier had the exact same price tag as the one we now had. Today, our house is worth four times what the original house is presently worth. The two houses cannot

O How I love Thy Law

be compared. It is ridiculous that we got this house for the price we did. God went above and beyond the call of duty for me simply because I believed His Word enough to rely on it alone.

Blessings Abound

I want to share with you the different ways that we were blessed by this home. I want you to understand the distance to which God will go when we obey Him with a willing heart, because we trust Him, not because we love, fear, or feel a sense of duty toward Him.

1. The address of our home was 316.
2. The tenant before us was a pastor by the name of John.
3. My next-door neighbor was a beautiful, elderly Christian woman who was a daily encouragement and a true bright spot in my young Christian life.
4. This dear lady's name was Mrs. Pew and her telephone number had 316 in it.
5. Although we were surrounded by dilapidated homes, no more than three months went by before they started coming down one after the other. In total eight homes that had surrounded us were torn down over the next few years.
6. All that was torn down was replaced by new construction.
7. When we moved in I stared out my kitchen window at bathroom plumbing on the outside of the neighbor's house. Now I look out into a beautiful shade garden with cascading trees against the backdrop of a new home.
8. When the children were small, we put up a fence and bought a combination lock. The correct combination was 3164.
9. Inside the home God had been a very present help in time of need. For all the years that we struggled financially, God gave us a handy man that refused to take money when we needed him for a repair. From plumbing to electricity this man always helped and never took a dime. The only payment he received were the friendly conversations we shared whenever he visited. This man, Dorance Pew, was the nephew of my neighbor, Mrs. Pew. I believe this blessing was a direct result of how I gladly submitted to Mrs. Pew as my spiritual authority. Whenever I was in her presence, I was looking for guidance. My authorities are ministers of good to me.
10. I love to decorate, though we have always been on a shoestring budget. Whenever I tackled a room I looked to

God for assistance. He amazed me at what He could do with very little money. I simply cannot do justice to what He has accomplished.

11. When Mrs. Pew went to be with the Lord, her home was torn down and there was talk of using the property to build condominiums. If that had happened, we would have been hemmed in. The property changed hands a couple of times and truckloads of dirt were incorporated into the landscape before it settled into its use. For the last several years only one fifth of it is used as a parking lot for the beautiful apartments behind us while the rest of the property is a nice open space. The yard adjacent to this lot is very large and open. It almost looks like a park.

12. The man who owns the property has generously allowed us to use this space. Because we heat our home with a wood stove, we always need space for cutting and stacking wood. This lot has provided the necessary space. This space also offers us a large area for a vegetable garden and allows us to share vegetables with our neighbors in the apartments. When we have parties, we play volleyball and Badminton and throw the football and baseball in that lot. Mrs. Pew's lot continues to be a blessing to us every day.

13. Although our home is conveniently located within walking distance of absolutely anything we may need, somehow it is situated in such a way that our yard is very peaceful and beautiful. No matter where you look, the view is very nice.

That list could have been twice as long; I spared you. Our home and our situation changed dramatically because I dared to believe that God would minister good to me through my ordained authorities. I was not under the law of submission as *"all things are lawful to me"*, however it would not have profited me to ignore my authorities, *"all things are not expedient."* I look at every opportunity to submit as an opportunity to be blessed. I am a peculiar person who is zealous of good works because I know what is in it for me.

What Not To Do

I did not submit to Roger, Roger's parents, Roger's boss, and the homeowner so that God would think well of me. I didn't submit to them because I was afraid that God would punish me if I didn't. Nor

O How I love Thy Law

did I feel it was my due service to submit to them. I submitted to them because of what was in it for me. I trusted God to perform that which He promised and knew that my authorities had no choice but to be ministers of good to me as long as I stayed under them.

When we couldn't get a co-signer for the house, I didn't beg and plead and try to make that happen. I didn't worry and fret and try to figure out another way. I submitted to the wishes of the one I had asked and believed God would honor that. When I told the seller the decision was up to him, I was submitting to him and his place of authority as seller of this home. When we function in this way, all stress is removed from the situation. I look to God to take care of me and prove that trust by obeying with the proper motivation.

Not only does the anointing of an authority work to bless us as it flows down over us; it also works to protect us. God is saying, "There's a storm coming...everyone take cover! When we are safely under our authorities, we are protected from many of the fiery darts of the evil one.

Giving Spiritually

Recently my sons mentioned to me that they missed an opportunity to receive some needed furniture. We agreed that what Satan had taken must be returned to them. Meanwhile, my son, Devon, had been asking God how he would like him to sow into His kingdom.

One day shortly thereafter, Devon felt led to give their mop to a neighbor lady. Submitting to his elder, Devon ran the idea past big brother Nathan. Nathan said, "She's rich; she can buy her own mop." So Devon asked me what he should do. I told him that his job was done. He had been willing to give that mop, and would have, if his authority had allowed. The authority did not allow the mop to be given in the natural realm, however, Devon, through his willingness, had already given the mop in the spiritual realm in his heart, *"Whereas it was in thine heart to give the mop, thou didst well that it was in thine heart."*

Only one week after Devon had been nothing more than *willing* to give a simple mop, the woman to whom he was going to give it gave them several items of furniture that they needed. They don't know why she gave them this furniture. She had found the items at estate sales, which are very popular in Florida, and simply brought the furniture to the boys. To their knowledge she had never done anything like this before.

Devon didn't want to give that mop because he loved, feared, or felt a sense of duty toward God. Devon had asked God how he should sow to secure a harvest. God showed him how to sow and Devon was glad to do it because of what was in it for him. The positive and willing attitude on the inside matched the positive gesture on the outside and a miracle happened.

Abraham never had to kill his son; he only needed to be *willing* to kill him. This is proof that it is never about the act; it is always about the believing heart that is motivating the act. Had Abraham continued to plunge the knife into his son's chest after the angel stopped him, his act would have been murder: Same act; different heart.

Watch Your Attitude

When I submitted to my husband, I *was* submitting to the Lord. This is what kept me in the game when the going got tough. Had I been doing it because it was the "right thing to do" I would have missed the blessing of it, and having no grace for the act, I would have failed miserably. While I begrudgingly submit to my husband out of a sense of duty, I am being a Pharisee. I may look good on the outside, but within are dead men's bones.

When we obey because we trust that God will be good to perform what He has promised, we are obeying by faith. That is the only kind of obedience God recognizes. God is not interested in our laboring and toiling; He only desires that we trust Him so that He can work miracles in our every day lives. When we obey expecting a return, we receive a return and God is glorified. It is in this way that we stay genuine in our relationship with God. When we obey with the wrong motivations of love, fear, and a sense of duty, at times we find ourselves obeying on the outside while we disobey on the inside.

When one does not expect a reward, the act becomes nothing more than a work. Look around; work with no reward produces bad attitude. When we find ourselves grumbling our way through our service to God it is because we are improperly motivated. The Pharisees were always grumbling about something.

Whited Sepulchers

The very educated Pharisees couldn't get enough of the law. The Mosaic Law wasn't enough for them. They added their own laws to God's laws and made it virtually impossible to do justice to any.

O How I love Thy Law

Although they took great pains to look pretty on the outside what with their tithes and their public prayers, the weight of their labors was trashing them on the inside:

> *"Woe unto you, scribes and Pharisees, hypocrites!*
> *for ye are like unto whited sepulchres,*
> *which indeed appear beautiful outward,*
> *but are within full of dead men's bones,*
> *and of all uncleanness.*
> *Even so ye also outwardly appear righteous unto men,*
> *but within ye are full of hypocrisy and iniquity."*
> *(Matt 23:27-28 KJV)*

These Pharisees did not do what they did for God's reward; they did it for man's reward. This is why they could always be seen praying loudly in the streets. It was all show and the world gave them their reward. However, that is the only reward they received. Because the Pharisees did not obey from a willing heart expecting God's reward, their behavior was nothing but a cover up for their self-reliant hearts.

When our outside behavior does not match the devotion of our heart, we are hypocritical. When I go about my duties for the praise of man because it is the proper thing for a Christian to do, my deeds are flesh powered and I am a hypocrite. I may be doing good acts, but I am not doing them joyfully and with a glad heart, for the abundance of all things. When we find ourselves trying to impress people on the outside instead of impressing God on the inside, we are hypocrites.

When we get real, we go about our duties the way one goes about a treasure hunt. We zealously do our works while we look for the treasure of blessing. It is always there.

Giving in Faith

For years I wondered about the idea of giving. I had tithed in the past and found myself in a financial mess as a result Add to that the fact that I am not a giving person by nature. Some people just love to give things to others. I only hoped for such a thought. I was selfish and frugal and this meant that if I were to give, my only motivation would have been because it was "the right thing to do" and not from a willing heart.

Although I was not willing to give, I was willing to be made willing and I knew this is what God promised to do for me. So I began to believe for willingness. Then I had to stand in my faith and have patience. A couple of years went by without any sign of "willingness." But then something happened inside my heart. I didn't even notice it at first; I just found myself writing checks whenever I saw someone in need. I noticed that I was glad to write those checks. I suddenly found it easier to give my money away than to spend it on myself. Although I said "no" to myself on many occasions, I never said "no" when it came to giving to others. I found it easier to give to others than to give to myself. This was a miracle of untold proportions, *"Thy people will be willing in the day of Thy power....*

The next thing I knew I was being blessed in my giving. I noticed that when I would give to others my bank account seemed to grow but when I went for a spell without giving I watched that same account wane. This was another miracle. Years before I had tithed myself into the poor house because my heart was not in it. Now that my heart was involved, I was being blessed, *"...and they shall eat the good of the land."*

A Difference

Christians are supposed to be different from the world. The people of God should stand out as the race that has the One True God. This is exactly why we had all the splash and dance in the deliverance of the children of Israel from Egypt. God said it Himself:

"And there shall be a great cry
throughout all the land of Egypt,
such as there was none like it, nor shall be like it any
more. But against any of the children of Israel
shall not a dog move his tongue, against man or beast:
that ye may know how that
the LORD doth put a difference
between the Egyptians and Israel."
(Ex 11:6-7 KJV emphasis mine)

In this particular incidence, God was telling the Israelites that death was going to move through the region and that there would be a great cry throughout the land of Egypt while not even a dog makes a sound against the children of Israel. Why is God going to do this? *"That ye may know how that the LORD doth put a difference between the Egyptians and Israel."*

O How I love Thy Law

God wanted the world to know that He puts a difference between the Egyptian and Israel. As well, the Lord puts a difference between the believer and the unbeliever. The difference is staggering. While there is a great cry heard throughout all the world, the children of the Most High God will be in perfect peace:

> *"Thou wilt keep him in perfect peace, whose mind is*
> *stayed on thee: because he trusteth in thee."*
> *(Isa 26:3 KJV)*

Perfect Peace

Christians are benefactors of perfect peace when they trust the Most High God. It is when our minds are stayed on Him and His provision that we have perfect peace. Translated, that means there should be nothing missing, nor broken in the life of a Christian. However, when I look around I see no difference between the average church attendee and the non-Christian. These days everyone looks the same. I see little peace, little love, and little power...and that on both sides!

In the early church, thousands were saved and radically changed while miracles were commonplace:

> *"And now, Lord, behold their threatenings:*
> *and grant unto thy servants,*
> *that with all boldness they may speak thy word,*
> *By stretching forth thine hand to heal;*
> *and that **signs and wonders** may be done*
> *by the name of thy holy child Jesus.*
> *And when they had prayed,*
> *the place was shaken where they were assembled together;*
> *and they were all filled with the Holy Ghost,*
> *and they spake the word of God with boldness."*
> *(Acts 4:29-31 KJV)*

Although it sounds like it, this was not the occasion when the Holy Spirit first came upon man on the day of Pentecost. This was down the road apiece. From the moment the Holy Spirit came to dwell in men, a new dispensation began and continues to this day. Part of that dispensation includes signs, wonders, and speaking the Word of

God in boldness. If we have read about it in the book of Acts, we are aware of what the church can, and *should* look like.

If the church functioned the way it is supposed to, the carnal world would take notice just as it did in the book of Acts. The world knew what was going on in Christian circles back then. These days we don't have that kind of renown. Churches minister to the struggling Christian, while the carnal world barely notices them.

Fame

In the land of Canaan dwelled many different pagan dynasties. These lands and people, with no quick form of transportation, were anywhere from days to months away, yet they had all heard about the Israelites:

> *"... if thou shalt kill all this people as one man, then the*
> ***nations which have heard the fame of thee***
> *will speak, saying,*
> *Because the LORD was not able to bring this people*
> *into the land which he sware unto them,*
> *therefore he hath slain them in the wilderness."*
> *(Num 14:15-16 KJV emphasis mine)*

These foreign people had heard the "fame" of God. They were not tolerating a religious people; they were hearing of miraculous ways of power and favor toward a particular people. Does the world hear of the power and favor God has toward a Christian? Is our God famous to the pagan world?

How in the world did these people, who were months away from each other, know what was going on with the Israelites? Word spreads fast when there is something to talk about. Signs and wonders are God's way of making His children famous. Moses was deeply concerned about God's fame in the world.

So the World will Know

When we orchestrate and try to work out our lives motivated only by love, fear, or a sense of duty toward God we are missing the power of God and the world watches the Christian try and fail. God wants us to look to Him to supernaturally invade our lives with blessings. When our lives are impacted with such glory, the world will notice:

> *"And the glory which thou gavest me I have given them;*
> *that they may be one, even as we are one:*

O How I love Thy Law

I in them, and thou in me,
that they may be made perfect in one;
*and **that the world may know** that thou hast sent me,*
and hast loved them, as thou hast loved me. "
(John 17:22-23 KJV emphasis mine)

God has given us glory through Jesus so that we can be perfectly at one with Him *so that the world would know* that God sent Jesus and has loved us just as much as He loved Him. When God loves a person, he blesses that person. We will be noticed by the blessings in our lives.

It is by signs and wonders that our Lord makes Himself known. How are we to receive signs and wonders if we do not believe for them? If we just go about our business trying to do the right thing, we are standing as a wall against the signs and wonders God hopes to shower upon us.

But when we obey God joyfully and with a glad heart, for the abundance of all things, we will be showered upon. Others will notice. Some people in my life think I am a special child of God. I am not. I simply trust Him to do what He says He will do. That is all. My God has fame. Everyone who knows me knows that my God is alive and working in my favor.

David

David loved God's law. Although the author of Psalm 119 is not expressly known, I believe, as do many commentators, that David wrote this Psalm. Probably the very best example of a person wholly submitted to his God ordained authorities, David was spot on in this department. David ever and only saw human beings in relation to who they were to God. David stayed under King Saul's authority the entire time he pursued him to kill him! David had ample opportunity to kill Saul but he refused to lift his hand against Saul because God had anointed him.

David won God's heart through that ordeal and his life was more than just a little bit blessed as a result. In the very last chapter of the Bible Jesus says:

"I Jesus have sent mine angel
to testify unto you these things in the churches.
I am the root and the offspring of David,
and the bright and morning star. "
(Rev 22:16 KJV)

Free to be Holy   189

Wow. What a commentary on a life, *"The root and offspring of David."* We know all about David's mistakes, however, his life was extraordinary. David trusted God. He feared nothing so long as God was on his side. David respected God's Word so much that he continually meditated upon it:

> *"O how love I thy law! it is my meditation all the day."*
> *(Psa 119:97 KJV)*

One does not meditate upon something all the day unless one is completely and utterly into it. David loved this practice as we see where he says, *"O how I love thy law!"* David meditated on God's Law because he had grown to love it. One does not love God's law to this extent unless this law has somehow earned that kind of devotion. David knew how to be blessed through the law. Take some time to read through Psalm 119 and see exactly how David perceived God's law.

It is more than obvious that David obeyed God joyfully and with a glad heart, for the abundance of all things. David was blessed. When we can change our perception about the law, release ourselves from the burden of it, and just see it as the pipeline of blessing that it is, our lives will change.

Time to Get Real

We are without excuse with this thing. God has made Himself perfectly clear about this. He wants obedience, and He wants it to come from a willing heart for the abundance of all things. Nothing else will do. David loved God's law because he understood the tremendous blessing that was the result of obedience. David knew that if he obeyed God, God would take good care of him.

It is expedient to be obedient. The Bible has clearly shown us how to be blessed through obedience. These blessings are to exist as signs and wonders in the earth. We no longer need to look for ways to get around the law; rather we look high and low for opportunities to show God that we trust Him completely to honor His Word. When this practice is employed, we will be singing with the Psalmist, *"O How I love Thy law."*

*Wherefore as the Holy Ghost saith, Today if ye will hear his voice,
Harden not your hearts...*

9

THE VOICE
OF GOD

When we begin
to trust God and obey Him with a willing heart,
we will enter into a place with Him that defies
reasoning. In this place, we learn how to follow
His still, small voice. You see, once God knows
that He can trust a person to obey Him, He is
quick to give personal instructions.

"*And he came thither unto a cave, and lodged there;
and, behold, the word of the LORD came to him,
and he said unto him, What doest thou here, Elijah?
And he said, I have been very jealous
for the LORD God of hosts:
for the children of Israel have forsaken thy covenant,
thrown down thine altars,
and slain thy prophets with the sword;
and I, even I only, am left;
and they seek my life, to take it away.
And he said, Go forth,
and stand upon the mount before the LORD.
And, behold, the LORD passed by,
and a great and strong wind rent the mountains,
and brake in pieces the rocks before the LORD;
but the LORD was not in the wind:
and after the wind an earthquake;
but the LORD was not in the earthquake:
And after the earthquake a fire;
but the LORD was not in the fire:
and after the fire a still small voice.
And it was so, when Elijah heard it,
that he wrapped his face in his mantle,
and went out, and stood in the entering in of the cave.
And, behold, there came a voice unto him, and said,
What doest thou here, Elijah?*"

1 Kings 19:9-13

The Voice of God

God wants nothing more than to be intimately involved in His children's lives and hearts. God shrouded everything about Him in mystery because He is mysterious. It is through the process of unveiling these mysteries that we become intimate with God. We picture God as this large man in heaven who has a big clan that He desperately tries to form into beings like Himself. We do not see Him as the very personal and romantic Lover that He is.

We forget that He knit us together in the womb. God became intimately aware of us as He formed every cell of who we would become. We must not only think of Him in terms of how He loves the world, but also about how He loves us as individuals. God knew us before we were formed. How can God know a person who does not exist? God had to have known us before we were formed of Hell dust. God knew us when we had no sin. We were eternal beings before we were ever natural beings. God is in love with the real us and He wants us to live in that reality with Him.

A Moment with God

We love intimacy. One time I was sitting in a very packed waiting room when the woman sitting next to me got up to go to the bathroom. In the meantime a nice, older gentleman entered the waiting room and unknowingly took her seat.

He seemed like the kind of guy who would want to know, so I leaned in a bit and discreetly explained that the woman who had been sitting in his seat had gone to use the restroom. The gentleman leaned back toward me and with a slight nod of his head said, "Oh, thank you."

A couple of moments later, without looking up from my reading material, I said, "You gellin'?

Without looking up from his reading material, he said, "Like Magellan." We both smiled and that was the only thing we said to one another until the woman came back from the bathroom and was given her seat. There was nothing to add. It was a perfectly played moment. The gentlemanly stranger gave me a smile and the tip of his hat as he left to find another seat.

So we had both seen the same commercial...so what? Nothing big, it was just a fun moment that I am sure we will both remember. We enjoy intimacy no matter how small its package. God created us in such a way that we would crave intimacy in all we do. If we can ever release ourselves from the burden of the law for any length of time, we will begin to have special moments of intimacy with God.

I love the way my relationship with God has grown since I have learned to respect His voice. People say, "God doesn't talk to me like that." Yes He does. It is we who need to learn how to listen.

Oh, Man

If you are a man…remember that God, Elohim, is not a man, nor is He even human. You mustn't let this be a stumbling block for you. God gave us loving relationships to help us understand the joy of loving God. It is not a male-female thing with God.

We are God's counterparts in the exact way Eve was Adam's counterpart. Yes, it is an amazing thing; He calls us the bride of Christ. God has made us His counterpart…of course He wants to be intimate with us.

God has emphatically stated that He is not a male and He is not a human. Therefore, He is not looking for a "female" counterpart. That is good because:

> *"For as many of you as have been*
> *baptized into Christ have put on Christ.*
> *There is neither Jew nor Greek,*
> *there is neither bond nor free,*
> ***there is neither male nor female:***
> *for ye are all one in Christ Jesus."*
> *(Gal 3:27-28 KJV)*

In Christ we are just as genderless as God. These genders we have been given are only to show us how to relate to God. We are God's counterparts and He wants very much to be intimate with us. As well, God created us to long for intimacy with Him. We cannot argue the fact that we all want intimacy with God.

As a matter of fact, when we speak of salvation, we speak of having a "personal" relationship with God. We all want this personal relationship with God; we simply do not know how to attain it. Christians commonly complain of that "brass ceiling" that stands in the way of their communication with God.

However, when we obey Him joyfully and with a glad heart, for the abundance of all things, God will begin to trust us with His voice and lead us even more intimately through our lives.

Intimacy Gone Awry

Sexual relations between a man and his wife were intended to be a physical manifestation of the heart of their union. We are living in a day when sex has become the entire essence of the union. That is why sexual relations have lost their beauty. Back in the day, wives enjoyed sexual relations as much as husbands.

In today's world sexual relations are commonly employed outside of true intimacy. The secular world has made its statement loud and clear: Everyone must enjoy sex all of the time, with or without intimacy. Unfortunately when sexual relations are employed without intimacy, the act can become compulsory, especially for the woman. We see this played out in modern day marriages and accurately depicted on our television shows.

It is commonplace for a husband to expect to have sexual relations with his wife even when there is no true intimacy between them. Their wives agree to have limited sex with them because they feel they owe them that much. These wives are not truly interested in sexual intimacy because they need emotional intimacy to the very degree that their husbands need physical satisfaction.

When we take these roles into our relationship with God, we can see that God, our Husband wants to be very physical with us, His bride. He wants to bless our natural physical lives. He wants to bring His love for us into full manifestation. He wants us to be in ecstasy with Him. We cannot ignore the fact that in the Old Testament, God absolutely showered individuals with untold blessings.

However, God well knows the needs of His bride. God made us specifically to crave intimacy with Him. The curse that was placed on woman was that her desire would be for the man. As well, we, as the bride of Christ, desire the Lord in an intimate way.

This is why God will not shower us with His natural physical blessings until He has first satisfied our emotional needs. God respects the physical relationship He shares with us enough to make sure our spiritual union with Him is intimate and solid.

Neither Male nor Female

Does a man have to act like a woman to be in an intimate relationship with God? Yes…to a certain degree. As I explained in *Hell Bent*, women are to teach men how man is to respond to God and men are to teach women how God responds to man.

A woman trusts her husband to take care of her and love her just as he loves himself. A man must trust his God to take care of him and love him just as He loves His very own Son. A woman submits to her husband because she respects his authority in her life and she knows that if she follows him she will be blessed. A man must submit to his God because he respects his authority in his life and he knows that if he follows God he will be blessed. When Paul spoke of marriage, he made the same connection:

"For this cause shall a man leave his father and mother,
and shall be joined unto his wife,
and they two shall be one flesh.
This is a great mystery:
but I speak concerning Christ and the church."
(Eph 5:31-32 KJV)

God came into us just as a man comes into his wife and the two become on flesh. What else can we make of the words of Jesus, *"I in You and You in them so that we can be one..."*. One need only look at Moses, Joshua, Elijah, David, Solomon, Jeremiah, Peter, and Paul to know that it is possible for a man to have deep intimacy with God. God is our loving Counterpart Who is primarily interested in meeting the needs of our heart *and then* meeting our physical needs. Not as male and female, but as God and human.

Seek and Ye shall Find

When we are looking for ways to get under the blessing of the law through our authorities, our enemies, and our trials, this pulls our attention from our problems and focuses it upon our God. When our focus changes like this, we begin to see and talk with God face to face. You see, God has always been looking our direction, when once we turn toward Him we will be looking at one another. That is an amazing thing. All of our Bible heroes heard distinct directions from God that were not found in the pages of the Bible.

God is far from silent and He really enjoys being the Sailor of our ship. He will speak to those who can be trusted with His voice. The law that was written in stone is taken away, but the voice of the God of the Law will always be speaking to His sheep:

"...he goeth before them, and the sheep follow him:
for they know his voice.
And a stranger will they not follow,
but will flee from him:
for they know not the voice of strangers."
(John 10:4-5 KJV)

The Voice of God

Relevant Voice vs. Mosaic Law

There is a story in the Old Testament that shows us how God feels about the Mosaic Law written in stone as compared to His specific voice in the present situation.

Moses gave one last sermon to the children of Israel before he went back up Mount Sinai for the final time. In this sermon, Moses reiterated the entire Mosaic Law. Following this, Joshua led the Israelites over the River Jordan to take the city of Jericho.

This is where the story gets peculiar. God gave specific instructions to Joshua concerning the capture of Jericho:

"And ye shall compass the city, all ye men of war,
and go round about the city once.
Thus shalt thou do six days.
And seven priests shall bear before the ark
seven trumpets of rams' horns:
and the seventh day ye shall compass the city seven times,
and the priests shall blow with the trumpets."
(Josh 6:3-4 KJV)

On the seventh day, the horns blasted and Joshua gave specific instructions to the men of war concerning the saving of Rahab the harlot and her family:

"...Joshua said unto the people, Shout;
for the LORD hath given you the city.
And the city shall be accursed,
even it, and all that are therein, to the LORD:
only Rahab the harlot shall live,
she and all that are with her in the house,
because she hid the messengers that we sent."
(Josh 6:16-17 KJV)

In the capture of Jericho, two Mosaic Laws were cast aside: Thou shalt not lie and thou shalt rest on the Sabbath. As well, one of the Mosaic transgressions concerned a harlot, who, under the Mosaic Law, should have been stoned. What do we say to this? Why did God instruct against the Law? Why was it okay for Rahab to testify falsely against her neighbors? Moses had just laid down the very meticulous Mosaic Law to these people. Part of this law said:

The Sin within

*"Keep the sabbath day to sanctify it,
as the LORD thy God hath commanded thee.
Six days thou shalt labour, and do all thy work:
But the seventh day
is the sabbath of the LORD thy God:
in it thou shalt not do any work,
thou, nor thy son, nor thy daughter,
nor thy manservant, nor thy maidservant,
nor thine ox, nor thine ass, nor any of thy cattle,
nor thy stranger that is within thy gates;
that thy manservant and thy maidservant
may rest as well as thou...
Do not testify falsely against your neighbor...
Neither shalt thou commit adultery."
(Deut 5:12 – 15&18 KJV & 20 NLT)*

A Broken Sabbath

First God says rest on the seventh day, now He is telling the Israelites to work *seven times as hard* on the seventh day! According to our verses above, *"in it (the Sabbath) thou shalt not do __any__ work."*

I'm thinking traipsing completely around a city is classified as work; traipsing *seven times* around a city has to be downright laborious. In these instructions, God was saying: Not only are you to work on this Sabbath; you are to work seven times harder than you did on the previous six non-Sabbath days.

By saying this, God was going a very long way to make His point: My relevant voice is more important than My written law. Astounding? Yes. True nonetheless. There are many, many examples of just this sort of thing in the Old Testament. God has always wanted to lead His people very personally. The apostle Paul taught us that the law came so that sin would abound; however, when God's voice comes, sin is abolished.

A Harlot Who Testified Falsely

Rahab was a harlot and there is no Biblical testimony of her changing her ways. In the New Testament, she is referred to *still* as *"Rahab the harlot."* As there is no other Rahab in the Bible, it was not necessary to distinguish her from others by using this description. Rahab transgressed the seventh commandment with her very livelihood. Yet, above everyone else in Jericho, Rahab is saved and

The Voice of God

immortalized because she lied to her own people about the enemy spies. Rahab "testified falsely against her neighbor", *"I know not where they have gone"* and because of this, these very neighbors were going to die.

The Sabbath was cast aside and the children of Israel took the land. Rahab the harlot testified falsely against her neighbor and was saved. The Mosaic Law would have had the Israelites resting on the seventh day and stoning Rahab the adulteress, but the law was replaced by the voice of God that is always supreme.

His Voice Speaks Louder than Words

What is the lesson? There must be a lesson. The Bible is inscribed in a very particular way. Every nuance must be measured. God gave a very specific law and then proceeded to give very specific instructions that forced the Israelites to break those very laws. So what is God trying to tell us?

For God, life with Him has never been about rote obedience to a law written in stone. God is in a relationship with us, not a business partnership. As we walk with Him in His Truth, we will learn to perceive the sound of His voice.

God is far from silent; He speaks to His children today just as He did in the Old Testament. Then He used prophets and angels in a very outward fashion, now, most often, He simply uses His own voice from His own Spirit Who resides within us. We must look at the natural to understand the spiritual. God wants to personally lead us through this life.

The Israelites had to leave the Mosaic Law behind at the moment they heard the voice of God. If they had not, they would have been prevented from taking the city of Jericho. Rahab had to leave her sin behind and follow her faith and bear false witness against her neighbor. If she had not, she would have died with the rest.

Decisions of the Heart

There will be times when we aren't really sure how to obey God. This Christian life can be confusing and it is then that we must remember to check our hearts. We cannot fool God. If we have a heart of faith we cannot go wrong. At one point Paul and Barnabas disagreed about whether the apostle Mark could be trusted on a missionary trip. You see, Mark had been with Paul and Barnabas on a former missionary trip:

The Sin within

"And Barnabas and Saul returned from Jerusalem, when they had fulfilled their ministry, and took with them John, whose surname was Mark." (Acts 12:25 KJV)

However, Mark had bowed out early and Paul was taking this into consideration as they prepared to set out again:

"And Barnabas determined to take with them John,
whose surname was Mark.
But Paul thought not good to take him with them,
who departed from them from Pamphylia,
and went not with them to the work."
(Acts 15:37-38 KJV)

Barnabas wanted to trust Mark to come with them while Paul clearly did not:

"And the contention was so sharp between them,
that they departed asunder one from the other:
and so Barnabas took Mark, and sailed unto Cyprus;
And Paul chose Silas, and departed,
being recommended by the brethren unto the grace of
God." (Acts 15:39-40 KJV)

We don't know who was right and who was wrong. Maybe Mark needed Paul to hold him accountable. Maybe Mark also needed someone to believe in him. Although Paul and Barnabas contended sharply with one another and even broke fellowship in that they headed out in separate directions, God used them both. Mark matured as a result of this contention and regained Paul's respect. In his letter to Timothy, Paul makes a special request for Mark:

"Only Luke is with me. Take Mark, and bring him with
thee: for he is profitable to me for the ministry."
(2 Tim 4:11 KJV)

Now Mark is profitable to Paul for the ministry. How could this good thing be born of contention? Paul and Barnabas clearly disagreed about what was right and what was wrong concerning Mark. They both followed their hearts, went their separate ways, and God used each of them to bless Mark.

Free to be Holy

The Voice of God

There are no apologies or corrections because in following their hearts both Paul and Barnabas were "right". We can follow our hearts and trust God because He promises to lead us and guide us and honor the condition of our hearts.

Obedience is Better than Sacrifice

God has given us a glimpse of how He feels about laws written in stone. In another example, King Saul was deposed of his throne because he ignored the voice of God in order to sacrifice animals according to the Mosaic Law. Saul stood to benefit nothing from this act. All the animals that were taken were the best of the bunch and used solely to be sacrificed to God. However, the fact is, Saul had been instructed through the prophet Samuel to leave none alive. Saul may have been obeying the Mosaic Law but he was disobeying the voice of God and therein lie the sin:

> *"And Samuel said, Hath the LORD*
> *as great delight in burnt offerings and sacrifices,*
> *as in obeying the voice of the LORD?*
> *Behold, to obey is better than sacrifice,*
> *and to hearken than the fat of rams.*
> *For rebellion is as the sin of witchcraft,*
> *and stubbornness is as iniquity and idolatry.*
> *Because thou hast rejected the word of the LORD,*
> *he hath also rejected thee from being king."*
> *(1 Sam 15:22-23 KJV)*

God, flat out tells us that He delights more in obedience than He does in sacrifice. That means there is a difference between listening and obeying, and sacrificing and offering, *"Behold, to obey is better than sacrifice, and to hearken than the fat of rams."* God delights more in our obedience and hearkening than He does in our sacrifices and offerings.

When we strive for God we should not be laboring and offering Him sacrifices; we should be obeying His voice and trusting Him. That is what will delight our God. When we do this thing the wrong way it is seen as rebellion to God. This is serious business. Through our rebellion and stubbornness we are guilty of iniquity and idolatry and our sin is as the sin of witchcraft. God is forcing our hand. In order for us to be truly obedient, we are going to have to allow Him to hold a very personal and intimate place in our lives.

Spare None

I think we need to remind ourselves of Saul's sin that forced this heinous accusation upon him. Saul was still getting fitted for his crown when the prophet Samuel came to him with a word from the Lord:

"Samuel also said unto Saul,
The LORD sent me to anoint thee to be king
over his people, over Israel:
now therefore hearken thou unto the voice
of the words of the LORD.
Thus saith the LORD of hosts,
I remember that which Amalek did to Israel...
Now go and smite Amalek,
and utterly destroy all that they have, and spare them not;
but slay both man and woman, infant and suckling,
ox and sheep, camel and ass."
(1 Sam 15:1-3 KJV)

It was time for a bloody war and none were to be left alive. King Saul did everything right except to obey the voice of God. Obviously very enthusiastic over a victorious battle, Saul slaughtered everyone and everything except the best of the sheep and the oxen to offer a huge offering to the Lord and Saul kept alive Agag, the king of the Amalekites as a war trophy. Saul clearly respected God's Laws more than His personal voice.

The prophet Samuel, forewarned by God, came to see Saul and upon hearing the herds of sheep, casually asked him what all the bleating was about. This was Saul's answer:

"And Saul said, They have brought them from the
Amalekites: for the people spared the best of the sheep and
of the oxen, to sacrifice unto the LORD thy God; and the
rest we have utterly destroyed." (1 Sam 15:15 KJV)

Samuel loved King Saul and this is evidenced in the way he tried to show Saul his sin:

"Then Samuel said unto Saul, Stay, and I will tell thee
what the LORD hath said to me this night.

The Voice of God

And he said unto him, Say on.
And Samuel said,
When thou wast little in thine own sight,
wast thou not made the head of the tribes of Israel,
and the LORD anointed thee king over Israel?
And the LORD sent thee on a journey, and said,
Go and utterly destroy the sinners the Amalekites,
and fight against them until they be consumed.
Wherefore then didst thou not obey the voice of the LORD,
but didst fly upon the spoil,
and didst evil in the sight of the LORD?"
(1 Sam 15:16-19 KJV)

The prophet Samuel was trying to remind Saul that he was not chosen because he had it all together. It was when he was little in his own sight that he was anointed to be king over Israel. Now that Saul was king, he was getting full of himself and was not hearkening unto the voice of God. Saul was sacrificing instead of obeying. Saul was so busy trying to be the war hero that he was not listening to the voice of God.

After being told that his sin was as the sin of witchcraft and that his stubbornness is as iniquity and idolatry, King Saul is informed:

"Because thou hast rejected the word of the LORD,
he hath also rejected thee from being king."
(1 Sam 15:23 KJV)

Saul exalted the Mosaic Law over the voice of God and he was stripped of his throne. How important do you think it is to tap into the still small voice of the living God?

Form and Function

Placing more emphasis on the written law than the voice of God is what got Saul into trouble. God's Word is not rigidly perfect in form; however, it is rigidly perfect in function. God never intended for us to be so perfectly led by words on a page that we would have no need to consult the Spirit of those words. God wants to be intimately involved with us. God's Word is supposed to lead us *to* God, not supplant Him. When God is intimately involved in our lives we will hear His voice and see miracles: Jericho fell.

God had told the Israelites to march for seven days in a row around Jericho. There is no arguing the fact that the Israelites either had to disobey the Mosaic Law, which was given by God, or disobey the voice of God concerning the present situation.

One command was written in stone while the other was the living voice of God. Joshua led his troops by disregarding the Mosaic Law in order to obey the voice of God and he was victorious and commandeered the nation of Israel for several years.

God had told Saul to leave none alive. Saul could either disregard the Mosaic Law and obey the voice of God, or he could disregard the voice of God and take the best of the oxen and sheep and offer them to God according to the Mosaic Law. Saul led his troops by disregarding the voice of God in order to keep the Law. Saul was dethroned, the Spirit of the Lord was taken from him and an evil spirit was sent to trouble him.

Talk About Your War Crimes

Just as an interesting note to further make this point, let us go back to King Saul's story for a moment. We remember that Saul had brought back King Agag as a war prisoner after the prophet Samuel had told him to leave none alive. Samuel still had this business to attend to:

> *"Then said Samuel, Bring ye hither to me Agag the king of the Amalekites. And Agag came unto him delicately. And Agag said, Surely the bitterness of death is past."*
> *(1 Sam 15:32 KJV)*

Agag came to Samuel delicately; he tiptoed in knowing his life was on the line. Seeing the prophet Samuel, Agag appealed to him, *"Surely the bitterness of death is past!"* No Agag, not so much:

> *"And Samuel said, As thy sword hath made women childless, so shall thy mother be childless among women. And Samuel hewed Agag in pieces before the LORD in Gilgal."* *(1 Sam 15:33 KJV)*

Samuel hewed Agag in pieces. Bad day Samuel? This wasn't murder; it was brutal murder. Thou shalt not murder. Hmmm. A simple killing of an enemy is one thing; cutting him in pieces just doesn't seem right. Was Samuel wrong in doing this? Evidently

The Voice of God

not. It is impossible to put God into any kind of a box, Mosaic or otherwise.

A Mysterious Union

We keep trying to figure out a God Who defies comprehension. It is insulting to even think we can get Him figured out. The Bible does not afford us this luxury. That is a good thing. If a woman overheard her husband saying, "Oh yeah...I have her all figured out", the wife would be deeply, and rightfully offended. As a matter of fact, she would probably respond by thinking, "Oh yeah? You think you have me all figured out? We'll see about that." We do not get our loved ones "all figured out"; we walk with our loved ones and enjoy the mystery that is them.

Let us walk with God with a pure heart and let His mysteries unfold as He sees fit to reveal them. Yes, this will involve a very real and vulnerable relationship, which seems out of our reach at times, but that is what God requires and it is the only way He will work with us. Everything else is just religion.

The best we can hope to do in this life is follow God with a perfect heart, according to what we believe He is truly telling us in the moment. We can see the benefit to the Mosaic Law, but we must see a bigger benefit to hearing God's still, small voice.

Well, I Don't Know. . .

Although obedience should be our best friend in time of need, sometimes we don't know how to be obedient. Surely God has proven Himself a faithful Lord Who stands by His Word in every occasion, but what do we do when we don't know exactly how to be obedient?

Do we send little Johnny to the Christian preschool? Should we financially help our teenager get a car? Do we buy that house? Do we send money to that ministry? Should we take in that orphan? Should we sit on that board? How much can we involve ourselves in politics? Do we take that job? Should be take that trip? Do we take that position in church? Every day we are met with decisions to be made that are not expressly covered in the Scriptures. What do we do in these circumstances?

It is in this place that we must remember what we learned in *The Heart of the Matter*. We saw where King Asa failed to remove all the high places, yet his heart was perfect all his days. And then we saw where King Azariah did what was right but not with a perfect heart. From this we learned that behavior was secondary to the condition of the heart.

When we are not sure, we pray for wisdom and guidance, examine the Scriptures, and then we must act out the persuasion of our heart. At times we will be correct; at other times we will be incorrect. That is secondary. At all times we must have a perfect heart.

Do Something ... Anything

It is important to do something rather than nothing. Sometimes we wait so long for a "sign in the sky" that we do not move on a thing soon enough. Certainly we must seek God through the Scriptures, prayer, and godly guidance, but when we have exhausted these, we must choose according to the leaning of our heart knowing that God will bless accordingly. Not to worry, someone who may try to exploit this aspect of God to get his own way is only fooling himself.

In all things, we must find a way to be obedient. Obedience is nothing more than following the loving guidance of a Father Who has promised to lead us into tremendous blessing. It matters not whether we are right or wrong, so long as our hearts are perfect toward God. If, to the best of our knowledge, we are leaning in a particular direction, we must be obedient to obey from our heart.

When we are obedient, we are exercising faith. Faith is what brings blessing. So rather than do nothing and live in limbo, we must do something according to our heart! Get in there, do it, and believe it to be blessed. God looks at the heart and knows whether we are trusting Him to take care of us or whether we are trusting in ourselves. We cannot fool Him.

The Auto Show

I will give you an example of how this works. Back before my husband began to walk with the Lord, he had terrible mood swings. It could be difficult to submit to him because often he would change his mind about things. I wanted to be able to land on something so that I could be blessed. I did not enjoy living in limbo.

This changed for me several years ago. Roger and I had made plans to go to the Chicago Auto Show while the boys spent the day with their grandparents. When the weekend came, Roger got into a snit and decided we weren't going to go. This was a shame because I knew he would eventually snap out of it and then regret not going. I looked up to God and asked, "I want to submit, but which Roger do

The Voice of God

I submit to?" God answered and told me to submit to the heart of my husband.

The "law" would have me respond to Roger in the moment and give up on the auto show, but the voice of God told me do the opposite. That settled it. I knew in my heart that Roger wanted to go to that auto show so I continued to plan the trip. All the while he remained difficult and insisted that he wasn't going to go. I held on to my faith and when the morning came, I woke up early, got ready to go and went to the front door. Roger was tailing behind me, grumbling all the while. Before we left town, he was so close to turning back he could taste it. I prayed. He set out for Chicago.

As we continued down the highway, the tirade continued. I had brought my Bible and had it open on my lap as I silently communed with God in His Word. Roger continued to foam away while he drove to Chicago. Well, it wasn't really *Roger*...

Getting the Attention of the Devil

"For we wrestle not against flesh and blood, but against principalities, against powers, against the rulers of the darkness of this world, against spiritual wickedness in high places." (Eph 6:12 KJV)

You see, I had made a decision to trust the voice of God. Satan knew that if I broke step, I would lose my blessing. He was doing everything he could to intimidate me. It wasn't working. Although my husband was hurling insults, making threats, and trying to bring me into condemnation, I was so involved with the Holy Spirit I hardly noticed him. Finally he gave up on words and blasted the stereo in hopes to get to me. It still didn't work.

All the way through the parking garage and into the McCormick Place he ranted. Upon entering the building, I debated whether we should get something to eat. It was at this point that Roger became so upset that he grabbed me by the arms and began to really get in my face.

I stopped him and, in a low voice, said, "Are you wanting to go to jail?" Roger stopped, looked around and saw the officers who were stationed by the doors. He immediately let go of me and that is when the real show began.

The Parting of the Sea

I know it sounds kind of crazy, but I just call them as I see them. After we got a bite to eat we began our walk through the Red Sea. You see, it was the final day of the show and the McCormick Place was packed. The sea of people bustling amidst one another did not look inviting but we ventured in. It seemed everyone was finding it difficult to get close to the specialty cars they wanted to see; however, I didn't have a problem at all. I strode right up to the cars I wanted to see without difficulty.

As I watched Roger, I saw that he was a part of the crowd of those who were fighting their way through purses and strollers so that they could stretch their necks to get a glimpse of a shiny automobile.

At some point, Roger took notice that I wasn't having this particular problem and he began to stick closer to me. We looked at a lot of cars before we came upon the real reason we were there: The Viper. Roger and I were Dodge fans and this was the year of the Viper prototype. Before now, the public had not seen this car. And, from all appearances, no one could see it now.

The mass of people around that car was astounding. While Roger was saying, "We will never get through that..." I was already on my way to the Viper. The crowd slowly began to disperse...Roger was silently on my heels. As we got closer, the crowd thinned. By the time we got to the Viper, we were close enough to smell it. We took our time as we walked completely around the shiny pink beauty. That was almost two decades ago, but I could still describe that car to you inside and out in detail. We left when we had seen enough and not a moment sooner.

God was showing me something that day. I had obeyed Him in faith with a willing heart and He was letting me see what that produced, *"That you may eat the good of the land."* God opened a way where there seemed to be no way. God went before me and cleared my path. All the while my cantankerous husband held a ringside seat. It was a wonderful day.

Not five minutes into the house that night, Roger says this to me: "It's too bad I was in such a bad mood...we could have really had a good time today." Oh that's right! *You didn't have a good time.* Pity; there was a good time to be had.

I assured him, "That's okay honey, I had a great time!" And that was pretty much the end of it.

The Voice of God

Auto Show...auto show...
Nope, No Auto Show

There is nothing in the Bible about auto shows, nonetheless, God instructed me. I didn't know for sure whether I heard from God. There was no audible voice telling me what to do. No finger wrote on my wall. But because I had a pure heart, God gave me direction and then blessed my deed as I followed Him.

When we act on what we believe God is telling us, we begin to live in a very blessed realm. It does not take long to convince us of this. God is in this for the relationship of love. He is madly in love with us and wants very much to bless us with His presence and His gifts. His Word proves this:

> *"Many, O LORD my God, are thy wonderful works which*
> *thou hast done, and thy thoughts which are to us-ward:*
> *they cannot be reckoned up in order unto thee:*
> *if I would declare and speak of them,*
> *they are more than can be numbered.*
> *Sacrifice and offering thou didst not desire;*
> *mine ears hast thou opened:*
> *burnt offering and sin offering hast thou not required."*
> *(Psa 40:5-6 KJV)*

If we have ever been in love, we know how this emotion can take over our mind so that all we can think about is the object of our love. David says that if he could speak something about the thoughts God has toward us, he would reckon them more than can be numbered. Evidently, God is head over heels in love with us. He does not desire sacrifice and offering; He has opened our ears. He will lead us with His precious voice, just as His Word promises.

Is it possible for someone to exploit this freedom to serve his or her own purposes? Of course it is! Will they get away with it? Of course not. We can sometimes fool others and we can even at times fool ourselves, but we cannot fool God. God knows our heart and will deal with us according to that heart. No one "gets away" with anything where God is concerned.

10

PETER, PETER CROW EATER

Jesus went out of His way to pump up the law beyond all human reach. No one seems to take much notice of the radical nature of His words. Jesus said to pluck out our eye and cut off our hand if they cause us to sin.

Peter, Peter...crow eater

Say What?
Unlimited Forgiveness

The disciples were always asking questions trying to get the inside angle from Jesus. Because they were used to being held strictly to a law, they assumed Jesus would raise the bar. So when they came to Him, they would raise the bar some, only to watch Jesus raise it clean out of reach:

"Then came Peter to him, and said,
Lord, how oft shall my brother sin against me,
and I forgive him? till seven times?
Jesus saith unto him, I say not unto thee,
Until seven times: but, Until seventy times seven."
(Matt 18:21-22 KJV)

Jesus took the law and made it impossible to keep. If we think for one minute that we are capable of forgiving a person four hundred and ninety times we are delusional. In admitting this, we are saying that Jesus put a premium on the law that could not be paid in human terms.

Jesus proved this by the abstract way in which He answered; He took Peter's number and simply multiplied it by itself then took that number times ten. Jesus was not saying that we were allowed to be unforgiving the four hundred and ninety *first* time; He merely purposed to place an unattainable number in Peter's head.

And so, Jesus was not telling Peter how many times he should forgive a man; He was telling him that it didn't matter because he was not capable of satisfying the requirement. If the requirement is that we forgive in this unlimited way, then the power for that kind of forgiveness is going to have to come from God because the task is humanly impossible.

Sins of the Heart

In the fifth chapter of Matthew, Jesus went on a rampage concerning the true weight of the law. This, the pinnacle of His speech, was probably met with silent awe:

"Ye have heard that it was said by them of old time,
Thou shalt not commit adultery: But I say unto you,

The Sin Within

That whosoever looketh on a woman to lust after her hath
committed adultery with her already in his heart. "
(Matt 5:27-28 KJV)

I'm surprised these guys didn't get whiplash. They went from being able to have several wives with no penalty under the Mosaic Law, to not being able to even think about it according to the words of Jesus. When a man looks at another woman to lust after her in his heart, Jesus says, "Don't do it and don't even *think* about doing it."

If one is walking in the flesh, this is an impossible task. I have read enough books and talked with enough people to know that a man struggles daily, if not hourly, with sexual thoughts. Truth be told, under this perspective of the law, every one of us is guilty of adultery. Again, Jesus made it humanly impossible to obey this law.

Thou Shalt Not Get Angry

"Ye have heard that it was said by them of old time,
Thou shalt not kill;and whosoever shall kill
shall be in danger of the judgment:
But I say unto you,
That whosoever is angry with his brother
without a cause shall be in danger of the judgment:
and whosoever shall say to his brother,
Raca, shall be in danger of the council:
but whosoever shall say, Thou fool,
shall be in danger of hell fire. "
(Matt 5:21-22 KJV)

Crime: Being angry with our brother without just cause and calling our brother names like "Worthless" (Raca) and "Fool". Punishment: We are in danger of the judgment, of the council, and of hell fire. Does this not scream "impossible"? Jesus raised the bar high out of human reach. The following is a story that puts the icing on the cake. A rich, prominent, and good man came to Jesus to receive salvation. Well, if anyone can get in...

Excuse me, Good Master, What must I do?

I have always been amazed by some of the things that Jesus said. He really had a shock factor thing going on. The following is the story of an upstanding man who was looking for salvation. Jesus proved time and again that He could understand the thoughts of a man and this was no exception:

> *"And a certain ruler asked him, saying, Good Master, what shall I do to inherit eternal life?"*
> *(Luke 18:18 KJV)*

We have a man who, we find later, is a very prosperous man, he holds a position of authority, he sees Jesus as his Master, and he is looking for honest salvation. I see nothing wrong with this picture. Nonetheless, rather than hand out a simple "salvation by grace" message, Jesus looks to see how this man reacts to the law with this smattering of commandments:

> *"Thou knowest the commandments, Do not commit adultery, Do not kill, Do not steal, Do not bear false witness, Honour thy father and thy mother."*
> *(Luke 18:20 KJV)*

The man responds oddly, *"And he said, All these have I kept from my youth up."* *(Luke 18:21 KJV)* Hold the phone there, Johnny. Do you mean to tell me that you have not transgressed one iota of the law from the time you were a child?! Liar, Liar, pants on fire. What? Do we look like idiots?

> *"If we say that we have no sin, we deceive ourselves, and the truth is not in us."* *(1 John 1:8 KJV)*

Now we know why Jesus brought the law into play. Jesus knew this man thought he had it all figured out. He was so good he thought he was a "10" in God's book. This was a modern day "Job" for Jesus. So what does Jesus do with Boy Wonder? He ups the ante. Jesus gave this very self-reliant man an impossible task:

> *"Now when Jesus heard these things, he said unto him, Yet lackest thou one thing: sell all that thou hast, and distribute unto the poor, and thou shalt have treasure in heaven: and come, follow me."* *(Luke 18:22 KJV)*

You've Got to be Kidding Me!

This is funny if you think about it. I can see the look on this guy's face, "Whhhhhaaaaaat?" He had expected to come strolling out to get a quick pat on the back and a sure trip to heaven, when instead, he lost everything he owned! A tornado would have been more merciful. Someone…quick…hit reverse!

Can you imagine, before you had secured salvation, looking Jesus in the eye and saying, "Good Master, what must I do to be saved seeing I have been perfect from my youth until now?" In other words, "I really don't need your salvation; I do pretty good on my own but is there some sort of fine print I need to know about?" This man was lying. If it were possible for any man to do what this man claimed to have done, the crucifixion of Christ was cruel and unnecessary, *"There is none righteous, no not one."*

Jesus had to strike this guy where he lived…right in the pocket book. Jesus had to give this man an impossible task to show him that he was incapable of earning salvation: Give up everything or go to Hell. What does one say to this?

"And when he heard this, he was very sorrowful: for he was very rich." (Luke 18:23 KJV) This is what Jesus knew about this guy: He was very rich. Jesus needed to make it impossible for anyone to work his way into heaven and this guy's belongings held the key to impossibility.

He Knows What We Need

Can you imagine if everyone who wanted to be saved had to sell all they had, give it to the poor, and just start roaming the countryside spreading the Gospel? This was a ridiculous request. When Jesus called His disciples, He did not tell them to go and sell all that they had before they followed Him. Why would Jesus make this request? Mark's Gospel says it was because He loved him:

> *"Then Jesus beholding him loved him, and said unto him, One thing thou lackest: go thy way, sell whatsoever thou hast, and give to the poor, and thou shalt have treasure in heaven: and come, take up the cross, and follow me." (Mark 10:21 KJV)*

Jesus is never about the things of this life. All He is concerned with is eternal consequences. God works from and for eternity. This man was rich and a ruler. What this means is that he conducted himself very well. He was self-sufficient. Jesus needed this rich young ruler to see himself as self-deficient: Not able to rise to the occasion.

It is true, *"And he was sad at that saying, and went away grieved: for he had great possessions." (Mark 10:2 KJV)* However, this man had been given something to think about. I am sure Jesus did not waste His love and words on this man. Personally, I stayed distant from the Lord for four years after I was given something to think about. The process had only just begun for this rich young ruler; there are some who believe this man was Barnabas.

What's the Big Secret?

Why didn't Jesus just come right out and say that we are incapable of fulfilling the law instead of confusing us by giving us impossible tasks? Because we are stubborn and that makes it difficult to convince us that we cannot do whatever we set our minds to do. We must admit that our first inclination is toward self-effort and that is what Jesus attacked. It is not until we give up on ourselves that we are ready to receive from God.

Peter was being generous when he offered to forgive his enemy seven times. More importantly, Peter actually thought he had the power to accomplish this task; otherwise he would not have made the suggestion. If Jesus had said, "Peter you do not have the power to forgive even one time", Peter would have responded, "Oh, yes I do!"

So, Jesus accomplished His goal by placing the law well out of Peter's reach. Peter needed to see that he was a failure at keeping the law.

God -- or someone -- Forbid!

Peter is an excellent example of carnal vitality in that he really did think he was a good bloke. The following is another instance when Peter thought more highly of himself than he ought. Jesus, speaking to his disciples, explained what was about to take place concerning His crucifixion:

"From that time forth began Jesus to show unto his
disciples, how that he must go unto Jerusalem,
and suffer many things of the elders
and chief priests and scribes,
and be killed, and be raised again the third day."

Upon hearing this ghastly news, Peter immediately took Jesus aside and began to chide Him:

"Then Peter took him, and began to rebuke him, saying,
Be it far from thee, Lord: this shall not be unto thee."
(Matt 16:21-22 KJV)

The Sin within

Although I am sure they were well intended, Peter's words contained the message of Satan. Peter put himself in a place so high that he actually thought he knew better than Jesus. Lest we think that Peter is confused about Who Jesus is, notice what Peter said just seven verses before this:

> *"...Jesus...asked his disciples, saying,*
> *Whom do men say that I the Son of man am?*
> *...they said, Some say that thou art John the Baptist:*
> *some, Elias; and others, Jeremias,*
> *or one of the prophets.*
> *He saith unto them, But whom say ye that I am?*
> *And Simon Peter answered and said,*
> ***Thou art the Christ, the Son of the living God.***"
> *(Matt 16:13-16 KJV)*

Evidently, Peter knew exactly Who Jesus was. In light of this, Peter was way out of line in taking Jesus aside and correcting him. Jesus called Peter out on it:

> *"But he turned, and said unto Peter,*
> *Get thee behind me, Satan:*
> *thou art an offence unto me:*
> *for thou savourest not the things that be of God,*
> *but those that be of men."*
> *(Matt 16:23 KJV)*

Jesus spoke correctly; Peter was not interested in what God could do for man; he was interested in what man could do for God. In warning His disciples, the story Jesus had told ended with a resurrection from the dead, *"...and be raised again the third day."* I don't think Peter even heard that part; he was too busy sewing a big "S" on his robe to notice. Peter, playing superhero, thought it would be a good idea to talk Jesus out of what He was born to do. Them's Satan's words.

Eating Crow

Jesus knew Peter was high on the mountain peak of self-reliance. This will never work. Satan will have us when we become self-reliant. Dear Peter is a good example of the average, self-reliant Christian. Each one of us must come to that place in time when we completely understand our wretchedness and begin to look to God

Peter, Peter...crow eater

for all things good. Until then, we will be bumbling about with all kinds of effort and show while we go nowhere, just as was the case with Peter.

Peter's problem comes to a head on the night of Jesus' betrayal. Quoting the Old Testament, Jesus told His disciples:

> *"... All ye shall be offended because of me this night:*
> *for it is written, I will smite the shepherd,*
> *and the sheep shall be scattered.*
> *But after that I am risen,*
> *I will go before you into Galilee.*
> *But Peter said unto him,*
> *Although all shall be offended, yet will not I.*
> *And Jesus saith unto him, Verily I say unto thee,*
> *That this day, even in this night,*
> *before the cock crow twice, thou shalt deny me thrice.*
> *But he spake the more vehemently,*
> *If I should die with thee,*
> *I will not deny thee in any wise.*
> *Likewise also said they all."*
> *(Mark 14:27-31 KJV)*

Although the very Son of God was quoting an Old Testament prophet, Peter had no problem arguing with Jesus. Surely the prophet Zechariah was wrong. Not only did Peter argue, he argued vehemently. Smoke blew out of Peter's ears at the very thought that he would deny His beloved Lord.

If this is not proof that self-reliance has no power and love is not a sufficient motivator, I don't know what is. The fact that Peter adamantly vowed he would not do a thing proves that he thought he had ultimate power over sin. The fact that Peter was motivated by love was irrelevant because we are told to serve God joyfully and with a glad heart, for the abundance of all things; not because we love God.

This does not mean we do not love God; it means we do not let that be the motivation for our behavior. Peter's love for Jesus wanted to stand in the way of God's Word. This is why love is not a good motivator.

Sifting

This is where the story gets interesting. Jesus, calling him Simon, took Peter aside and said the following:

The Sin within

"And the Lord said, Simon, Simon, behold, Satan hath desired to have you, that he may sift you as wheat: But I have prayed for thee, that thy faith fail not... when thou art converted, strengthen thy brethren."
(Luke 22:31-32 KJV)

Many assume that Jesus was saying the following to Peter:

"Simon, behold, Satan is going to try to get you to deny me so that he can sift you as wheat, but I have prayed for you to stand this test. However, if you do fail, when you are converted, strengthen your brethren."

What kind of a lame prayer is this? I do not believe this is what Jesus was saying.

1. First of all, if Jesus (Who is God) prays for something, He gets what He prays for. Therefore, if Jesus had prayed that Peter would stand up to this test against the devil, then Peter would have stood this test.

2. Secondly, Jesus would not have prayed against prophecy, *"for it is written, I will smite the shepherd, and the sheep shall be scattered."* If Jesus knew the Scriptures prophesied that His sheep would scatter, why pray for the opposite to happen?

3. Thirdly, if Jesus had prayed in belief that Peter would stand this test, why would He go on to prophesy of Peter's failure and conversion in the very same prayer? It is as though Jesus is saying, "I have prayed for you that your faith fail not, but that probably won't work, so when you come back to your senses, strengthen the brethren." This would not make sense.

4. If Jesus had told Peter that he was going to fail, why did He then pray that he not fail? Had Peter withstood the "test", Jesus would have had to say, "Gosh, I guess I was wrong." (Don't try to say those words out loud as you may choke on your tongue.) Jesus was and is never wrong. If Jesus said Peter would deny Him three times before the cock crowed... well...that is exactly what was going to happen no matter what anyone had prayed. It was prophesied.

Peter, Peter...crow eater

So if this is not what Jesus was referring to when He said He would pray for Peter, what was He referring to? Let's look again at what Jesus says to Peter:

Satan Desires to Have You

"And the Lord said, Simon, Simon, behold, Satan hath desired to have you, that he may sift you as wheat: But I have prayed for thee, that thy faith fail not: and when thou art converted, strengthen thy brethren."

Jesus begins by making a statement: Satan desires to have you that he may sift you as wheat. Satan desires to sift everyone as wheat; evidently Peter had been cooperating with him somehow. We saw a bit of Peter's self-reliance when he presumed to have the power to forgive, when he tried to prevent Jesus from going to the cross, and now when he is arguing strenuously against the Holy Prophets. And, being the leader of the gang, the other disciples had followed him.

I Have Prayed for You

Next Jesus had told Peter that He had prayed for him. When Jesus prays for a person, I cannot imagine God not responding. Whatever Jesus was going to pray was going to come to pass.

Thy Faith Fail Not

So what did Jesus pray? *"...that thy faith fail not...".* Jesus did not pray for Peter's behavior; He prayed for his faith. Peter was not exercising faith when he offered to forgive seven times. Peter was not exercising faith when he rebuked Jesus. Peter was not exercising faith when he swore he would not deny Jesus. Peter was not exercising faith when he cut off the ear of the soldier when they came to seize Jesus. In all of these, Peter was exercising the strength of Peter.

Peter was tremendously self-reliant; therefore, we know that Peter had to get in touch with his inner sinner before he could possibly understand what it meant to live by faith.

When You are Converted

Jesus goes on to tell Peter that he will be converted. What this literally means is to do an about-face. What does an about-face look like to Peter? Stop trusting in yourself and learn to trust in God. This is what is required.

The Sin within

Peter thought he had power in and of himself to perform the acts of God. Peter needed to be converted from this thinking…he needed to turn completely away from it. So how does one go about losing self-confidence? Sin generally comes in handy for this purpose. Peter *needed* to deny Jesus the way Adam needed to eat that fruit.

Strengthen the Brethren

Finally, Jesus makes a request of Peter, *"when you are converted, strengthen your brethren."* The word "strengthen" in Greek is *sterizo* and means, *to turn resolutely in a certain direction.* All the disciples had agreed with Peter when he said he would not betray Jesus, which means that the disciples looked to Peter as a leader. Jesus prayed that Peter's faith fail not and that when he was turned from himself he would then turn the other disciples from themselves as well. Jesus saw Peter as a leader and this is why, and how He dealt with him.

In essence, Jesus had said this to Peter:

> *"Simon, Satan has had your number for some time.*
> *He wants to get rid of you entirely,*
> *but I have prayed for you.*
> *You are about to fail miserably in your flesh*
> *and when this happens*
> *you will finally realize how incapable you are.*
> *I have prayed for you that your faith*
> *would not fail through this.*
> *When you are converted*
> *(have done an about-face from yourself),*
> *strengthen and encourage your brethren to do likewise."*

Peter needed to exchange his self-confidence for faith in God. This is why Jesus had prayed in particular that Peter's faith would not fail. Each man is given a measure of faith and Peter was no exception. Jesus prayed that Peter's faith would get him through the death of his flesh. I believe it did.

Tasting the Valley

Let us look and see what happens after Jesus is taken prisoner:

> *"…And when they had kindled a fire in the midst of the*
> *hall, and were set down together,*

Peter, Peter...crow eater

Peter sat down among them.
But a certain maid beheld him as he sat by the fire,
and earnestly looked upon him, and said,
This man was also with him.
And he denied him,
saying, Woman, I know him not.
And after a little while another saw him, and said,
*Thou art also of them. **And Peter said, Man, I am not.***
And about the space of one hour after
another confidently affirmed, saying,
Of a truth this fellow also was with him:
for he is a Galilaean.
*And Peter said, **Man, I know not what thou sayest.***
And immediately, while he yet spake, the cock crew.
And the Lord turned, and looked upon Peter.
And Peter remembered the word of the Lord,
how he had said unto him,
Before the cock crow, thou shalt deny me thrice.
And Peter went out, and wept bitterly."

Jesus had said that Peter would deny Him three times before the cock crowed twice. This is exactly what happened. I think this is ample proof that Jesus was not praying that Peter would not deny Him; rather Peter proved the accuracy of the prophecy Jesus had quoted.

Peter somehow had to get over himself and learn to look to God. There is no questioning the fact that he was way out of line at least three major times. Not only did Peter deny Jesus three times, but on the third time it is written, *"Then began he to curse and to swear, saying, I know not the man..."(Matt 26:74 KJV).* It seems that Peter was as vehement about denying Jesus as he had been about refuting the *very idea* that he would deny Jesus. When we squeeze the balloon on one end it will only blow out on the other. Apparently it mattered not what direction Peter was heading, he was going there with a vengeance.

Looking Into the Face of Love

I find it fascinating that when the cock crowed and Peter denied Jesus for the third time, *"the Lord turned, and looked upon Peter."* Can you imagine what that moment was like for Peter? What an eye-opening experience. This forsaken Prisoner, Who had warned him of exactly what he would do, was looking into his eyes at the moment of his most vehement betrayal. Peter looked back and saw himself for the first time; he was ashamed and wept bitterly.

Peter loved Jesus. This wasn't just an act for him. As Peter looked into those eyes and realized what he had done, horror filled his soul. He had denied his beloved Lord and that right in front of Him. It is a miracle that Peter lived through this experience. Judas took his own life after his betrayal. I am sure this is why Jesus had prayed for Peter. The bigger they are, the harder they fall.

Peter loved Jesus deeply but seemed to be unable to receive the basic message of what Jesus had been spelling out to him. Peter was not easily brought down. However, the promised Holy Ghost was coming and He only fills empty vessels. The disciples abandoned Jesus because they needed to lose all faith in themselves before they could be used of God. I cannot even imagine the thundering in his mind as Peter looked into the eyes of his beloved Lord, *"And Peter remembered the word of Jesus, which said unto him, Before the cock crow, thou shalt deny me thrice."*

What Pain. . .

…what agony. Peter's thoughts were racing. The words of Jesus, all that He had said to him about Satan sifting him and when he is converted, came rushing into his head as he tried to sort it all out: "What went wrong? I loved Him. I would do anything for Him. How could I fail Him this way? What is wrong with me? I cannot possibly continue as a disciple. Can I? I don't know what to do. He said that I would be converted. He said my faith would not fail. He said He would pray for me. He said He was coming back. I don't know what to do. I will wait for Him."

Peter's gospel maintained that one must play the hero and be super Christian. Now he had failed at this task and he didn't know what to think of it. Unfortunately, Peter seemed to miss a lot of what Jesus was saying because he was too busy ministering to Jesus to allow Jesus to minister to him; a trap we all fall into from time to time. Although the disciples had been given the score:

"From that time forth began Jesus to show unto his
disciples, how that he must go unto Jerusalem,
and suffer many things of the elders and chief priests and
scribes, and be killed, and be raised again the third day."
(Matt 16:21 KJV)

Peter, Peter...crow eater

Peter still felt it necessary to save Jesus from having to be a Savior. Chances are, Peter didn't retain much of what Jesus had to say. This explains why everyone was so confused by the foretold empty tomb. It was obvious the disciples just didn't get it.

One Long Day

It is interesting because when we look at this sequence of events from the Gospel of John, we see that Jesus warned Peter that he would deny Him in the thirteenth chapter. In the fourteenth chapter Jesus commissions His disciples. In the fifteenth chapter Jesus taught His disciples for the last time before His crucifixion. In the sixteenth chapter Jesus encouraged His disciples for the last time before His death. In the seventeenth chapter Jesus prayed for His disciples for the final time before they took Him away. In the eighteenth chapter Jesus is betrayed and taken prisoner. In the nineteenth chapter Jesus is crucified.

Seven chapters describe what took place in the space of one day. It was the night before His crucifixion that Jesus broached the subject of the betrayal of His disciples, *"...All ye shall be offended because of me this night..."* Therefore, when we look at the events that take place at the tomb of Jesus and forward, we must keep in mind that the occurrence of Peter's vehement betrayal in front of the eyes of Jesus was only three crazy days old. It was still raw.

On the Third Day

So we know we have a shaky Peter on our hands. He is not sure what to think. He has failed his own self-administered test. And so we come to the tomb in the twentieth chapter. It was a Sunday, or the first day of the week, when Mary Magdaline came to the tomb where they buried Jesus and found the stone rolled away. Mary thought that someone had stolen the body, *"For as yet they knew not the scripture, that he must rise again from the dead." (John 20:9 KJV)* Mary immediately, *"...runneth, and cometh to Simon Peter, and to the other disciple, whom Jesus loved." (John 20:2 KJV)*

I don't know what was up between Peter and *"the disciple Jesus loved"*, but there seemed always to be a contest of sorts between the two. This was no exception, *"Peter therefore went forth, and that other disciple, and came to the sepulchre. So they ran both together: and the other disciple did outrun Peter, and came first to the sepulchre." (John 20:3-4 KJV)*

This other disciple, whom many believe was John, outran Peter to the tomb. This was written in the Bible for a purpose. The last we heard about Peter he was weeping bitterly over his very flagrant betrayal. Peter was discouraged. I believe that John outran Peter because Peter had lost his gusto. Just three days ago Super Peter would have outran a cheetah to that tomb.

When they got to the tomb, *"Then cometh Simon Peter following him, and went into the sepulchre, and seeth the linen clothes lie, And the napkin, that was about his head, not lying with the linen clothes, but wrapped together in a place by itself." (John 20:6-7 KJV)* Peter actually went into the tomb and found these things.

Mary had thought that the body of her Lord had been stolen, but Peter and John saw something in the tomb that said otherwise, *"Then went in also that other disciple, which came first to the sepulchre, and he saw, and believed."* Mary had not gone into the tomb so she did not see the linen clothes lying there as though a body had disappeared from within them.

Walking Away

However, although Peter and the disciple Jesus loved believed when they saw the linen cloths emptied of their host, *"Then the disciples went away again unto their own home." (John 20:10 KJV)* Peter knew Christ had risen, but he went home. The others followed Peter, so they went home. They were still feeling the sting of the betrayal.

Although Jesus made three personal appearances after His resurrection, Peter remained discouraged. You see, Peter did not think any of it mattered anymore because he had failed. Jesus rising from the dead is great for others, but he had failed and was out of the game. Peter believed his gospel and he failed his gospel. Now he had no gospel.

The last time Jesus had spoken to them before He went to be with His Father in heaven He reprimanded and commissioned the disciples again:

"Afterward he appeared unto the eleven
as they sat at meat, and upbraided them
with their unbelief and hardness of heart,
because they believed not them
which had seen him after he was risen.
And he said unto them, Go ye into all the world,
and preach the gospel to every creature.
He that believeth and is baptized shall be saved;
but he that believeth not shall be damned.

Peter, Peter...crow eater

And these signs shall follow them that believe;
In my name shall they cast out devils;
they shall speak with new tongues;
They shall take up serpents;
and if they drink any deadly thing,
it shall not hurt them;
they shall lay hands on the sick,
and they shall recover."
(Mark 16:14-18 KJV)

Then said Jesus to them again, Peace be unto you:
as my Father hath sent me, even so send I you.
And when he had said this, he breathed on them,
and saith unto them, Receive ye the Holy Ghost:
Whose soever sins ye remit, they are remitted unto
them; and whose soever sins ye retain, they are retained."
(John 20:21-23 KJV)

Although Jesus was clearly addressing a group of traitors, He commissioned them as though they were stalwartly spiritual. The sin of betrayal didn't change a thing about God and His calling. Jesus had just paid the penalty for sin and wasn't going to let it stand in the way of God's calling.

A Personal Visit

In all of this, we see no intimate interaction between Jesus and Peter, which is unusual. Rather than receive Jesus' commission, the very confused and discouraged Peter went back to fishing. And that is why Jesus had one more stop to make before returning to God.

The next thing we see is Peter out on the boat with his buddies, *"Simon Peter saith unto them, I go a fishing. They say unto him, We also go with thee. They went forth, and entered into a ship immediately; and that night they caught nothing." (John 21:3 KJV)*

Peter the leader had given up. Yes, it was obvious that Jesus had risen from the dead just as the Scriptures foretold, but it did not matter; Peter had failed and denied His beloved Lord. Now here he was failing at his worldly profession; they caught nothing that night.

Peter's gospel allowed for no mistakes. One must forgive four hundred and ninety times, cut out his own eye if it offends him, save Jesus from having to suffer the crucifixion, and stand by the Lord in

His worst moment even if it means that, in process, we turn the Word of God into a lie.

Peter may as well go back to fishing, as he obviously failed at being a disciple…oops, he failed as a fisherman too. Now that Peter has fallen headlong off of the mountain of self-reliance and plummeted face first into the valley, he is primed to begin eating fish instead of crow.

A Fisher of Men

Jesus had originally chosen Peter while he was at work, *"And Jesus, walking by the sea of Galilee, saw two brethren, Simon called Peter, and Andrew his brother, casting a net into the sea: for they were fishers. And he saith unto them, Follow me, and I will make you fishers of men. And they straightway left their nets, and followed him." (Matt 4:18-20 KJV)* One can go from a fisher of fish to a fisher of men, but one cannot go from a fisher of men to a fisher of fish.

Jesus is so sneaky as he catches Peter in the act, *"But when the morning was now come, Jesus stood on the shore: but the disciples knew not that it was Jesus." (John 21:4 KJV)* I think this was a very special time for Jesus, not to mention for Peter. God's toughest job is getting us to admit we are failures. The valley is a very temporary dwelling. Now comes the good part.

I was talking to a Marine once and he said the following about his sixteen weeks of basic training: "It didn't matter where you came from, how much money you had, the color of your skin, or the shape of your body…everyone was treated the same and brought to the same place – the bottom. They have to break you down before they can lift you to a higher place." It is the same with God. Peter was useless until sin broke him down. Now that he is down, let's see what happens:

"Then Jesus saith unto them, Children,
have ye any meat? They answered him, No.
And he said unto them, Cast the net on the right side of the
ship, and ye shall find. They cast therefore, and now they
were not able to draw it for the multitude of fishes."
(John 21:5-6 KJV)

Jesus, staying incognito at this point, provided a miracle by filling their net with so many fish that they could not haul them into the boat. This was His way of letting Peter, and the rest of the disciples know that He still loved them and was there for them. Of course, His plan was perfect:

> *"Therefore that disciple whom Jesus loved*
> *saith unto Peter, It is the Lord.*
> *Now when Simon Peter heard that it was the Lord,*
> *he girt his fisher's coat unto him, (for he was naked,)*
> *and did cast himself into the sea."*
> *(John 21:7 KJV)*

True Nakedness

Gosh, I don't know...is there a reason we had to know that Peter was naked? *"And Adam and Eve were naked and not ashamed."* Peter had been spiritually naked for a long time. He was just at this moment being clothed for the first time as he realized salvation was from God...not man.

Peter could not have been happier. He had convinced himself that Jesus had forsaken him, and with good reason. I'm sure he had felt a mixture of love and condemnation every time Jesus came around. I can imagine that Peter had worked up a Judas complex on the inside.

Peter had probably meditated many times over the fact that Jesus made appearances and did not speak to him personally as in the past. Satan was trying to convince Peter that Jesus did not see him as valuable anymore and wouldn't be able to use him. But now, this Man/God Whom Peter had vehemently denied three times was standing on the shore of "where he was" and blessing him. Jesus came to the valley to rescue Peter and place him on the mountain of God.

Jesus forgave him. Oh I can only imagine the wash of relief that ran over this man, *"he girt his fisher's coat unto him, (for he was naked,) and did cast himself into the sea."* Peter wasn't waiting for the ship to come in; in his eyes, his ship had already come in. He jumped into the water and swam to shore.

> *"As soon then as they were come to land, they saw a fire of*
> *coals there, and fish laid thereon, and bread. Jesus saith*
> *unto them, Bring of the fish which ye have now caught."*
> *(John 21:9-10 KJV)*

I Love You

What kind of a message is this? I L O V E Y O U. What did Peter find when he got to the end of himself? Did he receive a, *"Get thee behind me Satan"*? No, that is what Peter got when he was full of himself. Peter is no longer full of himself and so instead of a reprimand, Peter got a warm meal from a loving Lord. Jesus was making Himself very clear. While valiant Peter was relying on himself, he was a tool of the devil. When Peter ceased to rely upon himself, he became the apple of God's eye and the center of His concern.

The message of love continued when they took up the haul:

> *"Simon Peter went up, and drew the net to land full of great fishes, an hundred and fifty and three: and for all there were so many, yet was not the net broken."*
> *(John 21:11 KJV)*

Jesus is not just saying, "I love you and I will take care of you." He was also saying, "I will give you great abundance, yet, you will supernaturally be able to contain it." The last known intimate interaction between Jesus and Peter was when Peter denied Jesus and Jesus looked at him. Now Jesus makes a personal appearance and chooses Peter again just as He had at the start. This time Peter understands what it means to be chosen.

> *"Jesus saith unto them, Come and dine. And none of the disciples durst ask him, Who art thou? knowing that it was the Lord. Jesus then cometh, and taketh bread, and giveth them, and fish likewise."* (John 21:12-13 KJV)

A Clear Message

Here we have the Bread of Life serving fish and bread to His chosen ones. How could Peter miss this message? How could he ever again depend upon himself? Jesus had encouraged him earlier by saying, *"when thou art converted, strengthen the brethren."*

Jesus had told Peter what he needed to hear. Essentially Jesus told Peter, "I am keeping you from being sifted by getting rid of you and all of your mighty efforts. Now you will live by faith in what *I*

Peter, Peter...crow eater

can do instead of empty confidence in what you can do. And when you are converted, I want you to lead the others likewise."

Peter got an up close and personal look at what was in it for him when he trusted God: Abundance and mercy. Peter changed courses on the spot, *"when thou art converted, strengthen thy brethren."* The next time we see Peter he is not on a boat, but in the upper room with the other disciples waiting for the promised Holy Ghost.

And Then There Were Twelve

Now since the Holy Ghost had not yet come, these disciples had not yet been empowered to walk in their calling:

> *"**But ye shall receive power, after** that the Holy Ghost is come upon you: and ye shall be witnesses unto me both in Jerusalem, and in all Judaea, and in Samaria, and unto the uttermost part of the earth."*
> *(Acts 1:8 KJV emphasis mine)*

Peter was back in the game all right, but the Holy Ghost had not yet come to change his "act before you think" mentality. Peter felt it necessary to fill the shoes of Judas before the Holy Ghost came. Jesus had told all of His disciples, *"But the Comforter, which is the Holy Ghost, whom the Father will send in my name, he shall teach you all things, and bring all things to your remembrance, whatsoever I have said unto you." (John 14:26 KJV)*

This should have been an indication to Peter that the Holy Ghost would guide them in these sorts of decisions. But Peter wasn't waiting for the Holy Ghost; he rose up and addressed the congregation:

> *"And in those days Peter stood up in the midst of the disciples, and said...For it is written in the book of Psalms, Let his habitation be desolate, and let no man dwell therein: and his bishopric let another take... And they appointed two, Joseph called Barsabas, who was surnamed Justus, and Matthias. And they prayed, and said, Thou, Lord, which knowest the hearts of all men, show whether of these two thou hast chosen, That he may take part of this ministry and apostleship, from which Judas by transgression fell, that he might go to his own place.*

The Sin within

And they gave forth their lots; and the lot fell upon
Matthias; and he was numbered with the eleven apostles."
(Acts 1:15&20&23-26 KJV)

The casting of lots was an Old Testament ritual that was used to receive guidance from God. However, these men were entering a new dispensation of time when rituals would be replaced by relationship. God Himself, in the person of the Holy Ghost, has come to live in man and comfort and guide him through his life. Jesus belabored this point over and over. He told His disciples to not depart from Jerusalem but to wait for the Holy Ghost to come upon them. That doesn't sound like the time to be making major decisions about prophecy and apostleship.

I think the Scriptures make it abundantly clear that Saul, surnamed Paul, was to be the twelfth disciple/apostle. Jesus called him in the same fashion that He called all the others: Personally. As far as the lot-elected *Matthias*, we never hear of him again.

The Day of Thy Power is Today

However, shortly thereafter, the Holy Ghost came upon them:

"And suddenly there came a sound from heaven as of a
rushing mighty wind, and it filled all the house where they
were sitting. And there appeared unto them cloven tongues
like as of fire, and it sat upon each of them. And they were
all filled with the Holy Ghost, and began to speak with
other tongues, as the Spirit gave them utterance."
(Acts 2:2-4 KJV)

And then Peter, emptied of self and filled with the Holy Ghost, rises once again:

"But Peter, standing up with the eleven, lifted up his voice,
and said unto them, Ye men of Judaea, and all ye that dwell
at Jerusalem, be this known unto you,
and hearken to my words:" (Acts 2:14 KJV)

What followed was a sermon the likes of which no one had heard before. Peter had lived salvation and knew exactly what it meant. Peter was no longer religious; now he was righteous in Christ. With passion, Peter began by explaining the miracle of the presence of the

Peter, Peter...crow eater

Holy Ghost and the gift of speaking in tongues, went on to speak of Who Jesus was and what happened to Him, and ended with what all this meant to mankind. The people responded favorably:

> *"Now when they heard this, they were pricked in their*
> *heart, and said unto Peter and to the rest of the apostles,*
> *Men and brethren, what shall we do?" (Acts 2:37 KJV)*

The Altar Call

Peter was clearly a new man who was speaking with power and anointing. No more casting of lots; now we have Holy Ghost guidance:

> *"Then Peter said unto them,*
> *Repent, and be baptized*
> *every one of you in the name of Jesus Christ*
> *for the remission of sins,*
> *and ye shall receive the gift of the Holy Ghost.*
> *For the promise is unto you,*
> *and to your children, and to all that are afar off,*
> *even as many as the Lord our God shall call.*
> *And with many other words did he testify and exhort,*
> *saying, Save yourselves from this untoward generation."*
> *(Acts 2:38-40 KJV)*

Reaching Thousands

Now what is the result when a man finds that he is worthless in and of himself and instead receives the power of the Holy Ghost?

> *"Then they that gladly received his word were baptized:*
> *and the same day there were added unto them about three*
> *thousand souls." (Acts 2:41 KJV)*

Silver and Gold Have I None. . .

Peter's speech brought in *three thousand souls*; those were big numbers back then. This is a changed man. So much so, as a matter of fact, that we see Peter perform signs and wonders:

> *"Now Peter and John went up together into the temple*
> *at the hour of prayer, being the ninth hour.*

The Sin within

> *And a certain man lame from his mother's womb*
> *was carried, whom they laid daily at the gate of the*
> *temple which is called Beautiful,*
> *to ask alms of them that entered into the temple;*
> *Who seeing Peter and John*
> *about to go into the temple asked an alms.*
> *And Peter, fastening his eyes upon him with John,*
> *said, Look on us. And he gave heed unto them,*
> *expecting to receive something of them.*
> *Then Peter said, Silver and gold have I none;*
> *but such as I have give I thee:*
> *In the name of Jesus Christ of Nazareth rise up and walk.*
> *And he took him by the right hand, and lifted him up:*
> *and immediately his feet and ankle bones received*
> *strength. And he leaping up stood, and walked,*
> *and entered with them into the temple,*
> *walking, and leaping, and praising God."*
> *(Acts 3:1-8 KJV)*

The people in the vicinity of this miraculous healing were amazed:

> *"And all the people saw him walking and praising God:*
> *And they knew that it was he which sat for alms at the*
> *Beautiful gate of the temple: and they were filled with*
> *wonder and amazement at that which had happened unto*
> *him. And as the lame man which was healed held Peter and*
> *John, all the people ran together unto them in the porch*
> *that is called Solomon's, greatly wondering."*
> *(Acts 3:9-11 KJV)*

Don't Look at Me!

Peter knew the power to heal did not come from him. He was running under an entirely different Gospel these days. Peter no longer looked to himself:

> *"And when Peter saw it, he answered unto the people, Ye*
> *men of Israel, why marvel ye at this? or why look ye so*
> *earnestly on us, as though by our own power or holiness*
> *we had made this man to walk?" (Acts 3:12 KJV)*

The old Peter would have just assumed the man was healed because of Peter's power and holiness. But now, Peter knew whose power

Free to be Holy

Peter, Peter...crow eater

and holiness was responsible for this act. Peter answers them:

> "...*the God of our fathers, hath glorified his Son*
> *Jesus...And his name through faith in his name hath made*
> *this man strong, whom ye see and know: yea, the faith*
> *which is by him hath given him this perfect soundness in*
> *the presence of you all." (Acts 3:13a&16 KJV)*

That's right...your God...the God of Abraham, Isaac, and Jacob. This God has glorified His Son Jesus and faith in this name is what made this man strong. Wow. Peter learned his lesson; he could not *earn* anything, though he must *receive* everything. Peter affected thousands in person; over the centuries, untold numbers have been influenced by his words. Look how Peter opens up his first letter to the church:

> *"Wherein ye greatly rejoice,*
> *though now for a season, if need be,*
> *ye are in heaviness through manifold temptations:*
> *That the trial of your faith,*
> *being much more precious than of gold*
> *that perisheth, though it be tried with fire,*
> *might be found unto praise and honour and glory at the*
> *appearing of Jesus Christ"*
> *(1 Pet 1:3-7 KJV)*

Peter is encouraging those who are going through what he went through the night he betrayed Jesus, *"Wherein ye greatly rejoice, though now for a season, if need be, ye are in heaviness through manifold temptations."* Peter gives them hope because he was in that trial and his faith carried him, *"That the trial of your faith, being much more precious than of gold that perisheth, though it be tried with fire, might be found unto praise and honour and glory at the appearing of Jesus Christ"*

You see, Satan desired to sift Peter, but he did not sift Peter because Jesus had prayed for him that his faith would fail not. We now see Peter walking in a lot of faith. Jesus had also asked Peter to strengthen his brethren. Peter, most assuredly, was doing that very thing. Jesus foretold of a betrayal, a faith, a conversion, and a strengthening. All of these came to pass.

Peter is a perfect example of someone who got a good enough look at himself to see his nakedness. Now he is clothed with Christ and walking like a god. This portrait of a self-reliant man must be a daily lesson to us. Peter was useless until he got rid of himself. Laboring in the flesh produces absolutely nothing.

In Summary

We take away many things from what we have learned in *The Sin Within*:

1. We are born hopelessly in bondage to sin
2. We are dead in Adam
3. We receive this death by faith and act accordingly
4. We do not judge ourselves better than others
5. We watch our heart to see that it is willing
6. We obey, looking for what is in it for us
7. We see the Ten Commandments as God sees them
8. We become peculiar people who are zealous of good works
9. We draw close to God and listen for His still, small voice.
10. We keep in mind that a lot of pomp and circumstance doesn't amount to a hill of beans. We must get to the end of ourselves.

The Abrahamic Covenant

r e i n s t i t u t e d

The next book in the *Free to be Holy* series, *The Abrahamic Covenant*, focuses on Abraham's life and ways. We have learned that we are participants in the Abrahamic Covenant and that it is an eternal covenant, which means we are forever in this covenant with God. Abraham's life was interesting to say the least. The single noteworthy thing we know about Abraham is that he lived by faith. Abraham is called our Father of Faith. As we study his life we will learn how faith works in every area of our lives.

Although it is fairly easy to follow the precepts we just learned in *The Sin Within*, there are certainly areas that will give each of us great difficulty. Strongholds have been built into each of our lives and these must be conquered before we will be free to manifest holiness. *The Abrahamic Covenant* will teach us how to deal with the strongholds of sin. Within the Abrahamic Covenant is all the persuasion anyone could ever need to embrace true holiness under the worst possible circumstances.

1781881

Made in the USA